Online Child Sexual Abuse

Grooming, Policing and Child Protection in a Multi-Media World

Elena Martellozzo

Routledge
Taylor & Francis Group

LONDON AND NEW YORK

First published 2012
by Routledge
2 Park Square, Milton Park, Abingdon, Oxon OX14 4RN

Simultaneously published in the USA and Canada
by Routledge
711 Third Avenue, New York, NY 10017

Routledge is an imprint of the Taylor & Francis Group, an informa business

First issued in paperback 2013

British Library Cataloguing in Publication Data
A catalogue record for this book is available
from the British Library

Library of Congress Cataloging in Publication Data

ISBN: 978-0-415-61821-2 (hbk)
ISBN: 978-0-415-73272-7 (pbk)
ISBN: 978-0-203-12411-6 (ebk)

Typeset in Times by
RefineCatch Limited, Bungay, Suffolk

Online Child Sexual Abuse

Online Child Sexual Abuse: Grooming, Policing and Child Protection in a Multi-Media World addresses the complex, multi-faceted and, at times, counter-intuitive relationships between online grooming behaviours, risk assessment, police practices and the actual danger of subsequent abuse in the physical world. Online child sexual abuse has become a high profile and important issue in public life. Understanding how sex offenders use the internet and how the police and the government are responding to their behaviour is central to the development of preventative measures. Based on her extensive ethnographic research conducted with the police and a specialist paedophile unit, Elena Martellozzo presents an informed analysis of online child sexual abuse: of the patterns and characteristics of online grooming and of the challenges and techniques that characterise its policing. Connecting theory, research and practice in the field of policing, social policy, victimology and criminology, this book adds significantly to our understanding and knowledge of the problem of online child sexual abuse, the way in which victims are targeted and how this phenomenon is, and might be, policed.

Elena Martellozzo is a lecturer in Criminology at Middlesex University. Her research includes the analysis of online sex offending, online sexual abuse, children's online behaviour and police practice in this area. She collaborates with a number of national and international agencies and works closely with the London Metropolitan Police.

Endorsements

'This incisive study is an essential read for all practictioners combating child abuse in a digital age. Developed from a unique partnership between law enforcement and academia, with unprecedented access to police systems and processes, it combines the investigators' experience with academic rigour and will ensure a greater understanding of the dynamics and anatomy of child abuse online. It will benefit those who work with victims and offenders and enhance their ability to provide a professional service to our society in one of the most challenging arenas.'

Peter Spindler, Commander, Metropolitan Police Service

'In this book, Martellozzo consolidates her standing as one of the world's leading criminologists in the field of online child sexual abuse. The Metropolitan Police deserve a great deal of credit for allowing such detailed access to their files and their staff. However, the real value in this work is created through the elegance of Martellozzo's highly accessible writing which, when combined with her compendious knowledge of and unique insights into the subject, presents the reader with a privileged entrée into what remains a huge challenge for modern policing and child protection professionals.'

John Carr, OBE, Adviser to UK Government

'*Online Child Sexual Abuse: Grooming, Policing and Child Protection in a Multi-Media World* is a welcome addition to a growing number of publications on technology mediated child victimisation. Continuing interest in the area is in part related to the number of convictions for offences related to grooming and the possession, distribution and creation of abusive images of children. This book is based on innovative empirical research and reviews existing knowledge to contextualise the findings. The importance of this book lies in its ability to use multiple sources of novel data, obtained during covert police operations, to further our understanding of online offending. In doing so it takes into account the voices of young people in relation to the offending process, as well as the importance of the medium itself. This book will be essential reading for all involved in the criminal justice and child protection services.'

Dr Ethel Quayle, Edinburgh University

For Ashley, with love and gratitude

Contents

Acknowledgements

Thank you to the London Metropolitan Police SCD5 High Technological Crime Unit and Paedophile Unit for recognising the importance of this research and granting me access to their staff and facilities. Conducting this research gave me the opportunity to meet and work with exceptionally dedicated and professional people. Thank you all for participating in this research, for your insightful comments and endless cups of coffee.

I would like to thank my colleagues and friends Daniel Nehring, Brian Kavenagh, Maggie Brennan and Noreen Tehrani for taking time to comment on draft chapters during the writing process. I also thank Melanie Fortmann-Brown from Routledge for her assistance in guiding me through the process of writing this book.

Thank you to all the other practitioners, academics, children and teachers whose views and research have been mentioned in this book.

Finally, this book would have not come to life without the endless support, love and encouragement of my husband and my family. To them, thank you.

Foreword

Internet use has grown considerably in the last decade. Information technology now forms a core part of the formal education system in many countries, ensuring that each new generation of internet users is more adept than the last. Research studies suggest that the majority of young people across the world have access to the internet on PCs and/or mobile devices. The internet provides the opportunity to interact with friends on social networking sites and enables almost unlimited access to information in a way that previous generations would not have thought possible. The internet provides a platform for peer communication previously unknown. Research suggests that digital media have become so central to young people's lives that the online-offline worlds have become a converged environment, where the young have developed their own language and social norms. Whilst the benefits of the internet undoubtedly outweigh negative aspects, it is clear that young people can be exposed to harm online. The nature of the risks encountered includes exposure to harmful or indecent material and exposure to harmful behaviour perpetrated by peers and by sex offenders. The idea that children might be 'groomed' on the internet by sex offenders is a relatively new one; the concept has been discussed in the sex offender literature for many years but has recently found its way into English law (Sexual Offences Act 2003) and is now part of an EU directive to Member States. Research in this area is embryonic and little is really known about the behaviour of those who use the internet to perpetrate sexual offences; still less is known about the way in which covert internet policing operates. In this book, Dr Elena Martellozzo confronts the emotive issue of online grooming of children. The book is based upon an extensive research study conducted by Dr Martellozzo, spanning several years spent with the Metropolitan Police High Technology Crime Unit, thus offering a unique insight into methods of covert police investigation. The behaviour of men who seek children online for the purposes of sexual abuse is extensively discussed, drawing upon observations of police practice, interviews with police officers and documentary analysis of offender chat logs and case files. The author also subjects the rapidly growing body of evidence on this emotionally fraught subject to a scrupulous and dispassionate analysis. This book is therefore a timely and much-needed assessment of the issues and evidence relating to the practice and policing of internet grooming and makes a significant contribution to our understanding of sexual abuse taking place on the internet.

Professor Julia C. Davidson, Kingston University

Introduction

'Just as the computer has begun to revolutionise social life, it will revolutionise crime and deviancy; especially the parameters of deviant sexual behaviour . . . in fact, it is doing so already'

(Durkin and Bryant 1995)

In 2007, Jack[1] was detained by the Metropolitan Police. An intelligence-gathering operation had revealed that Jack had been using a website with images of child sexual abuse. Jack's home was searched and the police found a number of digital memory cards containing further images. Notably, most of these displayed South East Asian girls and it was discovered that Jack had travelled to Thailand twice between 2002 and 2004. The images, however, only showed the hands of a white man violating the girls and the police had no direct means to attribute this abuse to Jack. Questions remained whether Jack was guilty only of the distribution of indecent images or whether he had sexually abused children himself. In response to this ambiguity, the police involved the Centre of Anatomy and Human Identification at the University of Dundee in the case. Members of the Centre developed an innovative forensic technique that made it possible to match skin patterns on Jack's hands against those shown in the photographs. Researchers examined, for example, the location of scars, knuckle skin creases, freckle patterns and the morphology of nail beds. The result was a convincing match between the studied pictures and Jack's hands. The following pictures (Black et al. 2009) display examples of this analytic procedure.

Jack was prosecuted under the 'sex tourist provision' of the Sexual Offences Act 2003. He was jailed for six years and will remain on the Sex Offenders' Register for the remainder of his life.

This case illustrates many of the concerns set out in this book. It highlights the connections between the real-life sexual abuse of children and the distribution and consumption of abusive images via increasingly sophisticated virtual networks. At the same time, it points to the need for police and other child protection agencies to develop innovative techniques to be able to trace the activities of sex offenders and establish connections between offences in cyberspace and in the

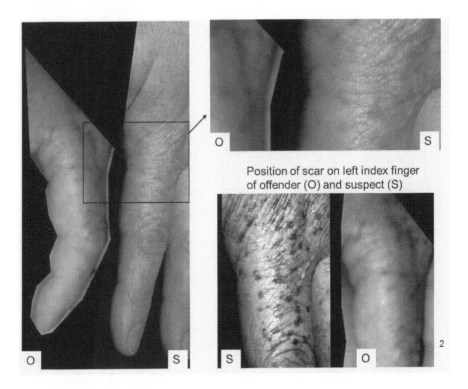

Position of scar on left index finger
of offender (O) and suspect (S)

real world. Just a short time ago, neither the technology required for Jack to make, store and distribute indecent images of children, eg digital cameras, digital memory cards, the internet, nor the techniques used by the police to prosecute Jack's actions, were available.[2] Finally, the case is indicative of the international scale of these problems. In this sense, there is a particular need for up-to-date academic research on online child sexual abuse, to account for the changing nature and growing scope of the problem. This book seeks to contribute to this project.

Drawing on unprecedented access to data of the Paedophile Unit of the Metropolitan Police Service in London, the following study seeks to understand and explain the problem of online child sexual abuse (CSA). More specifically, it presents a theoretical and empirical investigation of the current tactics and operational procedures employed by the London Metropolitan Police High Technological Crime Unit (HTCU) and Paedophile Unit, and it explores patterns and characteristics of online grooming.

Online child sexual abuse has become a high profile and important issue in public life. When the victims are children there is clearly intense public and political interest and concern. Sex offenders are society's most reviled deviants and the object of seemingly undifferentiated public fear and loathing. This may be

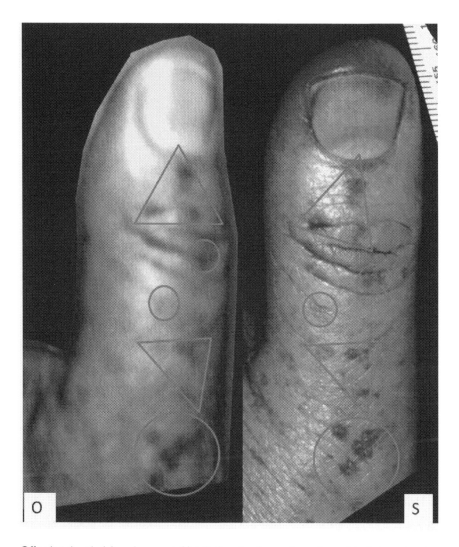

Offender thumb (o) and suspect (s) left thumb, after yellow channel isolation, showing distinct patterns of pigmentation that match the left thumb of the suspect.

evidenced from ongoing efforts to advance legislation, develop police tactics and educate children and their carers to engage safely with multi-media and the internet.

The internet has become a key tool in enabling us to 'make sense' of our world. Understanding how sex offenders use the internet and how the police and the government are responding to their behaviour is central to how we think about the development of preventative measures. There is no doubt that new information and communication technologies – the internet in particular – have opened up opportunities for perpetrators to abuse more victims in a less visible way. The internet allows for the expression of sexual behaviour with others that would not be feasible in the real world. The following chapters seek primarily to understand and explain the issue of online CSA and to explore patterns and characteristics of online grooming, policing and child protection in a multi-media world. The data presented throughout this book derive from empirical research conducted over the past seven years in the UK.

Data on grooming and policing child sexual abuse

I gathered data on online grooming and the online policing of online CSA through ethnographic research at the London Metropolitan Police HTCU and Paedophile Unit. I secured unprecedented access to these sites[3] and I was presented with an unique opportunity not only to engage with practitioners in the field but also anonymously to observe sex offenders' online behaviour and reflect on the development of police techniques and practices in response. Semi-structured interviews were undertaken with officers of varying rank and experience in the HTCU and Paedophile Unit. A total of 21 formal semi-structured interviews were conducted with police officers and forensic examiners working for the MET Police HTCU and Paedophile Unit. Those interviews basically involved all those officers who do play a significant role in the policing of cyberspace. The interviews focused primarily upon:

Indecent images

Internet sex offenders fall into two principal categories: those who produce and/or download indecent illegal images of children from the internet and distribute them (Quayle and Taylor 2002; Davidson and Martellozzo 2005) and those who use the internet to target and 'groom' children for the purposes of sexual abuse (Finkelhor et al. 2000).

Therefore, a descriptive account was sought from both officers working in the HTCU and forensic examiners regarding the nature and extent of indecent images encountered online. It is clear that sex offenders use the internet both to access child abuse images and to select victims for abuse. Gillan (2003) has suggested that the demand for child pornography through, for example, the use of file-sharing technology, has grown so rapidly that law enforcement agencies are now employed in an increasingly difficult global race to track down the child victims and the perpetrators involved. The approach adopted in the interview process allowed respondents to describe their views regarding the nature of the images, the pattern of escalation in the process of downloading and collecting the images, as well as their views about the offenders.

Grooming

Questions on grooming were addressed mainly in conversations with undercover officers of the HTCU. This component of the study sought to address the officers' views on sex offenders' *modus operandi*. This area proved to be the most difficult to explore, particularly given the lack of relevant previous empirical research. Since the introduction of the Sexual Offences Act 2003, the HTCU have placed undercover officers in teen and other chat rooms likely to attract children. Officers have been trained to act undercover and, through practice, have learnt how to pose as a child, as an adult or as a sex offender. They have learnt to mimic children's behaviour online, including their use of computer and mobile text language, in order to prompt and encourage conversation with child abusers seeking to groom a child.

The aim of this component was to ask respondents to describe and evaluate the process of online grooming, recounting any negative or positive impressions.

Innovations

It is clear that the internet is more than just a medium of communication (Castells 1996, 2004). It constitutes a new virtual reality or cyberworld with its own rules, identities and languages. It provides a supportive context within which the child sexual abuser is no longer a lonely figure, but forms part of a larger community that shares the same interests. The internet gives new meaning to the term 'paedophile ring', as the potential for offenders to organise child abuse is so considerable. However, the internet has also contributed to the development of innovative police tactics that make it possible to track down sex offenders who would otherwise have remained undetected.

Data on children's use of the internet

In collaboration with both the centre for Child Abuse and Trauma Studies (CATS) at Kingston University and the Metropolitan Police, I collected data on children's use of the internet through interviews with children, teachers and parents. Both pieces of research[4] aimed to explore young people's experience and awareness of internet use and other digital media safety and to understand their behaviour on social networking sites (SNSs). The resulting qualitative data were analysed using a thematic approach. A statement regarding confidentiality and anonymity was given to all respondents and a code is used to refer to each specific interview (Police Officer ID: 1; Girl ID: 2 etc).

Overview of the book

The intended purpose of this book is to construct conceptual and empirical bridges between child sexual abuse, the dynamics of grooming processes and online interactions related to sexual abuse. The emergence and increasing prominence in everyday life of mediated social interaction in cyberspace have had profound consequences for offenders' grooming behaviour, their underlying motivations and situational understandings, as well as their victims' responses and, in consequence, patterns of child sexual abuse in contemporary society as a whole. I therefore argue that it is necessary to unpick and re-examine grooming processes as they now occur online, with a view to achieving a better understanding of child sexual abuse today and formulating adequate policy responses.

Chapter 1 sets the scene, providing an overview of what we know and what we do not know about the nature and extent of child sexual abuse. It briefly reviews the existing academic literature to identify, define and critically evaluate the relevant key terms and concepts. This helps the reader gain a better understanding of the problem of child sexual abuse as it occurs both in the real world and in cyberspace. This chapter includes the definition of child sexual abuse in the new and much debated context of cyberspace. In this chapter, I also provide an overview of the international nature of online child sexual abuse and how there is increasing co-operation at policy level from government, law enforcement agencies and the charitable sector.

In Chapter 2, I present a sociological analysis of real and virtual abuse. More specifically, I explore the theories of the drivers that cause men and some women to deviate from the norm and engage in sexual activities with children. I will argue that there is no single theory that adequately explains why those who sexually abuse children (both on and offline) come to do so in the first instance and why they continue to offend over time. Nonetheless, sound theoretical explanations of child sexual offending are central to the development and implementation of policies, treatments and policing strategies sensitive to the range of motivations and behaviours underpinning abuse in the real world and in cyberspace. The chapter concludes by arguing that a key solution to the problem of child sexual abuse is to address all manner of potential offenders in the research – including men, women and children – and both worlds in which they may operate, namely the real world and cyberspace. It is only with a thorough examination of all such elements that it may become possible to increase awareness of the dynamics that occur between perpetrators and victims in the real world or in cyberspace.

Chapter 3 is concerned with the real protagonists of this e-era: young people and their use of the internet. In this chapter I turn my attention to the analysis of children's and young people's use of the internet and the risks they take when they are online. This chapter presents a critical review of relevant literature and recent research in this arena and links key findings to those from practitioners' and sex offenders' accounts presented in the two previous chapters.

Chapter 4 reviews the emergence of an international legislative framework to combat online child sexual abuse; from early laws prohibiting the sexual abuse and exploitation of children and initial manifestations of online child sexual abuse in the form of 'child pornography', through to more recent international legislative efforts to frame this problem as a form of 'cybercrime', a content-related offence associated with the production and circulation of illegal content in cyberspace. In particular, the chapter explores how the convergence of these socio-legal challenges with advances in the new technologies has resulted in the emergence of the grooming offence, a distinct category of criminal behaviour with a requirement for bespoke and broad-based legal intervention. The chapter then turns to the matter of law enforcement and supporting interventions, focusing on the UK policing response as an exemplar of how distinct policing specialisms have developed in response to recent grooming legislation and how policing practices have adapted to accommodate the provisions of these statutes. Finally, the chapter identifies new and emerging gaps and challenges in policing and child protection practice presented by the introduction of grooming legislation.

Chapter 5 explores the challenges that official agencies such as the police, educational and charitable sectors face in promoting and enforcing the protection of children against online CSA. The first part of this chapter seeks to identify and evaluate how the government and the police have reacted to the exponentially growing problem of the production and distribution of indecent images of children and the problem of online grooming. It will therefore provide an historical overview of how online CSA developed.

Chapter 6 focuses on day-to-day police activities. More specifically it presents empirical evidence of police officers' undercover online interaction with sex offenders. It discusses the context in which undercover policing takes place, explores the grooming process and the stages of police intervention. Here, police practice is considered in detail to ensure a better understanding of how the policing of online grooming occurs and how police assess the risk of offending. This chapter will be a reflexive account of the research process. Here I describe the real experience of conducting an ethnographic study of undercover operations targeting online groomers.

Chapter 7 considers practitioners' views about policing child sexual abuse. It is in this chapter where I draw together covert police activities and sex offenders' online behaviour. I analyse sex offenders' online *modus operandi*, from the creation of their online profile to the online grooming of undercover police officers who they believe to be children.

Chapter 8 brings together the key arguments presented throughout the book. The chapter concludes by proposing that law enforcement agencies, academics and internet service providers should continue to develop further co-operative dialogue geared to raising social awareness about the problem of CSA in an informative and, above all, useful way. The common media coverage of CSA occurring via new technologies promotes the perception that children are at greatest risk from online abusers. Therefore, there is a clear danger of over-prioritising online CSA over CSA that takes place in the home, where children are at greater risk of being abused by someone they know. Myths such as this should be challenged rather than reinforced and allowed to prevail.

Notes

1 All the names used in this book are pseudonyms.
2 To give another example, Facebook recently introduced a heavily promoted video chat facility on its website. This was not available when the fieldwork for this book was conducted and it has the potential substantially to alter interaction on one of the most widely used social networking websites. In turn, this will have an impact on both the online behaviour of potential sex offenders and attendant security measures and policing operations.
3 I was granted ethical approval by the University of Westminster Ethics Committee.
4 Ethical permission to conduct the research was granted by Kingston University and Middlesex University Ethics Committee in the UK.

References

Black, S. M., Mallett, X., Rynn, C. and Duffield, N. (2009) Forensic Hand Image Comparison as an Aid for Paedophile Investigations. *Police Professional*, 184.

Castells, M. (1996) *The Network Society*, Oxford, Blackwell Publishers.

Castells, M. (2004) *The Power of Identity*, Oxford, Blackwell Publishers.

Davidson, J. and Martellozzo, E. (2005) 'Policing the Internet and Protecting Children from Sex Offenders on Line: When Strangers Become Virtual Friends'; http://www.oii.ox.ac.uk/research/cybersafety/extensions/pdfs/papers.

Durkin, K. F. and Bryant, C. D. (1995) Log on to sex: Some notes on the carnal computer and erotic cyberspace as an emerging research frontier. *Deviant Behaviour: An Interdisciplinary Journal*, 16, 179–200.

Finkelhor, D., Kimberly, J. and Wolak, J. (2000) On Line Victimisation: a report on the Nation's Youth. Alexandria, Virginia, National Centre for Missing and Exploited Children.

Gillan, A. (2003) Race to Save New Victims of Child Pornography. *Guardian Newspaper* London, accessed on 20/09/07.

Quayle, E. and Taylor, M. (2002) Paedophiles, Pornography and the Internet: Assessment Issues. *British Journal of Social Work*, 863–75.

Chapter 1

Establishing the terrain

Introduction

Children are abused every day around the world: physically, emotionally and sexually, and sometimes with very severe consequences. There is a vast amount of academic research suggesting that prolonged neglect or abuse leads to children being placed in care and which can place them at serious risk of being socially excluded as adolescents and young adults. Such young people are more likely to engage in crime (Sir John Stevens 2002) and to continue to be victimised and abused in later life (Pritchard 2004). In particular, non-consensual sexual activities between a child and an adult[1] interfere with normal development processes and lead to maladjustment later in life. Abuse is often confusing, frightening and painful, and these negative effects may continue into adulthood. In fact, child sexual abuse has come to be widely regarded as a key cause of mental health problems in adult life (Mullen and Fleming 1998). Furthermore, abuse occurs during the critical formative time, when the child is learning by experience. Therefore, it should not be surprising that victims of sexual abuse may continue to suffer from debilitating effects, such as emotional distress, anxiety, rage, post-traumatic stress disorder, substance abuse and suicide attempts.

Arguably, the process of grooming represents the main method through which children are sexually abused. Mass media coverage seems to suggest that grooming is a new phenomenon that has developed recently with the advent of the internet (Gillespie 2008). However, this is clearly not the case. As will be argued later in this chapter, there is ample historical evidence of child sexual abuse, even though it has only been recognised as a social problem for just over two decades (Wells et al. 2007).

There is a limited but expanding literature on grooming in the cyber world. It is important to make clear from the start that with this book I do not intend to conduct a comparative analysis of online and offline grooming. On the contrary, this book is a focused case study of the process of online grooming, policing and child protection. We simply do not know enough about child sexual grooming in the real world to support a comparative analysis of grooming online and offline. Of course, where appropriate, comparisons will be made – in terms of theory, epistemology, policy and practice – regarding similarities and differences between grooming and child sexual abuse in the virtual and physical worlds. However, my analysis is firmly situated within the realm of cyberspace. In fact, what we may claim to know, however tentatively, about grooming in the physical world is so limited that it may even be counterproductive to attempt a thorough comparative analysis. Online and offline child sexual abuse take place within distinct but overlapping worlds. They are not hermetically sealed off from each other. The areas of overlap between online and offline grooming are manifold, substantive and significant. Moreover, these areas of overlap are neither straightforward nor easy to theorise or explore empirically. Because areas of overlap do exist, however, it is hoped that the generation of knowledge through sustained and focused engagement with the problem of online child sexual abuse will also contribute to a better understanding of child sexual abuse in the physical world.

It would not be possible to conduct any research exploring the problem of child sexual abuse (CSA) without defining key terms and establishing the social, political, cultural and legislative context within which this research fits. Given the ballooning interest in child sexual abuse among researchers with various disciplinary backgrounds, it is important to establish some conceptual order at the outset of this book and systematise key ideas. Therefore, it is the aim of this chapter to establish, first, what we know and what we do not know about the nature and extent of CSA. Secondly, this chapter will identify, define and critically evaluate the relevant key terms and concepts, so as to enable a better understanding of the problem of child sexual abuse as it occurs both in the real world and in cyberspace.

A necessary starting point of this analysis is the problematisation of the concept of childhood. Issues of childhood and child abuse are closely linked and, like most of the key terms addressed in this chapter, 'childhood' is a socially constructed and contested term whose meaning may vary significantly across space, time and context.

The second concept that deserves attention is 'sexual abuse'. This leads to the evaluation of more complex concepts, such as child sexual abuse, the issue of consent, as well as the British legislative and political context in which child sexual abuse is constructed and prosecuted.

Finally, this chapter defines child sexual abuse in the new and much debated context of cyberspace. It distinguishes between the production and distribution of indecent images of children and online grooming and explores the legislation created to prosecute these cyber crimes.

Defining 'childhood'

Common sense suggests that the notion of childhood is something that has been fixed and permanent throughout history. In fact, quite the opposite is true; childhood is a recent concept, which has been socially constructed over the years (Muncie 2004). The way in which society and law define childhood today is certainly different from the way it was perceived, for instance, in the European

Middle Ages. In fact, the concept of childhood was neither understood nor considered during the Middle Ages, where 'children', for example, were completely missing from medieval icons, and notions of childhood, as understood today, did not form part of Western culture (Aries in Skelton and Valentine 1998: 3; Aries 1962). Much of the work relating to the sociology of childhood has been inspired by the French social historian Philippe Aries' *Centuries of Childhood* (Aries 1962). Aries (1962) observes that this attitude towards the definition of childhood (or the lack thereof) was the outcome of interpreting children as young adults, rather than as conceptually different from adults. De Mause (1976) agrees with Aries's hypothesis that childhood developed as a separate category from the 16th century onwards but, unlike Aries, he sees this as a highly progressive move. De Mause perceives childhood as a:

'... [n]ightmare from which we are only recently begun to awaken. The further back in history one goes, the lower the level of the child care, and the more likely children are to be killed, abandoned, beaten, terrorised and sexually abused' (De Mause 1976: 11).

His despairing view of childhood in the past is further separated into stages, ranging from the 'infanticidal stage' in the 4th century to the 'helping stage' or 'child saving', which commenced in the middle of the 20th century. It was through these stages that we have progressed from seeing children as having no particular needs to a distinct social group with a particular set of rights. Anthony Platt (1969) in his book *The Child Savers: The Intervention of Delinquency* clearly highlights the horrific treatment that many children went through, particularly orphans and those that were poor. Stone (1977) supports de Mause and Platt's thesis and claims that adults did not invest in children prior to the 16th century because it was not considered worthwhile. Moreover, it was not until the late 16th century that childhood was 'discovered' as a distinctive stage in the life cycle and that children began to be seen as 'different' from adults, with distinct natures and needs. As Rousseau (1764 in Jenks 1996) once claimed:

'Nature wants children to be children before they are men. If we deliberately pervert this order, we shall get premature fruits which are neither ripe nor well flavoured, and which soon decay ... Childhood has ways of seeing, thinking, and feeling peculiar to itself; nothing can be more foolish than to substitute our ways for them' (Rousseau 1764 in Jenks 1996: 3).

But how did this process of differentiation between childhood and adulthood commence? The recognition of childhood started, albeit very slowly, through the placing of responsibility on natural parents to provide a safe environment and education before children could take on an adult role and responsibilities (Prout and James 1990 in Skelton and Valentine 1998: 3). Clearly, this produced great disparities amongst children coming from different social classes (Macfarlane

1979). On the one hand, affluent families could afford the 'luxury of childhood with its demands on material provision, time and emotion' (Jenks 1996: 6). On the other hand, the majority of children, that is, those coming from financially disadvantaged families, were seen as a vital source of income and were expected to work as soon as they were physically independent and strong. To highlight the disparities amongst the upper class and working class, Muncie (2004) looks at the industrial revolution and points out that the children of the poor formed the bulk of factory labour, as they contributed to maintaining the necessary basic level of income for their families and were a cheap source of labour for factory owners. Therefore, it should not be particularly surprising to find that this situation remained unquestioned for many years. Throughout the 19th century, young people became more separated from the adult world. However, there was an increasing tension between the middle class, which was constantly concerned about being in control in order to protect their children from troublesome undisciplined poor children, and the working class. Pearson (1983 in Skelton and Valentine 1998: 4) points out that this tension has been repeatedly mobilised in definitions of youth and youth culture over the last 150 years and has been the protagonist of 'moral panics' about delinquent groups (Cohen 1997; Hall et al. 1978; Waddington 1986), youth crime and violence (Muncie 2004: 49–50; Gillis 1975) and hooliganism (Pearson 1983).

During the 20th century, psychologists gradually clarified the stages of childhood development, with the psychoanalytical work of Sigmund Freud (1946) and Erik Erikson (1982, 1950) achieving a particularly lasting influence.[2] Freud's work during the early 20th century sought to systematise and develop an in-depth understanding of the process of human cognitive and moral development and the consequences of early-childhood experiences on later stages of the life cycle. In this context, Freud conceived of the human psyche in terms of the complex and only partially conscious interaction between three psychological instances, the ego, the id and the superego:

'In his early work, Freud conceived of the ego as differentiating from the id (the inchoate instinctual forces in the individual) as a result of interaction with the environment. It is during this early stage of development that cognition also develops as a primary process (primitive or irrational thought) which is replaced in consciousness by secondary process (rational logical thought). Primary process is not eliminated, but repressed into the unconscious. In his later work, Freud postulated the development of the superego. This component of the personality is the source of much of the motivation for moral judgement and decision-making' (Knowles and McLean 1992: 49).

Erik Erikson drew upon Freud's work, among others, to propose an elaborate stage theory of ego development over the life course, with strong implications for an understanding of the emergence and changes in human moral judgment and actions:

'He postulated a series of eight core developmental conflicts which occur over the life span. As these are resolved, the individual develops psychological virtues (hope, will, purpose, confidence, fidelity, love, care and wisdom). This developmental sequence differs from the psychoanalytic stages in that it focuses on virtue and moral effectiveness and is not limited to infants and children, and it has at its focus the explanation of behaviour which would be considered specifically moral' (Knowles and McLean 1992: 49–50).

What follows from the work of Freud and Erikson is the important insight that the stages of human psycho-social development do not coincide neatly and necessarily with age; rather, the development of the psyche and the interaction of its different instances with each other is shaped by a variety of social contextual factors. These are brought to bear upon the development of the psyche with particular force during early developmental stages in childhood, but continue to be of lasting influence over the life course.

It is clear that notions of childhood have been gradually discovered, identified and constructed throughout the centuries and that, despite all these attempts at constituting childhood as a clearly bounded social category, it still remains fluid and contested:

'... The boundary separating child and adult is a decidedly fuzzy one. Adolescence is an ambiguous zone within which the child/adult boundary can be variously located according to who is doing the categorising. Thus, adolescents are denied access to the adult world, but they attempt to distance themselves from the world of the child. At the same time they retain this link with childhood' (Sibley 1995 in Skelton and Valentine 1998: 4).

These boundaries are even more pronounced if legal classifications are taken into account, such as the age at which young people can smoke, drink, work, earn money, consent to sexual intercourse etc. In this context, James points out that 'the only boundaries which define the teenage years are boundaries of exclusion which define what young people are not, cannot do or cannot be' (James 1986 in Skelton and Valentine 1998). Lanning (2005) takes this analysis further and argues that terms such as 'sexual exploitation of children and youth' or 'sexual exploitation of children and adolescents' imply that a youth or an adolescent is not a child. This begs the question: At what age does a child become a youth or an adolescent? (Waites 2005: 145; Lanning 2005: 51). In answering this question, a number of conflicts emerge between the law and society's viewpoint that need to be taken into account. The difficulty is that, when children are between the age of 13 and the age of 17, they may often look like adults; they are able to reproduce and may have developed an early sex drive. However, within some societies, they may not be considered to be children in legal terms. National, cultural and ethnic variations exist in attitudes about who is a child (Waites 2005; O'Donnell and Minner 2007). In order to be able to define who is a child, the most straightforward way is to refer to the law. However, in doing so, investigators and practitioners must also take into account their own perception as well as those of other professionals, juries and society as a whole (Lanning 2005: 51). Every state and society has the moral obligation to protect children because they constitute a particularly vulnerable group (Fortin 2003; UNICEF 1989). However, the legal context to support child protection is sometimes absent. Therefore, the definition of childhood is vital, as it provides some general guidelines as to who is a child, when a child becomes an adult and, more importantly, when children acquire fundamental rights and when they lose certain protection measures. The approval of the International Convention on the Rights of the Child (ICRC)) in 1989 proved to be a significant step forward, as it radically changed the interpretation of what childhood is (UNICEF 1989). The child was rendered from 'a passive object to be protected and cared for' into 'an active social subject with rights, a person in the process of growing, whose evolutive capacity must be respected and protected' (UNICEF 1989). The Universal Declaration of Human Rights (1948) adopted by the United Nations (UN) on 10 December 1948 offers a set of core values that distribute freedom and authority. Although it is not the aim of this book to present the debate between universality and cultural imperialism of the Universal Declaration, the UN describes human rights as essential rights to live as human beings. In other words, human rights offer basic standards without which people cannot live or survive (UNICEF 1989). With the adoption of the Universal Declaration in 1948, the UN set a standard on human rights. Furthermore, the UN Convention on the Rights of the Child (CRC) makes it clear that children require rights specifically designed around their needs. Children require these 'tailor-made' rights because they 'need special care and attention that adults do not' (UNICEF 1989). The UN therefore acknowledges that children are more vulnerable. It follows that the issue of vulnerability is a key element of the rights discourse. In this book, the definition of 'child' from the UN CRC is adopted. Article 1 affirms that a child is understood as 'every human being below the age of 18 years unless, under the law applicable to the child, majority is attained earlier' (United Nations 1989). However, this definition was deliberately broad so as 'not to jeopardise universal acceptance of the law' (UNICEF 1989). Thus, it is the responsibility of legislators at the national level to establish and specify when childhood begins. Following the ICRC, childhood ends when an individual reaches 18 years of age 'unless, in virtue of any applicable law, the person has come of age before then' (ICRC 1986). That is to say, not all national legislation agrees that the end of childhood is at the age of 18. It may be earlier or later, depending on various civil, penal or other political aspects. However, 'the ICRC permits States where coming of age occurs before 18 years old to fix a lower age limit for certain purposes. What is required is that this be done coherently according to the spirit and general principles of the Convention' (www.UNICEF.org). In the UK the distinction between children and young people is believed to be significant (Statham 2004; Chase and Statham 2004; Beckett 2007), since age difference was incorporated into the Sexual Offences Act for the first time in 2003. This book, while adhering to the focus on under 18-year-olds (so as to incorporate in the research young people just under 18), also makes this distinction; that is to say, those in their teenage years are considered as 'young people' and those under the age of 13 as 'children'. Moreover, although there is still tension in agreeing that those between the ages of 14 and 16 are not capable of providing informed consent as they are still children, this book follows the new legal definitions and considers them as 'young people'.[3]

Defining sexual offending

After having explored definitions of childhood, it is necessary to understand how the term 'sex offending' is generally interpreted from the standpoints of society and legislation. This will contribute to a better analysis of the problem of CSA, which will be analysed subsequently.

In law,[4] a sexual offence is defined as any behaviour which is both illegal and sexual. The Sexual Offences Act 1956, subsequently replaced by the Sexual Offences Act 2003 (SOA 2003), was an overarching proscriptive statute since it attempted to cover for the first time the broader generality of sexual offending. This definition included a number of sexual offences that are clearly sexually motivated and violent against a child or an adult, such as gross indecency with a child, rape, indecent assault and USI. It also included offences which may be sexually motivated but do not involve the commission of a sexual act, including for example abduction. Finally, it incorporated offences where sexual abuse did not take place, for example indecency between males and bigamy. However, it excluded offences that are sexually motivated and may lead to sexual abuse, for example exposure and grooming. The limited and ambiguous use of these categories had major implications for both what came to be defined as a 'sexual offence' and for the measurement of the incidence of convicted offences.

Calder (2004) argues that the term 'sex offending' is a legal concept that refers to any sexual behaviour prohibited by the law. For example, as Davidson (2002) points out, the Sexual Offences Act 1956 provided a list of sexual offences that form the basis of the official Home Office statistics currently in use. Those include: unlawful sexual intercourse with a girl under 13; unlawful sexual intercourse with a girl under 16; gross indecency with a child; rape; buggery; indecent assault on a male; indecent assault on a female; indecency between males; procuration; abduction; bigamy; and incest.

However, whilst the term 'offending' (supported by the legal definition) implies that a criminal conviction is almost granted, it is widely recognised that many sexual offences remain unreported, and many that are reported do not always secure a successful outcome. The reasons for this can involve lack of corroborative evidence, the age of the child and the stress of participating in any criminal forum or false allegations (Jones 2003) and the issue of sexual consent.

Defining consent

In sex crimes, the fundamental legal difference between victimisation of an adult and a child is the issue of consent (Lanning 2005; Greer 2003). Generally, consent is 'based on the knowledge of the full consequences' (Calder 2005: 2) and it is difficult to accept that children are capable of giving informed consent to adults to engage in sexual activities. When children feel threatened or fear that they might be, they may consent. However, this form of consent does not involve full awareness of the consequences of their actions and certainly cannot be defined as a 'free' or 'true' form of consent.

At this point, what needs to be clarified is that 'true consent' is not necessarily the same as 'legal consent', as there can be consent to an unlawful sexual act, thus leaving legal and true consent in conflict (Calder 2004: 2). Adams et al. (1984) claim that 'consent is possible only when there is equal power. Forcing someone to give in is not consent. Going along with something because of wanting to fit in with the group is not consent: If you can't say "no" comfortably then "yes" has no meaning. If you are unwilling to accept "no" then "yes" has no meaning' (Adams et al. 1984: 2). Practitioners may find Adams at al.'s definition useful and straightforward if applied to two adults consenting to having sexual intercourse. However, difficulties may emerge when a child is involved in the consent process.

Lanning (2005) favours the term 'complaint' over 'consent' to describe those children who cooperate in or 'consent' to their sexual victimisation. He claims that 'because children cannot legally consent to having sex with adults, this compliance should not in any way alter the fact that they are victims of serious crimes' (Lanning 2005: 49). However, the sexual victimisation of a child, which might involve a full complaint or the complete absence of it, is the final 'product' of the process of grooming that comes long before the abuse. It can be argued that a complaint is directly proportionate to the relationship that the abusers manage to establish with their victims. The stronger the relationship and the level of trust established between the child victim and the abuser, the higher the level of consent. Lanning (2005) appropriately claims that child victims are human beings with needs, wants and desires and that their frequent cooperation to their victimisation needs to be viewed as an understandable human characteristic that should have little or no criminal-justice significance. However, it can be perplexing to find that a child victim 'could behave like an adult and respond to the attention and affection of offenders by voluntarily and repeatedly returning to the offender's home' (Lanning 2005: 49) for more of what they perceive to be 'love' and 'care'.

Throughout the research conducted at the High Technological Crime Unit (HTCU), it has been difficult to understand images of abuse depicting children smiling and laughing as if they were taking pleasure from being involved in sexual activities with adults. This clearly depends on the relationship of trust that the abuser has cautiously and patiently established with the child over a long period of time. Sex offenders conveniently justify their behaviour by claiming that children desire and often initiate contacts with them. They are not wrong in using those justifications because children do go back to their perpetrators for more attention. However, it is the motive that pushes them to return to the sex offenders that is wrongly interpreted by sex offenders (Gillespie in Quayle and Taylor 2005). Their explanation strongly contradicts the reality of the well documented dynamics involved on the seduction of children by manipulative sex offenders (Backer and Beech 1993; Calder 2004; Davidson 2002; Davidson and Martellozzo 2009).

The age of consent for engaging in sexual activities varies by jurisdiction across Europe. For example, in Spain the age of consent is 13, as specified by the Spanish Penal Code (Article 181(2)). In other countries, such as Austria, Croatia, Italy and Portugal, the age of consent is 14; in France and Sweden it is 15. In Andorra, Belgium, Germany, the Netherlands and Norway the age of consent is 16 and in Greece it is 17 (Waites 2005). The age of consent for heterosexual, homosexual and bisexual acts in the UK is 16 (17 in Northern Ireland). Thus, generally speaking, the median ranges from 14 to 16 years across Western Europe (Waites 2005).

There are a number of grey areas in the law about the age of consent. For example, in the UK under the SOA 2003, a person below the age of 16 and over the age of 13 may consent to sex, but it would still be illegal. However, it recognises that mutually agreed, non-exploitative sexual activity between teenagers does exist and that often no harm comes from it. Nevertheless, this does not apply to children who are under the age of 13 as, according to the SOA 2003, they lack the capacity to consent to any kind of sexual relations. This point is of particular relevance and extremely progressive as, prior to the SOA 2003, the Crown Prosecution Service (CPS) always had to debate and evaluate what constituted consent even with young children. Waites (2005) asserted that some of the grey areas, which make age of consent a confusing and debated subject, are due to unspecific and untried legislation, changes in social attitudes and conflicts amongst different legislations across countries. Indeed, as previously argued, it is difficult to adopt a universal definition of a socially constructed problem such as CSA, as it is strongly influenced by the culture and the historical time in which it occurs (Sanderson 2007). The lack of agreement in defining what constitutes CSA makes it even more complicated to have an internationally agreed age of consent.

One of the most important points to be established in UK law by the SOA 2003 is the age of sexual consent, as it seems to have reawakened the debate in this country. The main aim and responsibility of the SOA 2003 is not to protect teenagers against themselves, but to preserve the freedom of individuals while protecting them from harm and abuse (Waites 2005). Inevitably, the law about consent has a number of inconsistencies and anomalies, and it underlines the general problems that underpin the legislation about sexual behaviour. Thus, should the law have been more flexible about the age of consent rather than becoming even stricter?

On the one hand, those who are not in favour of lowering the age of consent believe that young people may run the risk of being encouraged to have sex earlier and consequently may be more at risk of abuse, unwanted pregnancies and sexually transmitted diseases (Phillips 2005). On the other hand, those who support the idea of decreasing the age of consent argue that young people engage in sexual activities from an early age, and this is verified by the high number of teenage pregnancies in the UK (Griffiths 2002). This is supported by the findings of the National Survey of Sexual Attitudes and Lifestyles (2001), which reveals that a quarter of women and nearly a third of men have sex under the age of 16 and that the average age of first sexual experience is now 14 for girls and 13 for boys. Leading researchers (Henderson et al. 2007) at the Medical Research Council's Social and Public Health Sciences Unit in Glasgow found that teenage pregnancy rates in the UK are higher than any other country in Europe. Although recent figures for England and Wales showed a slight drop in pregnancies for 16- to 18-year-olds, they claim that the number of pregnancies amongst 14- and 15-year-olds is rising. Campaigners such as Peter Tatchell (2003), writing in *The Guardian* newspaper, have looked at these figures pragmatically. Tatchell claims that: 'an age of consent of 16 criminalises more than half the teenage population. This is an odd way of protecting them. Consent at 14, for both gay and straight relationships would be fairer and more realistic' (Tatchell 2003, Channel 4).

However, the reality is that, where there is mutual agreement, children of the same or similar age are unlikely to be prosecuted. As pointed out by Beckett (2007), if two seven-year-old children engage in sexual activities, these acts cannot be considered abuse. Nonetheless, they would inevitably raise a certain preoccupation, as an excessive sexual play can be symptomatic of their having been abused by others (Ferguson and O'Reilly 2001; Ferguson 2004). However, problems may arise if there is an age gap, if for example one child is 13 and the other 17. Can this relationship be deemed abusive? According to the law, the young male person has acted illegally and could be labelled as a sex offender. In reality, as argued by Ashworth (Ashworth 1999), under the Sexual Offences Act 1956, the Crown Prosecution Service reserved prosecutions for cases where the relationship, particularly amongst adults, was evidently abusive. However, younger offenders were more likely to be cautioned and this problem needed to be tackled. Recently, the new SOA 2003 has recognised that children can and often do exploit and sexually abuse vulnerable children. As a result, although the age of consent remains 16, the SOA 2003 does not prosecute mutually agreed sexual activities between young people of similar age unless it involves abuse or exploitation.

Therefore, consent and the unequal power balance between victim and perpetrator are vital elements in understanding child sexual abuse, and must be incorporated in definitions. However, as Calder advocates, there is a need to differentiate between true consent and legal consent as there can be consent to an unlawful sexual act, thus leaving legal and true consent in conflict (Calder 2004).

Non-consensual sex is always deemed abusive but consensual sex between an adult and a child is perceived unacceptable and unlawful because of the power differential and lack of understanding between the two parties.

Defining CSA

The problem of CSA is not a new phenomenon; on the contrary, it has very deep roots and it has been researched, policed, defined and redefined throughout the years (Beckett, Beech et al. 1994; Morrison, Erooga et al. 1994; Marshall 1997; Corby 1998; Thomas 2000; Ashenden 2004; Pritchard 2004; Erooga and Masson

2006; Beckett 2007; Davidson 2008; Gillespie 2004). However, the starting point of this research is to deconstruct and critically evaluate some of the definitions established in the past with the expectation of being able to delineate and understand what constitutes CSA today.

Many researchers studying the area of CSA come from various methodological traditions and therefore differ in their definitions of abuse in terms of the abusive relationship and the nature of the abusive acts. For example, some researchers may define abuse as that which involves physical contact only; some include non-contact abuse, while others may include both (Carich and Calder 2003).

History

Normative definitions of sexual abuse rely on the values and beliefs of individuals, professionals and society at large (Dunphy 2000). With a wider scope than the research explanation, these definitions include concepts such as children's dependence and their inability to give informed consent to such acts. An example of a problem with these definitions can be seen in society's growing acceptance of teenage sex. Normative definitions imply that people who engage in underage sex are committing CSA, albeit unwittingly, but do not face any charges from the police. One only has to look at maternity wards for confirmation that underage sex is now widespread.

Thus, finding a balanced and coherent definition for this complex phenomenon is rather challenging, as definitions tend to be either too narrow or too vague. Calder (2004) recognises this challenge and suggests that, if definitions are too narrow, they may restrict practitioners' understanding and intervention, figures of incidence and prevalence. On the other hand, if they are too broad, they may include elements that possibly will distract practitioners from focusing on the most serious and high risk cases (Carich and Calder 2003). However, as Davidson (2002) suggests, the starting point of any investigation and research into CSA should represent an attempt to define what constitutes sexually abusing children.

In a process of distillation and elucidation, MacLeod and Saraga (1988) explore the key elements that shape the definition of CSA. Those are:

- the betrayal of trust or responsibility   *Contact/non contact*
- the abuse of power
- the inability of children to consent
- the violation of another's right.

All of these four elements should be considered when attempting to establish a coherent and adequately comprehensive definition of CSA. Numerous attempts have been made to incorporate all these elements into a definition. However, in what follows, it should be noted that the focus is on how CSA has been interpreted and defined, primarily within a legal framework.

For example, Chase et al. (2004) recognise the importance of defining the term 'commercial child sexual exploitation' and distinguish this term from sexual abuse. Commercial child sexual exploitation has been defined as:

'. . . a fundamental violation of children's rights. It comprises sexual abuse by the adult and remuneration in cash or kind to the child or a third person or persons. The child is treated as a sexual object and as a commercial object. The commercial sexual exploitation of children constitutes a form of coercion and violence against children, and amounts to forced labour and a contemporary form of slavery.' (The Declaration and Agenda for Action of the World Congress Against Commercial and Sexual Exploitation of Children 1996: 694).

important point →

This definition reveals an element that is often absent in definitions: the differentiation between contact and non-contact offences. It is important to recognise that even if non-contact offences do not cause physical harm and may be considered 'minor' compared with contact offences, they may have devastating and traumatic consequences for the victim. Carich and Calder (2003) classify the two types of offences as follows:

Table 1.1 Classification of offences

Non-contact offences	Contact offences
Obscene phone calling	Physical sexual harassment
Stalking	Fondling (frottage)
Peeping (voyeurism)	Paedophilia
Flashing (exhibitionism)	Date rape
Verbal sexual harassment	Sadistic rape
Unwarranted computer sex	Marital rape
Photography	Bestiality
Pornography	Sexual attempted murder
Mail/computer sex	Sexual murder
	Serial sexual murder
	Necrophilia (sex with the dead)

Source: Carich and Calder (2003).

It is therefore of significant importance for this research particularly when, later in this book, online sexual abuse (production of indecent images and online grooming) is discussed and evaluated.

Other definitions of what constitutes CSA have been provided by experts in the field of sex offending. Estes (2001) for example defines the sexual abuse of children as:

'. . . practices by which a person, usually an adult, achieves sexual gratification, financial gain or advancement through the abuse or exploitation of a child's sexuality by abrogating that child's human right to dignity, equality, autonomy, and physical and mental well-being, i.e. trafficking, prostitution, sex tourism, mail-order-bride trade, involvement in pornography, stripping, battering, incest, rape and sexual harassment' (Estes 2001 in Chase and Statham 2004: 6).

Whilst this definition includes serious issues such as child trafficking, prostitution and exploitation, it overlooks other important elements including age, consent and unequal power. The same problem lies in the definition more recently offered by the Department of Health and Education (2007), where CSA is defined as:

> '. . . forcing or enticing a child or young person to take part in sexual activities, including prostitution, whether or not the child is aware of what is happening. The activities may involve physical contact, including penetrative (e.g. rape, buggery or oral sex) or non-penetrative acts. They may include non-contact activities, such as involving children in looking at, or in the production of, sexual online images or watching sexual activities, or encouraging children to behave in sexually inappropriate ways' (DfES 2006: 38 in Beckett 2007: 66).

As suggested by Beckett, this definition lacks any reference to age or 'the question of unequal power which is central to sexual abuse and to other kinds of abuse' (Beckett 2007: 70). He claims that, whilst there is no doubt that consensual sex between two adults is not abuse, non-consensual sex is always a form of abuse. Also, consensual sexual activities between young children are not abusive, although they might cause concern. However, sexual activities between an adult [*power difference*] and a child are abusive independently of consent being granted, in so far as the power differential between adult and child constitutes a defining feature of this type of situation (Beckett 2007).

This official guidance distinguishes between physical and non-contact abuse, but fails to acknowledge the age of the perpetrator and that of the child or young person. This lack of precision may lead to several controversies. Under the SOA 2003, the age of perpetrators has been raised to 18 and over. However, as stated by Davidson (2007) this may raise debates about the difference in sexual maturity between individuals who are 17 and 18 years of age, although a legal line has to be drawn somewhere. Problems in fact tend to increase exponentially when the perpetrator is a person under 18.

Through the examination of these various definitions of CSA, it is possible to grasp the difficulties involved in exploring this complex issue. In this study, the legal definition contained within the SOA 2003, which includes both physical and non-physical contact, is used. It is generally agreed that the consequences of non-physical abuse meet those of contact abuse, and therefore it is important to include this element in the definition. *Non-contact just as important.*

Defining paedophiles and paedophilia

The terms 'child sexual offender' and 'paedophile' are often taken to be synonymous. However, there are important classificatory and behavioural distinctions which need to be clarified before proceeding to establish the legislative context within which this book is situated. Not all child sex offenders are paedophiles;

paedophiles are a sub-set of child sex offenders (Miller 1997). Some may have fantasies about sex with children, but they do not act them out with a child. Others may abuse children in different ways, including non-physical sexual abuse and exploitation (www.ecpat.net/temp).

The commonly cited *Diagnostic and Statistical Manual of Mental Disorders* describes paedophilia as 'the act or fantasy of engaging in sexual activity with prepubertal children as a repeatedly preferred or exclusive method of achieving sexual excitement . . . Isolated sexual acts with children do not warrant the [clinical] diagnosis of paedophilia' (ECPAT International 2008). This definition considers paedophilia as the act or fantasy of engaging in sexual activities with pre-pubertal children, but it is narrow in the sense that it does not state whether those acts involve violence or if there is any level of consent. According to Miller (1997), one of the most useful distinctions that needs to be made, for law enforcement purposes, is between the preferential and situational child sex offender: 'Preferential offenders are paedophiles and situational offenders are those who prefer adult sexual partners but who, at times of stress, convenience or curiosity, may engage in sexual activities with children' (Miller 1997: 33).

Bebbington (1979) provides a useful definition and analysis of the term 'paedophilia'. He argues that:

'. . . paedophilia is the condition of being erotically attracted to pre-pubertal children. Paedophiliacs fall into three groups: heterosexual, homosexual, and indiscriminate. The last group is rarer and tends to be more disturbed. Paedophilic acts rarely involve violence or coercion and usually take the form of immature sex play such as looking, showing, kissing and fondling. Coitus is uncommon. There are three age groups of adult participants: the adolescent (who may be looked upon as the upper end of a normal curve of immature sexual activity), the middle aged and the elderly. The middle aged group are mainly married, but with marital and social difficulties; the paedophilia may involve incest. The elderly paedophile is characterised by social isolation. The adult partner is usually known to the child and on one study the child was an active participant in two thirds of the cases. The age distribution of child partners is different for the two sexes. In boys, the distribution gradually phases into the curve for adult homosexual acts, but in girls it peaks at age seven to nine' (Bebbington 1979: 42).

Although this definition was written almost 30 years ago, it represents an important starting point for the deconstruction of the label 'paedophile', which seems to have become the bogeyman of our age (Davidson and Martellozzo 2009; Silverman and Wilson 2002). Popular misconceptions have been reinforced by the media, whose representations are 'emphatic and unrestrained in their vitriol, and occasionally border on hysteria' (Greer and Jewkes 2005: 19). The definition provided by Bebbington suggests that a paedophilic act is rarely violent or coercive, but involves much softer and effective tactics in order to obtain the child's consent. What made Beddington's definition so distinctive at the time it was written was its inclusion of the crucial element of consent or active participation. The fact that children voluntarily participate in sexual activities with their predators was rarely included in previous definitions (Silverman and Wilson 2002), perhaps because it represents an 'uncomfortable reality' (Lanning 2005) with which people, even academics and practitioners, were reluctant to engage. However, although it is confusing and uncomfortable to see children voluntarily responding to the attention of their predators, this notion should represent an important element for researchers and practitioners to gain a better understanding of sex offenders' grooming strategies, to manage them more effectively and to understand how to advance child protection. Although Beddington's definition includes the element of children's voluntary participation, it lacks precision in delineating the age of both victim and offender. Bebbington claims that there are three age groups of adult participants, the first one being the adolescent. However, he does not clarify the age of the adolescent and the fact that adolescents may be interested in other adolescents who have not matured past puberty.

This book has sought to avoid the term 'paedophile' and uses instead the term (child) 'sex offender', 'abuser' or 'suspect' as working labels. As argued above, the term 'paedophile' is very misleading as to the nature and causes of child sexual abuse.

Conclusions

In this chapter, I have established the definitional framework and mapped out the current legislative terrain upon which the present analysis is conducted. A number of issues have been raised, which are central to engaging with the problem of online grooming.

Considering the large increases in the reported incidents of CSA in the Western world during the past 30 years, one could be forgiven for thinking that CSA is a modern phenomenon. However, as this chapter has argued, there is nothing to indicate that CSA is a problem of the late 20th century. On the contrary, it has been occurring behind closed doors for centuries (Lalor 2001; Thomas 2000). CSA can be perceived as a socially constructed phenomenon, as it is heavily influenced by the culture and the historical time in which it occurs (Sanderson 2007). Therefore, it is difficult to adopt a universally agreed definition when different societies have different views of what constitutes 'abuse', what is a 'child' and at what age a child is capable of giving informed 'consent' to adults to engage in sexual activities (Calder 2005). The lack of consensus in defining what constitutes CSA makes it even more complicated for researchers to understand the scale of the problem. Thus, this book uses the legal definition contained in the SOA 2003 as a framework, which includes both contact and non-contact offences including the production and distribution of indecent images and internet grooming. In the next chapter, attention shifts to the theories with a view to adding further definitions to the legislative middle ground sketched out here.

Notes

1 Sex between an adult and a child is non-consensual and abusive, whether consensual or not, because of the huge differences in power and understanding between the two parties.
2 The seminal work of Jean Piaget may of course be said to have been equally lasting in psychology, education and other social sciences. Discussing it in detail is unfortunately beyond the scope of this book.
3 The Act applies to England and Wales. It also applies to Northern Ireland except that its age of consent remains 17, that is to say, the 'Child Sex Offences' sections will cover 17-year-olds. It does not apply in Scotland.
4 The socio-political construction of relevant legal frameworks, in turn, constitutes an important issue to consider. I will turn to this matter in Chapter 4.

References

Adams, C., Fay, J. and Loreen-Martin, J. (1984) *No is not enough: helping teenagers avoid sexual assault*, San Luis Obispo California, Impact.

Aries, P. (1962) *Centuries of Childhood*, London, Cape.

Ashenden, S. (2004) *Governing Child Sexual Abuse. Negotiating the Boundaries of Public and Private*, Law and Science, London, New York, Routledge.

Ashworth, A. (1999) *Principles of Criminal Law*, New York, Oxford University Press.

Backer, M. and Beech, A. R. (1993) *Sex Offenders: A Framework for the Evaluation of Community-based Treatment*, London, Home Office Publications Unit.

Bebbington, P. (1979) *Sexual Disorders*, Cambridge, Polity Press.

Beckett, C. (2007) *Child Protection. An Introduction*, London, Sage.

Beckett, R., Beech, A., Fisher, D. and Fordham, A. S. (1994) *Community-based Treatment for Sex Offenders: An Evaluation of Seven Treatment Programmes*, London, Home Office Publications Unit.

Calder, M. (2004) *Child Sexual Abuse and the Internet: Tackling New Frontier*, Lyme Regis, Russell House Publishing.

Calder, M. (2005) *Children and Young People who Sexually Abuse. New Theory, Research and Practice Developments*, Lyme Regis: Russell House.

Carich, M. S. and Calder, M. (2003) *Contemporary treatment of adult male sex offenders*, Dorset, Russell House Publishing.

Chase, E. and Statham, J. (2004) *The Commercial Sexual Exploitation of Children & Young People; an Overview of Key Literature and Data*, Thomas Coram Research Unit.

Cohen, S. (1997) *Folk Devils and Moral Panics: The Creation of Mods and Rockers*, Oxford, Basil Blackwell.

Corby, B. (1998) *Managing Child Sexual Abuse Cases*, London, Jessica Kingsley Publishers.

Davidson, J. and Martellozzo, E. (2009) Internet sex offenders: Risk, control and state surveillance, in M. Johnson and S. Scalter (eds), *Individual Freedom, Autonomy and the State*, Cambridge, Hart Press.

Davidson, J. C. (2002) The context and practice of community treatment programmes for child sexual abusers in England and Wales. *Department of Social Policy*, London, London School of Economics and Political Science.

Davidson, J. (2007) *Current Practice and Research into Internet Sex Offending*, Risk Management Authority Research, London, Department of Social and Political Studies, University of Westminister.

De Mause, L. (1976) *The History of Childhood*, London, Souvenir Press.

Dunphy, R. (2000) *Sexual Politics*, Edinburgh, Edinburgh University Press.

ECPAT International (2008) *Paedophilia*, http://www.ecpat.net.

Erikson, E. (1950) *Childhood and Society*, New York, Norton.

Erikson, E. (1982) *The Life Cycle Completed: A Review*, New York, Norton.

Erooga, M. and Masson, H. (2006) *Children who Sexually Abuse Others. Current Developments and Practice Responses*, London, Routledge.

Ferguson, H. (2004) *Protecting Children in Time: Child Abuse, Child Protection and the Consequences of Modernity*, Basingstoke, Palgrave Macmillan.

Ferguson, H. and O'Reilly, H. (2001) *Keeping Children Safe: Child Abuse, Child Protection and the Promotion of Welfare*, Dublin, A&A Farmar.

Fortin, J. (2003) *Children's Rights and the Developing Law*, London, Lexis Nexis, Butterworths.

Freud, A. (1993) *The Ego and the Mechanisms of Defence*, New York, International Universities Press (Original work published 1936).

Gillespie, A. (2008) *Child Exploitation and Communication Technologies*, Dorset, Russell House Publishing.

Gillis, J. R. (1975) The evolution of juvenile delinquency in England 1890–1914. *Past & Present 1975*, 67, 96–126.

Greer, C. (2003) *Sex Crime and the Media. Sex Offending and the Press in a Divided Society*, London, Willan Publishing.

Greer, C. and Jewkes, Y. (2005) Extremes of otherness: Media images of social exclusion. *Social Justice (Special edition on emerging imaginaries of regulation, control and oppression)*, 32, 20–31.

Griffiths, J. (2002) Sexually transmitted infections in H. O. Commons (ed).

Hall, S., Critcher, C., Jefferson, T., Clarke, J. and Roberts, B. (1978) *Policing the Crisis*, London, Macmillan.

Henderson, M., Wight, D., Raab, G., Abraham, C., Parkes, A., Scott, S. and Hart, G. (2007) The impact of a theoretically based sex education programme (SHARE) delivered by teachers on NHS registered conceptions and terminations: final results of cluster randomised trial. *British Medical Journal*, 334, 133–5.

International Convention on the Rights of the Child (ICRC) (1986).

Jenks, C. (1996) *Childhood: Key Ideas*, London, Routledge.

Jones, T. (2003) Child abuse or computer crime? The proactive approach, in A. Macvean and P. Spindler (eds), *Policing Paedophile on the Internet*, Eastbourne, East Sussex, The New Police Bookshop on behalf of The John Grieve Centre.

Knowles, T. R. and Mclean, F. G. (1992) *Psychological Foundations of Moral Education and Character Development: an Integrated Theory of Moral Development*, Washington D.C., CRVP.

Lalor, K. (2001) *The End of Innocence. Child Sexual Abuse in Ireland*, Cork, Oak Tree Press.

Lanning, K. (2005) Compliant child victims: Confronting an uncomfortable reality, in E. Quayle and M. Taylor (eds.), *Viewing Child Pornography on the Internet. Understanding the Offence, Managing the Offender, Helping the Victims*, Lyme Regis, Russell House Publishing.

Macfarlane, A. (1979) *The Origins of English Individualism: The Family, Property and Social Transition*, Cambridge, Cambridge University Press.

Macleod, M. and Saraga, E. (1988) Challenging orthodoxy. *Feminist Review*, 28.

Marshall, W. L. (1997) *The prevalence of convictions for sexual offending*, London, Home Office.

Miller, K. (1997) Detection and reporting of child sexual abuse (specifically paedophilia): A law Enforcement perspective. *Paedophilia: Policy and Prevention*, 12, 32–8.

Morrison, T., Erooga, M. and Beckett, R. (1994) *Sexual offending against children*, London, Routledge.

Mullen, P. and Fleming, J. (1998) Long term Effects of Child Sexual Abuse, Melbourne, National Child Protection Clearinghouse Australia.

Muncie, J. (2004) *Youth and Crime*, London, Sage.

National Survey of Sexual Attitudes and lifestyles (2001) http://www.ias.org.uk/resources/data-dictionary/dd-series16.pdf.

O'Donnell, I. and Minner, C. (2007) *Child Pornography*, London, Willan Publishing.

Pearson, G. (1983) *Hooligan: A History of Respectable Fears*, Basingstoke, Macmillan.

Phillips, A. (2005) It is time we adults grew up. *Guardian*, London.

Platt, A. (1969) *The Child Savers: The Invention of Delinquency*, Chicago, University of Chicago Press.

Pritchard, C. (2004) *The Child Abusers. Research and Controversy*, Maidenhead, Open University Press.

Quayle, E. and Taylor, M. (2005) *Viewing Child Pornography on the Internet*, Lyme Regis, Russell House Publishing.

Sanderson, C. (2007) *The Seduction of Children. Empowering Parents and Teachers to Protect Children from Child Sexual Abuse*, London, Jessica Kingsley Publishers.

Silverman, J. and Wilson, D. (2002) *Innocence Betrayed. Paedophilia, the Media and Society*, Cambridge, Polity Press.

Sir John Stevens (2002) Public Speech. Leicester University.

Skelton, T. and Valentine, G. (1998) *Cool Places: Geographies of Youth Cultures*, London, Routledge.

Statham, J. (2004) Effective services to support children in special circumstances. *Child: Care, Health & Development*, 30, 589–98.

Stone, L. (1977) *The Family, Sex and Marriage in England 1500–1800*, London, Weidenfeld and Nicolson.

Tatchell, P. (2003) http://www.channel4.com/health.

The Declaration and Agenda for Action of the World Congress Against Commercial and Sexual Exploitation of Children (1996) Stockholm.

Thomas, T. (2000) *Sex Crime: Sex Offending and Society*, London, Willan Publishing.

UNICEF (1989) United Nations International Convention on the Rights of the Child, 1989, http://www.unicef.org.

Waddington, P. A. J. (1986) Mugging as a moral panic: a question of proportion. *British Journal of Sociology*, 32, 245–59.

Waites, M. (2005) *The Age of Consent: Young People, Sexuality and Citizenship*, Palgrave Macmillan.

Wells, M., Finkelhor, D., Wolak, J. and Kimberly, J. (2007) Defining child pornography: Law enforcement dilemmas in investigations of internet child pornography possession. *Police Investigations Police Practice & Research: An International Journal*, 8, 269–82.

Chapter 2

A theoretical analysis of real and virtual child sexual abuse

Introduction

In this chapter I introduce the main theories that inform the analysis within this book and highlight significant themes and tensions that arise in the attempt to explain why child sexual abuse (CSA) occurs in both the cyber and the real world. I embark on the argument that in order to reduce the problem of CSA effectively, understand CSA in the context of online abuse and manage the risks posed by sex offenders' behaviour, it is important to understand why and how sex offenders get to the point of sexually abusing a child. However, explaining why men and women commit sexual abuse, and how best to rehabilitate them is always a work in progress (Gannon, Polaschek and Polaschek 2005) because, as explained by Finkelhor (1986), there are not 'single factor theories' to explain sexual interest in children. Furthermore, CSA is a genuinely multidisciplinary problem that requires the close cooperation of a wide range of professionals with different skills.

According to Cossin (2000), the central question that engages researchers of CSA is what motivates men to engage in sexual activities with children rather than with other adults. CSA is a problem of major concern to society and, as is true of many complex problems, has more than one cause. Indeed, there is no one single answer to why sex offenders engage in sexual abuse; nor is there only one type of sex offender. There are a number of theories that are useful for a better understanding of what drives men and some women to deviate from the norm and engage in sexual activities with children. However, there are clear and important areas of overlap within and between these theories. For the purposes of discussion in this chapter, they can be grouped under three main headings: biological, psychological (crucially including paradigmatically dominant cognitive behavioural approaches) and sociological.

In this chapter I intend, first, to map out the issues surrounding the problem of under-reporting CSA; secondly, critically to evaluate the key theoretical approaches to understanding CSA; and, thirdly, to situate the phenomenon of online CSA within this wider context. This chapter will thus provide a comprehensive discussion of current theoretical perspectives on CSA.

Explaining the under-reporting of CSA

What makes it difficult to determine the extent of CSA is that official statistics of sex offences are extremely unreliable as indicators of the true volume of deviant behaviour in society (West 2000b). In addition, they refer to the number of offences committed and not to the number of offenders. What is also important to consider is that statistics may vary widely according to how questions are framed and what is counted as abuse (West 2000a) (the definition of abuse is dealt with at length in Chapter 1). There has been considerable clinical work done on child sex offenders (Abel et al. 1987). In 1987, Abel et al. carried out a study with 232 child sex offenders to quantify how many sex offences they committed. From this study, it was hypothesised that offenders may abuse, over their lifetime, an average of 76 victims each. While these figures may appear disturbing, only a small percentage of child sex offenders come to the notice of law enforcement, and an even smaller proportion are convicted for their crimes (Miller 1997). There is no existing empirical research establishing the true extent of CSA and it is unlikely that such research will ever be carried out. It is believed that only 10 per cent of cases are reported (Judge W. Taylor 2004). However, whatever the true figure is, it is a serious problem and far greater than recorded crime statistics suggest.

There are at least two main obstacles impeding the development of a coherent and reliable overview of the nature and extent of CSA in England and Wales and across other jurisdictions: the lack of reporting of CSA and the definitional problems relating to the various legal and social frameworks within which CSA is defined, understood, policed and prosecuted. The reasons why CSA is reported so rarely to the relevant authorities have been well rehearsed in the research literature and will be outlined in the remainder of this chapter. The definitional and legislative complications related to ascertaining the nature and extent of CSA are more complex and merit a fuller analysis. For this reason these and other definitional problems have been addressed in Chapter 1.

The silent nature of the victims of abuse has been well documented in recent times and has been considered closely by charities specialising in child protection and the prevention of cruelty to children (NSPCC 2007). The reasons for this silence and therefore for the significant level of under-reporting are complex and varied. Cawson et al. (2000), in a study on child maltreatment in the UK, found that three-quarters (72 per cent) of sexually abused children did not tell anyone about the abuse at the time but that 27 per cent told someone later. Around one-third (31 per cent) still had not told anyone about their experience(s) by early adulthood.

LaFontaine (1990) suggests that this large percentage of unreported cases is a symptom of an enforced silence around the topic. It is important that the matter of silence is understood, as it relates to the issues of lack of understanding of sexual matters combined with feelings of guilt and embarrassment. Therefore, it may be useful to delineate some of the suggestions available that explain why sexual crimes are not reported to the same extent as others. This is not to suggest that other crimes such as physical assault and physical abuse are commonly disclosed. On the contrary, research suggests that we know very little also about the extent of domestic violence and child maltreatment in the UK. Official data advise us on what is known to the authorities, and many offences against children are known to go unreported.

What may help the formulation of a constructive answer to why children fail to report sexual abuse is the analysis and evaluation of the seduction or grooming process which begins much before any physical contact (Cawson, Wattam, Brooker and Kellyon 2000). It usually begins with the identification of the appropriate child victim and it continues, often for a long time, through careful and meticulous research about the interests, passions and weaknesses of the child.

Arguably, preferential sex offenders know how to select a child for potential sexual abuse: they are usually very good at obtaining cooperation and gaining control of the child through well planned seduction that employs adult authority, attention and gifts (Finkelhor 1994; Finkelhor et al. 1986). Thus, given the complex strategies that sex offenders employ to reach their aims, it is understandable that many victims fail to realise the ultimate goal of their perpetrators. Even when they do realise that attention, affection and gifts were only offered as a means toward exploitation, they may find it difficult to report the abuse. Difficulties may arise as a result of a strong bond created with the offender over time, or through feelings of guilt and a sense of compulsion to inform the offender of their decision first, thus placing themselves at risk of being persuaded to remain silent (Lanning 2005). Indeed, the offender may continue to manipulate the child even after disclosure has been made and an investigation has begun – for example, by making the child feel guilty or disloyal. The reasons why children do not report sexual abuse can be complex and varied in both the real and the cyber world. One of the reasons why online abuse tends not to be reported is because most children do not realise they have been abused and do not understand what constitutes virtual abuse (this concept is explored further in Chapter 3). Should online grooming at some point become physical abuse in the real world, then those reasons for not disclosing abuse to responsible parents or authorities already discussed above equally apply here. There are certain important spatial and temporal dynamics to the online grooming of children which will be discussed elsewhere in this book. Not least, there is the 'paradox of online intimacy', in which spatially distant strangers effectively abuse vulnerable children within the intimate surroundings of the child's home.

Physiological and biological theories of child sexual abuse

Biological and physiological theories have been used for centuries to explain why men commit sexual abuse. Historically, numerous theorists and researchers have sought to explain delinquent behaviour (both male and female) through reference to either biological or psychological abnormalities, paying scant attention to wider social and environmental factors (Lombroso 1835–1909; Ferri 1855–1929; Garofalo 1852–1934; Goring 1870–1919; Sheldon 1999; Pollack 1950; Marques et al. 2000). Although these ideas have subsequently been persuasively challenged and are now largely discredited in their crudest form, they still need to be recalled, since they have provided the starting point for many criminological debates. When considering the issue of male criminality, Lombroso and Ferrero (1985) applied their theory of the born criminal, thus focusing on so-called 'born male criminals', arguing that men who engaged in crime had a biological or physiological predisposition to crime. The environment was also taken into account but it was viewed as 'a potential trigger of the biological force' (Muncie 2004: 25).

The literature that covers this area of research tends to focus on the existence of brain abnormalities and testosterone levels in sex offenders (Marshall 1996). However, there is very little evidence to support the proposition that there is a relationship between sexually deviant behaviour and physiological or biological impairments. The focus should be placed on explaining why, if sexual offending is caused by biological or physiological factors, abusers choose to assault children. In general, it could be argued that traditional criminology has largely failed to answer this key question.

Managing sex offenders: a biological perspective

In an attempt to explain sexual abuse, biological theories are still widely applied, particularly when it comes to developing treatments for sex offenders. For example, biological theories have linked sexual behaviour to the dysfunction of the hormonal and nervous system. Some scholars, such as Flor-Henry (1987), believe that sexual deviations are, overwhelmingly, a consequence of the male pattern of cerebral organisation. That is to say, male offenders' sex drive is difficult to control because their level of sex hormones is too high. Marques et al. (2000) support Flor-Henry's arguments and claim that male sex hormones (androgens), which promote sexual desire and orgasm, are responsible for the regulation of 'aggression, cognition, emotion and personality' (Tallon and Terry 2004). Therefore, it is hypothesised that there is a strong correlation between aggression and high testosterone levels (Ehlers et al.; Rada et al. 1976) which, in the early 1970s, was believed to be controllable by using chemical castration. This is a chemical way of mimicking what is achieved by physical castration (the removal of the testicles), which produces about 95 per cent of all testosterone in the male body. It involves the regular taking of oestrogen drugs such as Cyprotene Acetate (which suppresses physiological sexual responses and libido) and Medoxyprogesterone Acetate (MPA), more commonly known as Provera in its pill form. There is also the option of taking Depo-Provera, in its intramuscular injection form, which is known for its ability to reduce the sex drive in less than two weeks (Murray 1987).

Setting aside obvious ethical considerations, chemical interventions do appear to have a substantial effect on recidivism (Bradford 1988: 194). Research in

Denmark and Switzerland found strong effects when using these types of measures, with very low recidivism rates (for a detailed critique see Baker (1984); Becker and Hunter (1992)). In his article on 'the antiandrogen and hormonal treatment of sex offenders', Bradford (1990) provided evidence that the treatment of sex offenders of this kind is clearly successful in reducing recidivism rates. However, he argues that CPA should have limited use in the correctional facility, as it may become part of a 'subtle coercion process involving the offender parole contingent on accepting treatment' (Bradford 1990: 301), as it does not provide the tool necessary to control his offending behaviour (see also Grubin (1998)).

For a number of reasons, it can be argued that the research evidence is very inconclusive. First of all, the clinical samples used for research are arguably very small, entailing a lack of validity and reliability. Furthermore, reconviction rates amongst this offender group are not indicative of the actual amount of reoffending; for example, with what certainty is it possible to claim that after treatment further offences were not perpetrated?

Chemical castration has also had its supporters in the UK. In 2007, a similar strategy was considered by the Home Office, which involved voluntary ingestion of libido-reducing drugs or anti-depressants, representing one of the new range of methods recently implemented by the Home Office to enhance the protection of children from sex offenders (http://news.bbc.co.uk/1/hi/uk/6746965.stm). Karen Harrison (2007), in her article 'The High-risk Sex Offender Strategy in England and Wales: Is Chemical Castration an Option?', argues that this method, which is currently used in a number of countries in Europe and worldwide, helps to control men's sexual urges and desire and therefore reduces the possibility of abuse. Also Donald Findlater (http://news.bbc.co.uk/1/hi/uk/6746965.stm) from the Lucy Faithfull Foundation, a child protection charity, believes medical treatments are only part of the package needed to tackle paedophilia and claims that 'some people need treatment such as biological or chemical measures to support psycho-logical treatment' (http://news.bbc.co.uk/1/hi/uk/6746965.stm). These treatments can only take place on a voluntary basis, as sex offenders need first to be able not only to recognise, but fully and openly to acknowledge the extent and nature of their behaviour towards children.

However, since sex offenders frequently deny the nature of their crime, very few are currently treated under this scheme. According to Home Secretary: 'a voluntary system of medication may well be useful in some cases' (House of Lords 2007), but the reality is that it deals with a small proportion of self-confessed sex offenders. Therefore, the great majority of sex offenders, including many of the most dangerous predators, who remain either unwilling or incapable of acknowledging their attraction to children, are overlooked entirely by the programme as it currently operates. In an attempt to increase the range and impact of chemical castration, former Home Secretary John Reid suggested offering convicted sex offenders a choice: either to take part in the programme or to remain incarcerated in prison. Such a development, if implemented, would of course fundamentally undermine the voluntary nature of the programme, and therefore the philosophical underpinnings upon which it has thus far been based.

Furthermore, the initiative has been welcomed by the UK Government after research conducted in Scandinavia showed that the use of drugs can reduce the risk of further offending. In countries such as Denmark, Sweden and eight states in the United States, similar schemes have already been adopted and, to date, have proved to be successful (Weinberger, Sreenivasan and Sreenivasan 2005). However, these studies highlight a common argument that sexual violence is not necessarily about sex but instead about control and power. Therefore, castration may be viewed as a fruitless intervention.

It seems likely that any biological intervention into offending behaviour, however minimal or drastic, would need to be supplemented with parallel and complementary interventions. The following sections consider those theories of sexual offending behaviour grounded primarily within the discipline of psychology.

Psychological theories of child sexual abuse

In this section, key current psychological theories that explain the causation of child sexual abuse are presented and analysed. These have been identified as psychoanalytical, learning and cognitive behavioural theories.

Finkelhor's precondition theory

David Finkelhor's contribution to the understanding of what motivates sex offenders to abuse children sexually has also been of great significance. Finkelhor believes that there was a pressing need for a new theory to understand child sexual abuse and, as a result, he created a new model which he defined as 'the four preconditions model' (Finkelhor 1984). He argued:

> 'What theory we have currently is not sufficient to account for what we know. Nor is it far-reaching enough to guide the development of new empirical research'. (Finkelhor 1984: 53).

Finkelhor believed that existing theories needed to be more comprehensive and cognisant of the fact that CSA is a widespread social problem that has a socio-logical dimension. Furthermore, in order to understand the problem effectively, he believed that the knowledge about the characteristics of the offender, victims and families could not be treated separately but needed to be collated and analysed together. Indeed, Finkelhor's empirical work on the development of his new theory is exhaustive, and worthy of review.

Finkelhor's theory suggests that four factors need to be met for CSA to occur. These are:

'1   A potential offender needed to have some motivation to abuse a child sexually.

2   The potential offender had to overcome internal inhibitions against acting on that motivation.

3   The potential offender had to overcome external impediments to committing sexual abuse.

4   The potential offender or some other factor had to undermine or overcome a child's possible resistance.'

(Finkelhor 1984: 54)

The theory supports the notion that, in order for a man to engage in the sexual abuse of a child, all four specific preconditions, namely motivation, internal inhibitions, external inhibitions and resistance, must be met. Thus, to abuse a child sexually, offenders need to be first sexually *motivated*. But, how does a person, whether an adult or an adolescent, become interested in having sexual contact with a child? To explain this, Finkelhor makes use of three components: emotional congruence, sexual arousal and blockage. He employs the term *emotional congruence* to refer to abusers who feel compelled to select children in preference to adults, as a consequence of emotional immaturity and low self-esteem coupled with an inability to relate to adults and possible early social deprivation. Therefore, the concept refers to feelings of 'emotional congruence' with children precisely because offenders cannot relate well to adults and have difficulty in building and maintaining adult relationships. As a result, they turn to children who are easily drawn into relationships and manipulated (see also Carich and Calder 2003; Glancy 1986; Smallbone and Dadds 1998). Secondly, sexual arousal refers to the origins of sexual attraction to children where children represent the source of sexual gratification for the abuser (Carich and Calder 2003). Thirdly, blockage refers to problems associated with the abusers' inability to meet their sexual gratification elsewhere. Finkelhor argues that these three components are not mutually exclusive:

'. . . an offender may sexually abuse a child without necessarily being sexually aroused by the child; he may do so simply because such abuse satisfies an emotional need to degrade' (Carich and Calder 2003: 55).

Motivation is only the first of the four steps that leads sex offenders to abuse children sexually. According to Finkelhor (1984), even if motivation is strong and persistent, in order to abuse the child sexually, offenders will need to overcome their *internal inhibitions*. That is to say, if the offender is inhibited by taboos, which antagonises his motivation, then he will not abuse (Carich and Calder 2003).

External inhibitions, such as the environment outside both the offender and the child, also need to be overcome in order to create a convenient situation for the offence to take place. According to Bottoms and Wiles (1997), these can refer to accessibility, which represents the physical qualities of the situation such as visibility, ease of access and lack of observation at the scene of the crime. This viewpoint bears a close resemblance to 'opportunity' theory (Cohen and Felson 1979), which argues that for a crime to occur there is a need for: a specific situation (time and location); a target (the potential child victim); and the absent guardians (parents' or carers' supervision). In reality, a child cannot be constantly supervised. However, clinical research suggests that lack of supervision and guidance may represent a contributing factor to online abuse (Davidson and Martellozzo 2004; Livingstone and Bober 2005).

Finkelhor's last precondition is about overcoming the *resistance* of the child. The preferential sex offender is usually very good at obtaining cooperation and gaining control of the child through well-planned grooming techniques that may employ adult authority, attention and gifts, and many sex offenders seem to know clearly how to select a child for potential sexual abuse. Research suggests that sexual offenders often target children with particular characteristics:

> '[c]hildren in the care of the state; children who have experienced prior abuse; emotionally immature children with learning difficulties and problems with peer friendships; children with strong respect for adult status; children from single parent families; children who will cooperate for a desired reward (such as money and/or computer games); children who have been sexually abused and are displaying learned behaviour which a paedophile will spot; and children with low self-esteem' (Stanley 2001:14).

However, as Lanning argues, '*any* child is vulnerable to seduction by *any* adult, but troubled children from dysfunctional families targeted by adults who are authority figures seem to be at even greater risk of being seduced' (Lanning 2005: 57; emphasis in original). When children realise they are in danger they may impose resistance. However, no matter how much resistance is manifested by the child, this may not necessarily prevent abuse (Finkelhor in Carich and Calder 2003: 21).

Ward and Beech (2006) find Finkelhor's model original as it looks at CSA as a multifaceted phenomenon incorporating both physiological and sociological variables. Furthermore, it emphasises the importance of socialisation, cultural norms and biological factors in offending behaviour (Ward and Gannon 2006). Fisher and Beech (1999) in their review of 'current practice in Britain with sex offenders' underline the influential work of Finkelhor by maintaining that cognitive behavioural therapy, with reliance on Finkelhor's four preconditions model and the offence cycle (which will be explained and evaluated later in this chapter), is found to be the most widely used method particularly by the National Probation Service and the Prison Service.

On the whole, through this theory, Finkelhor (1984) has created a framework which describes who is more at risk of offending in both a familial and extra-familial environment. Therefore, Finkelhor's theoretical model has contributed in an innovative and comprehensive manner to the understanding of CSA and has thus been used in this research as a theoretical framework to aid the understanding of the problem of online CSA.

Cognitive behavioural theories

According to Palmer et al. (2008) 'cognitive behaviour' theory emerged from combining two theoretical approaches in psychological research and psychotherapy. In other words, it is 'an amalgam of two previously separate theories: behaviourism and cognitivism' (ibid: 16). Whilst cognitive issues were directly brought into mainstream behavioural therapy in the mid–1970s (Marshall et al. 1999), behavioural theory, since its formulation, acknowledged the strong relationship that exists between the external environment and individuals' internal world. Therefore, behaviour is seen as the product of the interplay between personal/internal situations and situational/external factors (McGuire 2000). In the cognitive behavioural approach, the focus is upon confronting distorted thinking about children, developing victim empathy, increasing offender awareness about the harmful long-term consequences of action upon victims and enabling abusers to control their offending behaviour via behavioural modification techniques (Beckett 1994).

However, Quayle et al. (2006) argue that sex offenders do not form a homogeneous group of individuals and tend to be affected differently by situational/ external factors (McGuire 2000). It has been acknowledged that sex offenders tend to share similar distortions about their victims, the nature of the offences committed and their responsibility for their offending behaviour, and that they are often not cognisant of their wrongdoing (Middleton 2004) as they neutralise the consequences of their actions (Costello 2000). Sykes and Matza's (1957) seminal work, originally formulated to understand juvenile delinquency, explains this process of denial or deflection of blame primarily through five 'techniques of neutralisation':

1   denial of responsibility for the act
2   denial of the injury caused
3   denial of the victim
4   commendation of the accuser
5   appeal to higher loyalties.

Sykes and Matza (1957) argue that at some point in their early years most people engage in deviant behaviour. However, in order to route criminal behaviour towards becoming an habitual offender, individuals need to rationalise their deviance, in effect convincing themselves that their behaviour is not wrong. This can be interpreted as a process through which the individual neutralises the harmful and immoral aspects of his actions prior to carrying them out. Indeed, rationalisations for committing crime serve to neutralise psychological restraints, such as

guilt, against criminal behaviour (D'Ovidio et al. 2009). Neutralisation thus operates as an important feature of the motivation to commit criminal acts. Similarly,
techniques of neutralisation are routinely used by sex offenders in order to justify
or rationalise their abusive behaviour.

Whilst specific reference to Sykes and Matza is almost entirely absent from the
literature on CSA, a number of commentators have mobilised similar concepts to
Sykes and Matza's techniques of neutralisation in order to explain child sex
offending. For example, Scott and Layman (1968), in seeking to explain CSA,
differentiated between 'excuses', where offenders admit what they have done is
wrong but fail to take responsibility for their actions, and 'justifications', where
offenders admit what they have done but deny the seriousness of their actions. Such
explanations have also been used to explain how sex offenders avoid acceptance of
responsibility for their offending (Fisher and Beech 1999; Quayle et al. 2006;
Davidson and Martellozzo 2004). For example, Fisher and Beech (1999) observe
that many sex offenders may seek to abrogate responsibility for their behaviour by
insisting that it is a reflection of their love for and desire to nurture children.

Today, cognitive behavioural approaches are widely applied to intervening
with offenders but more specifically with sex offenders; indeed, the UK Sex
Offender Treatment Programme (probation and prison) is based upon this
approach. Of relevance to this cognitive behavioural perspective is the concept of
the 'cycle of offending' behaviours mediated by cognitions, an amalgam of two
previously separate theories: behaviourism and cognitivism (Wolf 1985).

The cycle of offending

'The cycle of offending' model developed by Steven Wolf (1985) has been one of
the most influential theories that has helped academics to understand the nature of
sexual offending and has aided practitioners in treating sex offenders (Wolf 1985;
Eldridge 1998; Finkelhor 1986; Sullivan 2002). Through the cycle of offending,
which traces the cognitive, psychological, learning and behaviour components of
sexual offending, Wolf created a comprehensive model that partly explains the
development and maintenance of sexually deviant behaviour. Furthermore, it
argues that fantasy-masturbation-orgasm may become an addiction and lead to
sexual deviant fantasy, which increases the possibility of moving on to contact
sexual offences (Wolf 1985; Finkelhor 1986; Eldridge 1998; Sullivan and Beech
2004). The strength of Wolf's addiction cycle is the detailed consideration of
fantasy, arousal and planning in sexual offending, and the clear cyclical structure
which the offender may allow once, or repeatedly.

Sullivan's spiral of sexual abuse

Sullivan's (2002) theory on the 'Spiral of Sexual Abuse' has expanded upon
Wolf's model and deserves close analysis. This theory was developed as a result
of clinical assessment and treatment work with a large number of sex offenders

and it helped practitioners to address some of the difficulties implicit in the clinical application of the previous models (see Eldridge 1998; Finkelhor 1986). Through the 'spiral', Sullivan (2002) explains how abuse develops and takes place: it starts with the initial motivation, which is immediately blocked by the internal struggle. However, this seems to decline as the motivation and sexual desire increases. It then moves on to the decision to offend and follows the steps taken to facilitate the abuse and deal with the result. It is important to note that not all offenders are linked to the same motivation to abuse sexually. Sullivan (ibid) explains that on average 65 per cent of sex offenders report that they have been sexually abused as children. Mullen at al. (1995), in their study of long-term impact on the abuse of children, reinforce Sullivan's explanation and suggest that:

> '. . . child abuse, and sexual abuse in particular, has come to be regarded by many clinicians as making a powerful contribution to adult pathology' (Mullen et al. 1995: 19).

That is to say, the cycle of abuse may continue when the victims of sexual abuse become parents themselves. However, this does not explain why some children who have been sexually abused would, in their adult life, abuse other children and others would not. This approach also fails to explain the highly gendered nature of CSA – that is, why the majority of perpetrators are male and the majority of victims are female? Nor can it explain why it is that so few females abused as children go on to become abusers in their adult lives but many more men do. The fact that they have been sexually abused might play a part in understanding the journey towards offending but this cannot be considered as the only factor.

As Finkelhor (1986) claims, factors such as sexual preference and emotional congruence or connection with children cannot be overlooked. Undoubtedly, this is not to suggest, for example, that those people who are in contact with children or are exposed to indecent images of children during the course of their work (such as police officers, therapists, researchers) may develop a sexual arousal to children or a desire to abuse them to feed this arousal. On the contrary; as Sullivan (2002) suggests, those people would be horrified or frightened by the experience of encountering a 'brick wall'. Furthermore, sex offenders find themselves having to face the 'brick wall' of guilt (for having fantasised about something immoral and illegal) or fear (for thinking of the consequences of getting caught if they were to abuse a child). While some may not be able to overcome the sense of guilt or fear and may go back to the initial stage of illegal fantasy, others may succeed in overcoming this 'wall'. Thus, they would allow the arousal to develop through a process of 'cognitive distortion' or by reassuring themselves that the act they intend to commit is 'not so bad overall' (Sullivan 2002). As a result, following Sullivan's model (Sullivan 2002: 18), sex offenders move forward in the spiral. This is the 'fantasy stage', where offenders have successfully overcome the guilt or fear and allow themselves to return to fantasies and fall into sexual stimulation or masturbation where they experience a fall in arousal after orgasm. However, the process of linking fantasy with masturbation, which is also recognised as a form of behavioural conditioning (only in the treatment sense where practitioners attempt to interrupt the cycle with behavioural modification techniques), develops the urge of sexually offending (ibid). This process has a powerful effect on the sex offender as it builds arousal towards desire to act out fantasy. This is when the grooming process begins to take place and the sex offender carefully selects the victims to groom, or the person who is close to the child for protection in order to access the victim.

As already discussed in the previous chapter, the grooming process consists of sex offenders socialising and grooming children over long periods of time as preparation for sexual abuse and will ensure that abuse will take place without being disclosed. However, grooming and offending tactics will vary amongst offenders depending on the situation, environment, urge for offending and response from the victim. For example, if a child shows distress, some offenders may not be able to continue with the abuse. On the other hand, other offenders may be even more aroused if distress and antagonism are shown. Therefore, it is important not to classify all offenders as behaving in the same way; on the contrary, each offender is motivated and acts in different ways. However, whilst the process of grooming is recognised as common practice, sex offenders' *modus operandi* is very similar across different cases where patterns do emerge. The manner in which the grooming process takes place over the internet is nevertheless significantly different, as the subsequent discussion of the findings will show.

The previous sections have engaged critically with the contributions of biological and psychological theories to our understanding of sexually abusive behaviour and, in places, to the various forms of intervention that have arisen from this type of understanding. Whilst psychological theories continue to dominate in practitioner-based interventions, sociological theories are crucial when seeking to locate abusive behaviour within a wider social, political, cultural or even economic context. Arguably, the specific gender dynamics and power relations that exist between abuser and abused can only be adequately detailed and addressed through a combination of micro-individualistic approaches (including those offered by psychology and psychoanalysis) and macro-societal approaches (like those offered by a fuller sociological approach). It is these macro-explanations of sexually abusive behaviour that we turn to in the final sections of this chapter.

Sociological theories of child sexual abuse

Feminist approaches

Feminist theories tend to explain the problem of child sexual abuse from a structural and cultural perspective. Child protectionists and feminists have had an enormous impact upon our thinking of child abuse (Jenks 1996); they have fought extremely hard to extend the definition of adult-child sexual contact as harmful and to make it more visible, contested and illegal.

It is now widely acknowledged that sexual contact between adults and children is not a new phenomenon (Foucault 1988; Corby 1998) and indeed a number of writers have pointed out that, historically, it was commonplace in certain communities, perhaps especially those in rural areas. Nevertheless, the issue was not identified as 'child sexual abuse' and targeted as a social problem until the early 1980s in the UK and the US (Best 1990; Kitzinger 1996; Smart 2000). Such concern has been brought into public consciousness simultaneously by incest survivors (cf. Plummer 1994), the wider and hugely influential second wave Women's Movement, as well as right-wing politicians in the context of broader neoliberal reforms of penal policy (cf. Wacquant 2009).

Key amongst feminist writers, Carol Smart (2000) in her paper 'Reconsidering the Recent History of Child Sexual Abuse 1910–1960' looks at four fields (medical, political, legal and psychoanalytical), in which definitions of and meanings of adult sexual contact with children were contested. In exploring how the medical profession fails both to explain and deal with children suffering the consequences of sexual abuse, Smart (2000) argues that, during the 1920s, the problem was so neglected, ignored or silenced that even when the evidence was clear there was no intervention. For example, *The Lancet* carried a report publicising that 17 girls between 6 and 10 years old, living in a well-administered institution, were notified as suffering from gonorrhoeal vulvo-vaginitis. The diagnosis focused on poor hygiene, the use of dirty towels or shared lavatory seats (*The Lancet* 1925 in Smart 2000). Such news did not create any public concern regarding sexual abuse; on the contrary, it probably made parents more aware of issues of hygiene rather than focusing on protecting their children from being sexually abused by people within the family or others in positions of trust. However, this is not surprising at all if one considers that after 'the Second World War the dominant medical discourse available to explain venereal diseases in children consisted of denial and lack of recognition' (Smart 2000: 59). However, according to the Departmental Committee on Sexual Offences Against Young Persons in 1925 (Smart 2000), this lack of recognition or denial was often imposed on doctors who were encouraged to remain silent or the child would have been removed from treatment. Smart (2000) stresses that this inability to intervene was linked to the power that fathers had over their own children during that time whereby, for example, fathers had to consent to the medical examination of a raped child.

Masculinities

As an extension and development of feminist thinking, Connell developed the notion of 'hegemonic masculinity' (Connell 1987, 1995) as 'the configuration of the gender practice which embodies the currently accepted answer to the problem of the legitimacy of patriarchy, which guarantees (or is taken to guarantee) the dominant position of men and the subordination of women' (Connell 1995: 77). However, this notion can also be used to investigate the dominant position that men had regarding children. Hegemonic masculinity is the socially dominant form of masculinity in any given historical period and is therefore historically mobile. Qualities associated with this include authority, physical strength, bravado, exclusive heterosexuality and independence. It is through the term 'hegemonic masculinity' that it is possible to highlight the multi-dimensional and socially constructed aspects of male dominance in modern society to explain CSA. As useful as this theory might be to understanding male sex offending, it has not made it possible to explain why women also abuse.

Women and child sexual abuse

Up to this point, I have evaluated some of the existing theories that contribute to the explanation of why people sexually abuse children, but it has not recognised offenders' gender difference. Arguably, in comparison with males, only a small percentage of females sexually abuse children (Matravers 2008). This common knowledge has fuelled the misconception that female sex offending is so rare that the problem simply does not exist (Bunting 2007). However, research suggests that, although rare in comparison with male perpetrated offences, females are involved in a significant minority of sexual offences. Given that the majority of reported child molestations is committed by men, the issue of the female sex offender has been virtually ignored (Elliott 1993; Finkelhor 1984; Mathews 1989). This is evident in the literature which dates back mainly to the late 1980s. Prior to that, scant attention was paid to the female sex offender, and this has made victims of female CSA feel 'more isolated than those abused by men' (Bass and Davis in Elliott 1993: 220). Research into the participation of women in CSA has varied widely from 0 per cent in research carried out by Jaffe et al. (1975), 24 per cent in the National Incidence Study (1981) to 70 per cent in research carried out by Fromuth and Burkhart (1989).

In their exploratory work on online female sex offenders, Martellozzo et al. (2011) argue that one of the reasons for the indifference shown by mainstream criminology towards gender differences in crime is the fact that women commit fewer crimes and less serious ones. However, in order to understand why people commit certain crimes, it is important to understand why others do not. Thus, it is necessary to analyse the various theories that have attempted to explain why women seem to be involved in CSA more rarely than men. But how much less are women involved in child sex offending in comparison with men?

Brian Corby (1998) found that women accounted for just over four per cent of sexual abuse perpetrators, with mothers accounting for two per cent of this number. However, it should be noted that, as with cases of sexual abuses in general, a large number of abuses carried out by women may go unreported.

Furthermore, the cultural taboo surrounding sexual abuse by women would make it more unlikely that children would report such crimes (Elliott 1993). This taboo is fuelled by society, which:

> '. . . romanticises and minimises the impact female molesters have on their young male victims. If a boy discloses abuse, he may not be believed. If he

physically enjoyed the molestation, he does not perceive himself as a victim, despite the fact that he may be suffering from the effects of abuse. Many will suggest that he should have enjoyed the experience. If he did not enjoy aspects of the abuse, he may fear he is homosexual. Either way the young male victim of the older female is placed in an untenable position' (Mayer 1992 in Bunting 2007: 256).

This quote suggests that there is a great lack of awareness and cultural assumption about the emotional damage that female sex offending can cause to the victims, which may also increase the risk of sex offending in adulthood (Salter et al. 2003). With such a small percentage of CSA cases being attributed to women, it is assumed that women are less likely to commit this crime against children. Many ascribe this to women's instinctive feminine protectiveness (Heidensohn 1987). In other words, societal perceptions of females as sexually harmless and innocent appear to have an impact on victim reporting practices (Denov 2003). However, as pointed out by Liz Kelly, 'even if arguments that there is a hidden iceberg of female abusers have some validity to them, to reverse the gendered asymmetry would require an iceberg of literally incredible proportions' (Kelly 1996: 46).

La Fontaine also suggests that the figures relating to women's abuse of children may be misleading. He argues:

'Women are permitted such a degree of physical familiarity with children that it is difficult to know when it becomes abuse [creating] . . . a double standard in these matters that favours women. Which would indicate that the abuse by women never come to light' (La Fontaine 1990: 106).

Other scholars have suggested that women commit few sexual offences against children because of the physiology of the act: a woman cannot have sexual intercourse with a man unless his penis is erect (Walters 1975). However, as Davidson (2007) argues, this explanation shows the lack of a clear understanding of CSA, given that most abuse does not involve penetration but masturbation, which can be as gratifying to a woman. O'Connor (1987) finds less ambiguous explanations, by using Finkelhor and Araji's 'four preconditions' model as an aid (see above). This model has helped to separate the various theoretical approaches available better to explain female sex offending. O'Connor (1987) found that females were motivated to abuse sexually by:

'. . . boredom after a broken marriage complicated by sedative alcohol abuse; . . . sex with a 13-year-old boy as a revenge against her husband for being unfaithful; punishment of a 13-year-old boy for breaking into her house by taking his trousers off and interfering with him (aided and abetted by her husband); fear of being beaten by her boyfriend if she did not aid and abet him indecently assaulting a 9-year-old boy' (O'Connor 1987: 617).

As the quote above suggests, an important factor that may motivate female sex offenders to abuse is related to their obsessive dependency on their partners (Mathews 1989). Research conducted by the Metropolitan Police (2007) found that 11 subjects out of 18 had long histories of poor and abusive relationships with men and yet continued to be involved with the partner. This shows the necessity to have a man in their lives, as highlighted by one of Mathews's respondents:

> 'I wasn't a whole person unless there was somebody else with me. That's pretty much what it's been like for a long time. There had to be a male in my life, otherwise I would think I was nobody' (Mathews 1989).

This dependency is so strong that it increases women's vulnerability to the point that they become easily manipulated by their male partners and may even be persuaded or coerced into engaging in inappropriate sexual acts against children, often their own children.

It is vital to stress that the theoretical views that explain the motivations that lead to female sexual offences should not be considered as mutually exclusive; rather, 'females who sexually abuse children may have a host of motivations that underlie their behaviour' (Jennings 1993: 224). Whilst empirical research suggests that 'the majority of reported victims are women, and the majority of reported sex offenders in our society are men' (Jennings 1993: 224), it should not be ignored that women do commit a small yet significant number of sexual offences. However, the literature that explains this phenomenon is new and lacks some basic information necessary for the development of research in this area. If female offenders were not incorporated in the theoretical framework that explains child sexual abuse, there would be a marginalisation not only of the female offender but also the exclusion of the victims who have been subjected to female CSA. This is also important on the internet.

Theories of CSA applied to cyberspace

With the advent of 'the information age', important questions arise regarding the extent to which sociological, biological and psychological theories of child sexual abuse can be applied to understand the abuse of children online. This issue is one of the core concerns of this book and thus deserves special consideration at this point. Therefore, it is necessary to understand how the internet has shaped people's lives and ways of communicating with each other. Nicholas Gane (2005) argues that the internet 'adds on' another dimension to existing social relations; a dimension that has revolutionised the 21st century:

> 'It would seem to me that the internet-related technologies *have* directly altered the patterning of everyday life, including the way we work, access and exchange information, shop, meet people, and maintain and organise existing social ties. These technologies have done more than "add on" to

existing social arrangements; they have radically altered the three main spheres of social life, the spheres of production, consumption and communication' (Gane 2005: 475, original emphasis). *Good quote*

For Gane, the internet has contributed much more to people's lives than simply adding on another dimension. It has radically changed the way people communicate, socialise and operate. Some of these changes may be regarded certainly as positive features of this new medium. However, if the same changes are related to crimes that take place in the realm of the cyber, in this case that of child sexual *← impact on society* abuse online, the detrimental impact that these changes have on society become immediately clear. The internet has altered both sex offenders' motivation and the way in which these crimes are perpetrated. As will be discussed in detail in Chapter 7, the internet has offered new opportunities to sex offenders to exploit children, find new victims to abuse and create a virtual community with whom to interact and find support.

Some commentators maintain that it is unnecessary to generate new theoretical tools in order to explain online child sex offending (Gillespie 2004). Others remain unconvinced that the full burden of explanation for offending in the virtual *Argue* world can be supported by theories which only seek to engage with offending in the 'real world' (Middleton in Calder 2004). As I demonstrated earlier in this chapter, some strong theoretical models have been developed to help understanding the aetiology of CSA and to help offenders identify and control their sexual attraction to children. However, some modifications are needed to make these models relevant for online CSA, mainly because they have been originally developed to understand the pattern of behaviour involved in 'hands-on' child abuse (Middleton in Calder 2004). Currently, the treatments available to practitioners to understand and control online child sex offenders are based on those that were developed almost 30 years ago. For example, Middleton (2004) uses Finkelhor's 'four preconditions' model and attempts to apply it online. However, *Model needs updating* this could not be achieved without a significant reconfiguration of the existing model. For example, when considering the viewing of indecent images online, Middleton suggests that Finkelhor's precondition of 'Overcoming External Inhibitors' could be adapted to ask: 'What steps did you take to make sure that no one close to you (or at work) knew what you were looking at?' Similarly, the precondition of 'Overcoming Victim Resistance' could be adapted to ask: 'What needed to happen to make the child participate in the image?' (Middleton in Calder 2004: 102).

Quayle et al. (2006) also apply existing theories to cyberspace, focusing mainly on cognitive behavioural approaches. Drawing on this theoretical perspective, Quayle and her colleagues created a model which proposes five classes of offending behaviour: downloading; trading; production of child abuse images; commission of contact offence; and engagement with the internet for the seduction of children (Quayle et al. 2006: 31ff). The model suggests that 'the classes are not discrete and each requires particular conditions for expression' (Quayle et al.

2006: 34). The person who collects indecent images does not necessarily move on to engage with internet seduction of children or to commit a contact offence with a child. However, there is considerable evidence to suggest that there is a strong relationship between pornography and sexual aggression (Quayle et al. 2006).

Whilst Middleton (2004) and Quayle at al. (2006) attempt to apply previous theories to cyberspace in order to explain the online production and distribution of indecent images, Gillespie (2004) uses the same strategy to explain online grooming. He recognises that the problem of online grooming has increased exponentially since the internet has become more popular, but this is not to suggest that it is a new form of crime and therefore new theoretical tools are needed to explain this phenomenon. On the contrary, grooming practices have been around for as long as CSA itself, and it takes place as much online as it does offline. He explains: 'The internet does not create any new stages in this cycle (see the cycle of abuse, Sullivan 2003) but does, arguably, allow the cycle to be quickened'(Gillespie 2004: 3).

Therefore, as suggested by Gillespie, a new theoretical framework is arguably not required. However, how can the same theories be used to explain online CSA when the environment in which such abuse takes place – cyberspace – is anonymous to the point that it is perfectly possible to be anyone, anywhere, anytime? Indeed, the empirical research on sex offenders using the internet presented later in this book has contributed to fill some of the gaps missing in the literature.

Conclusions

Overall, no one theory explains adequately why people who sexually abuse children, both on and offline, sexually abuse in the first instance, and why they continue to do so. Nonetheless, developing sound theoretical explanations of child sexual offending is central to the development and implementation of policies, treatments and policing strategies that are sensitive to the diversity of motivations and behaviours that underpin abuse both in the real world and in cyberspace. It is therefore important to acknowledge that there are gaps in the existing research literature that need to be addressed. The solution to the problem of CSA is to incorporate in the research potential offenders – crucially including men, women and children – from *both* worlds in which they may operate – the real world and cyberspace. It is only through a thorough examination of all elements that it may be possible to increase awareness of the dynamics that occur between perpetrators and victims in the real world or in cyberspace.

References

Abel, G., Becker, G., Mittelman, J. V., Cunningham-Rathner, J., Rouleau, J. L. and Murphy, W. D. (1987) Self-reported sex crimes of non-incarcerated paraphiliacs. *Journal of Interpersonal Violence*, 2, 3–25.

Baker, W. (1984) Castration of the male sex offender. A legally impermissible alternative. *Loyola Law Review*, 30(2), 377–99.

Becker, J. V. and Hunter, J. A. (1992) Evaluation of treatment outcome for adult perpetrators of child sexual abuse. *Criminal Justice and Behaviour*, 19, 74–92.

Beckett, R. C. (1994) Assessment of Sex Offenders, in M. Erooga and R. C. Beckett (eds), *Sexual Offending Against Children: Assessment and Treatment of Male Abusers* (pp. 55–79), London: Routledge.

Best, J. (1990) *Threatened Children*, Chicago, University of Chicago Press.

Bottoms, A. E. and Wiles, P. (1997) Enviromental Criminology, in M. Maguire, R. Morgan and R. Reiner (eds), *The Oxford Handbook of Criminology* (2nd edn), Oxford, The Clarendon Press.

Bradford, J. M. (1988) Organic Treatment for the Male Sex Offender. *Annals of the New York Academy of Sciences*, 528, 1993–2002.

Bradford, J. M. (1990) The Antiandrogen and Hormonal Treatment of Sex offenders, in W. L. Marshall (ed), *Handbook of Sexual Assault: Issues, Theories, and Treatment of the Offender* (pp. 297–310), New York, Plenum Press.

Bunting, L. (2007) Dealing with a Problem that Doesn't Exist? Professional Responses to Female Perpetrated Child Secual Abuse. *Child Abuse Review*, 12, 252–267.

Calder, M. (2004) *Child Sexual Abuse and the Internet: Tackling New Frontier*, Lyme Regis, Russell House Publishing.

Carich, M. S., and Calder, M. (2003) *Contemporary treatment of adult make sex offenders*, Dorset, Russell House.

Cawson, P. W. C., Brooker, S. and Kelly, G. (2000) *Child maltreatment in the United Kingdom: a study of the prevalence of child abuse and neglect*, London, NSPCC.

Cohen, L. E. and Felson, M. (1979) Social change and crime rate trends: a routine activities approach. *American Sociological Review*, 44, 588–608.

Connell, R. (1987) *Gender and Power,* Cambridge, Polity Press.

Connell, R. (1995) *Masculinities*, Cambridge, Polity Press.

Corby, B. (1998) *Managing Child Sexual Abuse Cases*, London, Jessica Kingsley Publishers.

Cossin, A. (2000) Masculinities, Sexualities and Child Sexual Abuse. *British Society of Criminology Conference: Selected Proceedings*, 3.

Costello, B. (2000) Techniques of Neutralization and Self-esteem: A Critical Test of Social Control and Neutralization Theory. *Deviant Behavior: An Interdisciplinary Journal*, 21, 307–29.

D'Ovidio, R., Mitman, T., El-Burki, I. J. and Shumar, W. (2009) Adult-Child Advocacy Websites as Social Learning Environments: A Content Analysis. *International Journal of Cyber Criminology*, 3(1).

Davidson, J. (2007) *Risk Management Authority Briefing. Current Practice and Research into Internet Sex offending*, Glasgow, Risk Management Authority, available on http://www.rmascotland.gov.uk/ViewFile.aspx?id=235 accessed 10/06/08.

Davidson, J. and Martellozzo, E. (2004) *Educating Children about Sexual Abuse and Evaluating the Metropolitan Police Safer Surfing Programme*, London, University of Westminster and Metropolitan Police.

Denov, M. (2003) The Myth of Innocence: Sexual Scripts and the Recognition of Child Sexual Abuse by Female Perpetrators. *Journal of Sex Research*, 40(3), 303–15.

Eldridge, H. (1998) *Therapist's Guide to Maintaining Change*, London, Sage.

Ehlers, C. L., Rickler, K. C. and Hovey, J. E. A Possible Relationship between Plasma Testosterone and Aggressive Behavior and Social Dominance in Man, *Psychomatic Medicine,* 36, 469–475.

Elliott, M. (1993) *Female Sexual Abuse of Children*, New York, The Guilford Press.

Finkelhor, D. (1984) *Child Sexual Abuse; New Theory and Research*, New York, Free Press.

Finkelhor, D. (1986) *A sourcebook on child sexual abuse*, Beverly Hills, Sage Publications.

Finkelhor, D. (1994) The Scope and Nature of Child Sexual Abuse. *Sexual Abuse of Children*, 4(2).

Finkelhor, D., Araji, S., Baron, L. and Browne, A. (1986) *A Sourcebook on Child Sexual Abuse*, California, Sage.

Fisher, D. and Beech, A. (1999) Current Practice in Britain with Sexual Offenders. *Journal of Interpersonal Violence*, 14(3), 240–56.

Flor-Henry, P. (1987) Cerebral aspects of sexual deviation, in G. Wilson (ed), *Variant Sexuality: Research and Theory*, (pp. 49–83), London and Sidney, Croom Helm Ltd.

Fromuth, M. and Burkhart, B. (1989) Longterm Psycological Correlates of Childhood Sexual Abuse in Two Samples of College Men. *Child Abuse and Neglect*, 13, 533–42.

Gane, N. (2005) An Information Age without Technology: a Response to Webster. *Information, Communication and Society*, 8(4), 471–6.

Gannon, T. A., Polaschek, D. L. L. and Polaschek, T. W. (2005) Social cognition and sexual offenders, in M. McMurran and J. McGuire (eds), *Social problem solving and offenders* (pp. 223–47), Chichester, UK, Wiley.

Gillespie, A. A. (2004) Tackling Grooming. *The Police Journal*, 77(3), 239.

Glancy, C. (1986) In D. Finkelhor (ed), *A Sourcebook on child sexual abuse*, California, Sage.

Grubin, D. (1998) Sex Offending against Children: Understanding the Risk. *Police Research Series*, 99.

Harrison, K. (2007) The High-risk Sex Offender Strategy in England and Wales: Is Chemical Castration an Option? *The Howard Journal*, 46(1), 16–31.

Heidensohn, F. (1987) Women and crime: Questions for criminology, in P. Carlen and A. Worral (eds), *Gender, Crime and Justice*, London; Milton Keynes, Open University Press.

House of Lords (13 June 2007). Child Sex Offender Review, http://news.bbc.co.uk/1/hi/uk/6746965.stm.

Jaffe, A., Dynneson, L. and Ten-Bensel, R. (1975) Sexual Abuse of Children. An Epidemiologic Study. *American Journal of Diseases of Children*, 129, 689–95.

Jennings, K. (1993) Female Child Molesters: A review of the Literature, in M. Elliott (ed), *Female Sexual Abuse of Children* (pp. 219–34), New York, Longman Group.

Jenks, C. (1996) *Childhood: Key Ideas*, London, Routledge.

Judge W. Taylor (2005) BBC Panorama 2215. Recorder Plymouth (William Gold).

Kelly, L. (1996) Weasel Words: Paedophiles and the Cycle of Abuse. *Trouble and Strife*, 33, 44–9.

Kitzinger, J. (1996). Media Constructions of Sexual Abuse Risks. *Child Abuse Review*, 5(5), 319–33.

Lanning, K. (2005) Complaint Child Victims: Confronting an Uncomfortable Reality, in E. Quayle and M. Taylor (eds), *Viewing Child Pornography on the Internet. Understanding the offence, Managing the Offender, Helping the Victims* (pp. 49–60), Lyme Regis, Russell House Publishing.

LeFontaine, J. (1990) *Child Sexual Abuse*, Cambridge, Polity Press.

Livingstone, S. and Bober, M. (2005) *Internet Literacy Among Children and Young People*, London, LSE.

Lombroso, C. and Ferrero, W. (1895) *The Female Offender*, London, Fisher Unwin.

Lombroso, C. and Ferrero, W. (1895) The Criminal Type in Women and its Atavistic Origin, in E. McLaughlin, J. Muncie and G. Hughes (eds), *Criminological Perspectives*, London, Sage.

Marques, J. K., Nelson, C., Alarcon, J. M. and Day, D. M. (2000) Preventing Relapse in Sex Offenders: What we Learned from SOTEP's Experimental Treatment Program, in D. R. Laws, S. M. Hudson and T. Ward (eds), *Remaking Relapse Prevention with Sex Offenders: A sourcebook*, Thousand Oaks, CA, Sage.

Marshall, W. L. (1996) Assessment Treatment and Theorizing About Sex Offenders: Developments over the Last Twenty Years and Future Directions. *Criminal Justice and Behavior*, 23, 162–99.

Marshall, W. L., Anderson, D. and Fernandez, Y. (1999) The Development of Cognitive Behavioural Treatment of Sex Offenders, in (pp. 9–31), Chichester, UK, Wiley.

Martellozzo, E., Dehring, D. and Taylor, H. (2011) Online Child Sexual Abuse by Female Offenders: An Exploratory Study. *International Journal of Cyber Criminology*, 4 (1 & 2), 592–609.

Mathews, R. (1989) *Femal Sexual Offenders: An Explanatory Study*, Brandon, Safer Society Press.

Matravers, A. (2008) Understanding Women Who Commit Sex Offences, in G. Letherby, K. Williams, P. Birch and M. Cain (eds), *Sex as Crime?* (pp. 299–320), London, Willan Publishing.

Matza, D. and Sykes, G. (1961) Juvenile Delinquency and Subterranean Values. *American Sociological Review*, 26(5), 712–19.

McGuire, J. (2000). *Cognitive-Behavioural Approaches: An Introduction to Theory and Research*, London, Home Office.

Middleton, D. (2004) Current Treatment Approaches, in M. Calder (ed), *Child Sexual Abuse and the Internet. Tackling New Frontier* (pp. 99–112), Lyme Regis, Russell House Publishing.

Miller, K. (1997) Detection and Reporting of Child Sexual Abuse (Specifically Paedophilia): A Law Enforcement Perspective. *Paedophilia: Policy and Prevention*, 12, 32–8.

Mullen, P., Martin, J., Anderson, J., Romans, S. and Herbison, G. (1995) The Long Term Impact of the Physical, Emotional, and Sexual Abuse of Children: A Community Study. *Child Abuse and Neglect*, 20.

Muncie, J. (2004). *Youth and Crime* (2nd edn), London, Sage.

Murray, J. B. (1987) Psychopharmalogical Therapy of Deviant Sexual Behavior. *The Journal of General Psychology,* 115, 101–10.

National Centre for Child Abuse and Neglect. (1981) *Study Findings: National Study of the Incidence and Severity of Child Abuse and Neglect*, Washington, DC, D.H.E.W.

NSPCC. (2007) Sexual Abuse. Retrieved 08/09/07, from http://www.nspcc.org.uk/helpandadvice/whatchildabuse/sexualabuse/sexualabuse_wda36370.html.

O'Connor, A. (1987) Female Sex Offenders. *British Journal of Psychiatry*, 150, 615–20.

Palmer, J. E., McGuire, J., Hatcher, M. R., Hounsome, C. J., Bilby, A. L. C. and Hollin, C. (2008) The Importance of Appropriate Allocation to Offending Behavior Programs. *International Journal of Offender Therapy and Comparative Criminology,* Sage, 52(2), 206–21.

Plummer, K. (1994) *Telling Sexual Stories: Power, Change and Social Worlds*, London, Routledge.

Quayle, E., Erooga, M., Wright, L., Taylor, M. and Harbinson, D. (2006) *Only Pictures?*, Dorset, Russell House Publishing.

Rada, R. T., Laws, D. R. and Kellner, R. (1976) Plasma Testosterone Levels in the Rapist, Psychomatic Medicine, 38, 257–256.

Salter, D., McMillan, D., Richards, M., Talbot, M., Hodges, J., Bentovin, A., et al. (2003) Development of Sexually Abusive Behaviour in Sexually Victimised Males: A Longitudinal Study. *The Lancet*, 361, 9356–471.

Scott, M. and Lyman, S. (1968) Accounts. *American Sociologiacal Review*, 33(10), 46–62.

Smallbone, S. W. and Dadds, M. R. (1998) Childhood attachment and adult attachment in incarcerated adult male sex offenders. *Journal of Interpersonal Violence*, 13(5), 555–73.

Smart, C. (2000) Reconsidering the Recent History of Child Sexual Abuse, 1910–1960. *Journal of Social Policy* 29(1), 55–71.

Stanley, J. (2001) *Child Abuse and the Internet*, Melbourne, Australian Institute of Family Studies.

Sullivan, J. (2002) The Spiral of Sexual Abuse: A Conceptual Framework for Understanding and Illustrating the Evolution of Sexually Abusive Behaviour. *NOTA NEWS*, 41, April, 17–21.

Sullivan, J. and Beech, A. (2004) *Are Collectors of Child Abuse Images a Risk to Children?*, London, The John Grieve Centre for Policing and Community Safety.

Sykes, G. M. and Matza, D. (1957) Techniques of Neutralization: A Theory of Delinquency. *American Sociologiacal Review*, 22, 664–70.

Tallon, J. and Terry, K. (2004) *Theories and Etiology of Child Sexual Abuse by Males* (http://www.bishop-accountability.org/reports/2004_02_27_JohnJay/LitReview/1_3_JJ_TheoriesAnd.pdf), New York, John Jay College Research Team.

Taylor, M. (2002) The nature and dimensions of Child Pornography on the Internet. Retrieved 7/11/05.

Wacquant, L. (2009) *Punishing the Poor: The Neoliberal Government of Social Insecurity*, Durham, NC, Duke University Press.

Walters, D. R. (1975) *Physical and Sexual Abuse of Children: Causes and Treatment*, Bloomington, Indiana Press.

Ward, T. and Beech, T. (2006) An Integrated Theory of Sexual Offending. *Aggression and Violent Behavior: A Review Journal*, 11, 44–63.

Ward, T. and Gannon, T. A. (2006) Rehabilitation, etiology, and self-regulation: The comprehensive good lives model of treatment for sexual offenders. *Aggression and Violent Behavior: A Review Journal*, 11, 77–94.

Weinberger LE, Sreenivasan S. and Sreenivasan, T. G. (2005) The Impact of Surgical Castration on Sexual Recidivism Risk among Sexually Violent Predatory Offenders. *Journal of the American Academy of Psychiatry and the Law Online*, 33, 16–36.

West, D. (2000a) Paedophilia: Plague or Panic? *The Journal of Forensic Psychiatry*, 11(3), 511–31.

West, D. (2000b) The sex crime situation: deterioration more apparent than real? *The Journal on Criminal Policy and Research*, 8, 399–422.

Wolf, S. (1985) A Multi Factor Model of Deviant Sexuality. *Victimology: An Internal Journal*, 10, 359–74.

Chapter 3

Young people's use of the internet

Introduction

In this chapter, I focus on the real protagonists of the internet: children and young people. Since they are our new 'digital generation', it is important that young people's use of the internet and their risk-taking behaviour is understood and critically evaluated, as this may provide a clearer picture of what attracts sex offenders to groom them in the first place. This chapter draws on a range of recent empirical research conducted with young people in the US (Wolak et al. 2008) and in Europe (Davidson et al. 2010; Livingstone and Haddon 2009; Martellozzo 2011; Shannon 2007). Here I present a critical review of relevant literature and link key findings from recent research[1] to those from practitioners' and sex offenders' accounts presented in other chapters of this book. Nationally and internationally, a number of scientific evaluations of young people's use of the internet have been conducted, with results that indicate that educational programmes have had a positive impact on children's attitudes towards various risks that they may encounter online (Chibnall et al. 2006; Crombie and Trinneer 2003; Davidson and Martellozzo 2004; Shannon 2007). I will argue that responsible internet use and online safety are considered essential skills for children and young people.

The popularity of social networking sites (SNSs)

Boyd and Ellison (2007) define SNSs as:

'Web-based services that allow individuals to (1) construct a public or semi-public profile within a bounded system, (2) articulate a list of other users with whom they share a connection, and (3) view and traverse their list of connections and those made by others within the system. The nature and nomenclature of these connections may vary from site to site' (Boyd and Ellison 2007; available at http://jcmc.indiana.edu/vol13/issue1/boyd. ellison.html).

The basic structure of SNSs consists of individuals who are linked to others in the same network. In a way, social networking is not a recent invention. According to the Department for Communities and Local Government (2008) examples of online social networking may be traced back to 1987 where people working for GreenNet in the UK started to collaborate with colleagues at the Institute for Global Communications (IGC) in the US and shared electronic material in a way that can be considered online social networking (Association of Progressive Communications (APC) 2008). As a result, this networking rapidly increased to include other organisations in countries such as Sweden, Canada and Brazil, leading to the creation in 1990 of the APC. Since then, and particularly since 2003, the year of the creation of MySpace and Hi5, the number of SNSs has increased dramatically.

ComScore, an internet marketing research company, reported that Facebook attracted 132.1 million visitors in June 2008, compared to MySpace, which attracted 117.6 million. These numbers are indicated below.

On 21 July 2010 Facebook reached over 500 million users worldwide (comScore World Metrix) and these numbers keep on growing every day. Facebook is available now in 70 different languages with 30 billion pieces of content (weblinks, news stories, blog posts, notes, photo albums etc) being shared each month (Clikymedia 2011).

However, what is even more impressive is that in recent years SNSs have moved from niche phenomenon to mass adoption, with enormous growth rates, making them the most visited sites on the web (Friedel and Kraus 2009: 6). According to Boyd and Ellison (2007), this growth has prompted many corporations to invest time and money in creating, purchasing, promoting and advertising

Table 3.1 Worldwide growth among selected social networking sites. June 2008 vs June 2007

Total Worldwide Audience, Age 15+	Total Unique Visitors (Child Online Protection Act 2000 (COPA) United States)		
	Jun-2007	Jun-2008	per cent Change
Total internet: Total Audience	778,310	860,514	11 per cent
Social Networking	464,437	580,510	25 per cent
FACEBOOK.COM	52,167	132,105	153 per cent
MYSPACE.COM	114,147	117,582	3 per cent
HI5.COM	28,174	56,367	100 per cent
FRIENDSTER.COM	24,675	37,080	50 per cent
Orkut	24,120	34,028	41 per cent
BEBO.COM	18,200	24,017	32 per cent
Skyrock Network	17,638	21,041	19 per cent

(*Source:* comScore World Metrix 12/08/2008)

SNSs. At the same time, more conservative companies and organisations are blocking their employees from accessing the sites. A number of debates are still taking place regarding what is the best policy to adopt in terms of SNSs, both in the private and public sectors. Gartner (6 August 2008), an American IT professional source for addressing IT issues, suggests for example that organisations should not ban web participation for fear of bad behaviour; instead, they should anticipate it as part of the social experience and formulate a multilevel approach to policies for effective governance.

Online SNSs are so popular that they have brought about a shift in traditional community dynamics. According to Boyd and Ellison (2007), whilst early public online communities were structured by topics, more current SNS are structured as personal networks, with individuals being placed at the centre of their own community. This reminds us of what Wellman suggested back in 1988 that 'the world is composed of networks, not groups' (Wellman 1988: 37). SNSs simply bring together, for the first time, pre-existing interactive technologies on a single service. Facebook, for example, allows people to make new friends, send emails, messages, post photos, music, blogs, videos etc and, at the time of writing, it is currently the most popular social network site. There are a multifaceted number of reasons why users join SNSs. On the one hand, Facebook for example helps people to keep in contact with family and friends in a way that a simple phone call or a short email would not be able to do. It also helps develop personal relationships and make new friends. On the other hand, LinkedIn helps people to build professional connections and develop personal profiles on a daily basis. Thus, SNSs may help individuals with difficulties in expressing either their skills or emotions on a face-to-face basis and to form close relationships with people they would otherwise never know exist. However, what should not be overlooked is the fact that 'the internet acts as voyeuristic space, in the sense that more and more of the self must be revealed in order to achieve online visibility and validation' (Cavanagh 2007: 124). Individuals may, as a result, feel the need to reveal more of the self in order to attract public attention, whether this is related to work or to one's personal sphere. A professional, for example, with a public profile in a well known network such as LinkedIn, in order to differentiate his or her profile from others, must be prepared to publicise as many aspects as possible about his or her professional life, including personal opinions on new facts and events, to the public audience. Also young people who have joined SNSs such as Facebook, in order to gain popularity among a group of friends, feel the need to add to their profiles as many friends as possible, including those they do not know; to post pictures (often sexy or 'cool' pictures) of themselves alone or with friends; and to publicise their hobbies and activities, without taking into account the risks that this public openness may cause. Allison Cavanagh (2007) in her book *Sociology in the Age of the Internet* uses an interesting simile to describe this 'voyeuristic enactment'. She compares the internet to a theatrical space where:

'... an online presence depends on making visible, on enacting the self for an audience, and thus we come to "play act" our own personas. In this sense we move from inhabiting identity to performing it, enabled by the low cost and low user requirements of web technologies' (Cavanagh 2007: 124).

Perhaps this strong desire of being constantly in the public eye is merely a symptom of the 'self-revelatory culture' (Bunting 2001) of modern life. Arguably, this cyber attraction to accessing and publicising personal information derives from the wider trend of the offline reality where the public is still keen to know what is happening in the 'big brother' house. Thus, it does not come as a surprise if SNSs are extremely popular in both Western and Eastern countries (Davidson and Martellozzo 2010).[2]

Internet use

As previously argued, social networks are popular and incredibly important for all users but in particular for young people. They provide opportunities to communicate, interact, share content, interest and find emotional support (Boeck et al. 2006). According to the Home Office Task Force some of the main reasons to use such services include:

'•   keeping in touch with friends and interests
 •   experimenting with their identity and opinions
 •   having a place or space where their parents or carers may not be present
 •   demonstrating their technical expertise and skills.'
      (Home Office Task Force on Child Protection on the Internet 2007: 6)

However, what is missing from this list is the unique feature offered by SNSs of 'making new friends'. The British Office of Communications (Ofcom) in its research on social networking, attitudes, behaviours and use (2 April 2008) found that the majority of children (53 per cent) reported that they had used social networking sites to make new friends. This was supported by the Byron Review (2008), which also showed that 59 per cent of children who used social networking sites claimed to do so to make new friends, without specifying whether or not these were people previously unknown to them. Although this was not the main reason for using SNSs and therefore was less important than other activities such as communicating with friends and family, or browsing profiles, it showed that many children saw this as an important use of social networking sites.

Clearly, there are concerns that these facilities, combined with children's own high risk behaviour, may lead them to become potential victims for sexual exploitation by adults or, sometimes, by other young people. What is most concerning is that, owing to the popularity of online interactivity in a group setting, people feel more comfortable sharing personal information that is widely accessible to anyone, including those who manipulate privacy and intimacy. This may represent a risk, particularly to children and young people.

Young people and online risk

Young people find the adult world fascinating, challenging and worth exploring. People are logging on every day, obsessively updating their profiles and checking the status updates of their online friends. One may argue that although it is fun to pass time and stay in touch, there is likely to be a negative effect on the impact that SNSs may have on young people or adults. In other words, can a person become addicted to social networking?

A number of studies (Banquil et al. 2009; Douglas et al. 2008) have already shown that the internet has an addictive power and that socialisation is one of the magnets behind this power. According to Grohol (2005), some individuals spend an excessive amount of time interacting online, be it through social networking sites, fora, chat rooms, online games etc. Whilst these facilities are exciting as they allow individuals to express themselves freely and widely, they are also socially isolating and have resulted in a small proportion of the population being affected by what has now been recognised and defined as Internet Addiction Disorder (IAD). Although it is not within the scope of this book to explore IAD in young people, it is important to state that some young people, particularly girls, showed a 'compulsive internet use' (Griffiths 1998).

It can be argued that young people, like adults, may suffer from a digital dependency on the internet. Many respondents claim that they are obsessed with their smart phones. They check their Facebook page as soon as they wake up, sometimes during the time they are at school or when they are back from school. Some young people that use the internet for more than four hours a day, particularly the older ones (14–15) claimed that they spent long periods on Facebook and feel they cannot stay calm without checking their friends' profiles regularly and updating theirs. This is illustrated by the quotes below:

'I spend so much time online I cannot even say. I am addicted to Facebook.' (Girl 12, Metropolitan Police Project).

'I don't know why but it (Facebook) is very addictive. I cannot stay away from it even when I go on holidays. I take my phone or my laptop where I have facebook.' (Girl 14, Metropolitan Police Project).

Girl: I am online pretty much all the time because now you can be signed on, on Facebook, chat on your phone and msn and all the other things that you need, all the time'
Interviewer: You say it as something worrying you?
Girl: Yes, it's really bad.
Interviewer: Why?

Girl:	I can't go that long without being on Facebook. I just hate it.
Interviewer:	It is interesting. We had other students that said the same: 'I think I am addicted, I can't stay without, I can't go on holidays without it, what do you do when you go on holidays, for example'.
Girl:	I take my phone, I take my laptop. I do and I sign in on Facebook. And if something doesn't work, there's normally like an internet café, so every 2 days I go on line and talk to my friends.

(Girl 14, Metropolitan Police Project).

A large number of young people (68 per cent) felt the need to be online to combat boredom and a small but significant number (23 per cent) claimed they would become nervous if they were not online. This finding supports other research findings where all respondents also felt that without the internet life would be dull, and 'became nervous if the internet connection was slow' (in Yellowlees and Marks 2005: 1450).

Of the most avid users (14 per cent), 44 per cent felt that the internet negatively influences their daily routine, particularly in relation to studying. Some students blamed various social networking sites for not being able to concentrate on their homework. As stated by this girl:

'The problem I have is that I spend hours checking stuff on Facebook and I don't do my homework. Sometimes I wish Facebook didn't exist' (Girl 14, Metropolitan Police Project).

'I have the laptop near me all the time so while I am studying whatever I can check stuff so I do it while studying' (Girl 13, Metropolitan Police Project).

This is supported by Banquil et al. (2009) and Young's (1998) findings, who claim that although the internet has been introduced in schools as a essential educational tool, its excessive use may affect young people's academic performance. Young's research showed that 58 per cent of students reported a decline in study habits, a significant drop in grades and missed classes, because of excessive internet use (Young 1996).

It is also common for adolescents to test the boundaries that this world has to offer. They may do so in a number of ways: lying about their age, exploring new sexual experiences, keeping or breaking secrets etc. This behaviour is to be expected to take place both online and offline. However: 'online, such practices may be spread, manipulated or shared in ways that are easier, quicker, and possibly unexpected in their consequences, compared with online practices' (Home Office Task Force on Child Protection on the Internet 2007: 10).

The internet has become an integral part of young people's social world. In a way, the internet makes their life simpler because what they were doing before offline they can now do it also online, at their convenience and much more quickly. Furthermore, in the area of relationships, for example, the internet may be perceived as an important source of knowledge for children to learn about sexual issues, a topic that may be difficult to discuss with parents or teachers, or with anyone else for that matter, in the context of more traditional social environments (Shannon 2007).

On the whole, the rise of easily accessible online communication tools has profoundly altered patterns of social interaction for many young people. Box 3.1 displays part of an online conversation between two 15-year-old girls from East London on Yahoo Messenger chat software. This conversation was recorded as part of an enquiry into online safety in schools I conducted with the Metropolitan Police in 2010/2011. The conversation highlights the intersection of emergent conventions of online interaction – such as the copious use of abbreviations and neologisms – with the linguistic complexities of life in multicultural London.

A young person's language is strictly related to the socio-historical, religious, cultural, socio-economic context in which that language is learnt. Therefore, it may be argued that the more diverse the environment in which a language develops, the more complex this may be. According to some teachers interviewed during the study, the way children communicate in Britain is becoming more complex to comprehend because of all this mixture of cultures. Moreover, it can be argued that online interaction is developing cultural features and patterns that are very much distinct from other forms of mediated and non-mediated communication.

Box 3.1 Online communication amongst 15-year-old girls

A: ARE U GNA BANG DOE? (are you going to have sex with someone?)
B: naah im alryttn (no I'm alright)
A: sik maaan (cool man)
B: RE YOU ALRYT MY SEXY BITCH (are you alright my sexy lady)
A: Jam ur hype fam LOL (calm down you are exited my friend, laugh out loud)
B: HOWS RK BBZ? (how is you random kid (boyfriend) baby (blowjob) baby makes more sense (Rk = Random kid/kill bbz = baby/s? Or blow job)
B: HUSH YUR MOUTH X (be quiet (the 'x' denotes the friendly tone))
A: wag1 every one yuu kw i need ur sexy numba (oh go on, everyone you know I need your sexy number)
B: :)(happy face)
B: You Slag. Piss Off U ASSWIPEEEEEEEE (you promiscuous girl, go away you ar*e wipe (toilet paper)
B: heey u uglii (hey you are ugly)
B: bitch (nasty girl)
A: why yuu callin us stuipd bruv calm dwn charlleeeeyyy (why are you calling us stupid brother just calm down Charlie (name)

```
A:     plz (please)
B:     Dat wernt Charlie u buttcrack. (that was not Charlie you a*se)
A:     Omg! (oh my God)
A:     U Evil Ppl (you are evil people)
A:     Jk (just kidding)
A:     Lets Talk Slang (let's talk slang)
A:     So Dey Wnt understand (so they will not understand us)
A:     Nuffin. (nothing)
B:     shut de fuk upp (shut the f*ck up)
B:     bye xx (goodbye)
```

It is perhaps owing to the novel and highly particular characteristics of online interaction among young people that attendant dangers are as yet incompletely understood. Whilst most children and young people use the internet positively, there are some that behave in ways that may expose them to risks. Hasebrink et al. (2009) provide a comprehensive classification of online risks to children. Table 3.2 shows that risk can be categorised in terms of the motivations of the online producers whether they are commercial, aggressive, sexual or value-related motivations.

Clearly the internet introduces new opportunities for young people to get access to inappropriate content, including pornographic and violent content. This content may include: nudity or other sexually explicit material; hate or racist websites; promotional material about tobacco, alcohol or drugs; graphic violence; information about satanic or cult groups; or even recipes for making bombs and explosives at home. Other internet dangers to children include sexual exploitation or

Table 3.2 A classification of online risks to children

	Commercial	Aggressive	Sexual	Values
Content – Child as recipient	Advertising, spam, sponsorship	Violent/hateful content	Pornographic or unwelcome sexual contents	Racism, biased or misleading info/advice (eg drugs)
Contact – Child as participant	Tracking/ harvesting personal information	Being bullied, stalked or harassed	Meeting strangers. Being groomed	Self-harm, unwelcome persuasion
Conduct – Child as actor	Gambling, hacking, illegal downloads	Bullying or harassing another	Creating and uploading pornography	Providing advice eg suicide/ pro-anorexic chat

(*Source:* EU Kids Online; Hasebrink et al. 2009)

enticement and online grooming. But it also provides an opportunity to young people to 'act out' and contribute to the production of inappropriate content such as 'sexting', bullying and developing dangerous content that may encourage vulnerable young people to self-harm.

Although a small minority of children encounter the worst of these risks, the type of risks that society and the media are generally more concerned with are those related to pornographic or unwelcome sexual content and meeting with strangers after being groomed. Given the purpose of this book, the remainder of this chapter seeks to explore research findings on how young people behave online and their experiences, which will shed some light on online sex-offending behaviour, evaluated in the following chapters of this book.

Research on sexual solicitation and exploitation

Before exploring the findings of recent research on the seriousness and the extent of sexual exploitation, it is important to clarify that this term is rather broad as it encompasses a range of different behaviour.

Exploitation may include:

- exposure to harmful content, including adult pornography and illegal child abuse images
- engaging in sexually explicit communications and conversations that may reduce children and young people's inhibitions
- manipulation and exploitation which can include being encouraged or paid to pose in sexually provocative ways and pose naked and/or perform sexual acts via webcams
- grooming and luring of children to meet offline to sexually exploit them.
    (Home Office Task Force on Child Protection on the Internet 2007: 14)

Furthermore, Wolak et al. (2006) define sexual solicitation as 'requests that involve sexual activities or sexual talk or give personal information' (ibid:14). This definition includes unwanted behaviour ranging from explicit requests for sexual activity to online interactions that resemble unwanted 'flirtatious approaches'. This broad term is, however, misinterpreted and used commonly in everyday speech (Biegler and Boyd 2010) and certainly by the media. As noted by Biegler and Boyd, it is important to bear in mind that while all interactions labelled as sexual interactions are problematic, the seriousness in terms of the harm that each interaction may cause varies widely.

Research on sexual exploitation of young people conducted in different countries across Europe and the US leads to similar findings. The Swedish National Council commissioned a survey to explore how common it is for young people to report experiences of sexual contacts from adults via the internet (Shannon 2007). The survey included a nationally representative sample of 7500 15-year-olds and showed that a large number of 15-year-olds report having been the subject of a sexual contact from an adult during the 12 months prior to the survey from a previously unknown person that they knew or believed to be an adult. Interestingly, the proportion of girls reporting the experience was much higher than the proportion of boys (48 per cent and 18 per cent respectively) and the vast majority of young people subjected to this experience claims that the contact took place via the internet. A further questionnaire was administered to approximately 1000 Swedish youths aged 15–17. It was found that almost 50 per cent of the female respondents reported having experienced unwanted sexual contacts during the 12 months prior to the survey. The girls in the sample also reported having experienced such contact at an earlier age than their male counterparts and 40 per cent of the girls in the sample reported that this contact had taken place before their 15th birthday. Furthermore, it was found that it is much more common for girls than boys to find these contacts experience as 'quite distressing' or 'very distressing' (Shannon 2007: 8). Similar findings were found in the UK. During the evaluation of the ThinkUKnow educational programme (Davidson et al. 2010) we found that one in five young people have received a 'threatening' experience online, described as being made to feel uncomfortable or online peer bullying experiences. Furthermore, girls appear to be at higher risk than boys because they use social aspects of the internet more (notably instant messaging and SNSs), and are slightly more willing to share some types of personal information and to interact with strangers.

The quote below illustrates that having a long list of friends is perceived as 'cool', even if some of these 'friends' have never been met in person:

> 'It is fun to add people you don't know from other countries for example. It is fun to have a lot of friends' (Girl 14, Evaluation of the ThinkUKnow project).

Most young people using SNSs had from 20 to 300 friends. However, not all of them know who their online friends are. As one of the young people claimed:

> 'No I only know about 100 of them and the other 500 of them I haven't got a clue who they are' (Girl 16, Evaluation of the ThinkUKnow project).

The quotes above highlight that interacting with strangers (that is, adding them as ISM or Facebook friends and exchanging messages) is becoming an accepted behaviour not perceived as 'risk-taking'.

It may be argued that, although it is difficult to establish with certainty the age of the person interacting online with a young person, technology and particularly the internet 'have become by far the dominant means by which adults attempt to establish sexual contacts with children' (Shannon 2007: 7). In the US, researchers such as Wolak et al. claim that chat rooms are by far the most common reported location of initiated sexual relationship (Wolak et al. 2008). These contentions may be applied to both the West and East showing even more clearly that the internet does not have geographical boundaries and may reach all citizens across the globe.

Online risk-taking behaviour

Research conducted in the UK and in the Middle East has focused on the extent to which young people engage in behaviour regarded as 'high risk' and the extent to which they have had negative experiences online. Broadly speaking Maria De Gutzman and Kathy Bosh (2007) define high risk behaviour as something that can have 'adverse effects on the overall development and well being of youth, or that might prevent them from future successes and development . . . Risk behaviours also can affect youth by disrupting their normal development or prevent them from participating in "typical" experiences for their age group (ibid 2007: 1). In relation to the internet, it would be appropriate to consider the sharing of a range of personal information with strangers[3] and interacting with strangers (eg by adding them as online friends) as risky behaviour. These types of behaviour have been of particular interest to academics and professionals because of their prevalence in youth today. The sharing of personal information with strangers and the easiness with which young people add strangers to their Facebook accounts and interact with them have proved, in some cases, to put young people at risk either physically, emotionally or both, and with very tragic consequences. In 2010, in the small town of Sedgefield in England, a serial sex offender was sentenced to life imprisonment for kidnapping, raping and murdering a teenager whom he met and groomed online after becoming her friend, using a false identity on Facebook.

Research conducted in the UK (Davidson et al. 2010) found that young people consider those whom they have talked to online for some time not strangers but as virtual friends. This affects the degree to which young people are willing to share information and interact with such 'strangers'. This is indeed an issue of concern. A substantial proportion of children reported having engaged in high risk behaviour online:

- 37 per cent had shared an email address
- 34 per cent provided information about the school they attended
- 23 per cent provided a mobile number
- 26 per cent provided a personal photograph.

The findings about risk-taking on the internet are summarised below:

- A high proportion of children reported having engaged in high risk behaviour online (defined by the degree to which they share information and interact with strangers).
- A significant proportion says they will continue with such behaviour (particularly 13+).
- Interacting with strangers (that is, adding them as ISM or Facebook friends and exchanging messages) is becoming an accepted behaviour not perceived as 'risk-taking'.

Some young people agreed that if they forge a relationship with a person they have met online, or were introduced to this person online by someone, they would consider a meeting. However, the young people who raised this point said they would meet with an online friend only if they were accompanied by a guardian or a friend:

> 'If I build up the friends and then you really, really want to go and see them I think you should definitely bring a parent or like a young adult, a responsible person someone who's responsible for you or something to act like a guardian for you' (Boy 13, Evaluation of the ThinkUKnow project).

Nevertheless, it was found that some students (particularly older students) would consider meeting a person they have not met before. Some students said they would meet someone if they have spent a considerable amount of time chatting online and if they could see their real face via a webcam. This finding is confirmed by Davidson and Martellozzo's (2008) study, where respondents indicated that they would be willing to meet virtual friends if they had been chatting online for some time and felt comfortable with them.

As making friends online is part of a wider social trend toward socialising online, there is no reason to expect young people to behave otherwise. This presents problems in terms of the effectiveness of safety messages regarding strangers. During the focus groups, when young people were asked what they know about safety online, they all seemed very knowledgeable. They could all list the messages they learnt from the TUK training and other internet safety awareness training. Some are illustrated below:

> 'Just there are people that you don't know and they can be on msn and not to talk to anyone you don't actually know' (Boy 13, Evaluation of the ThinkUknow project)

> 'Don't give away personal information like where you live to people you don't know' (Boy 12, Evaluation of the ThinkUKnow project)

It was interesting to note that, although most young people are knowledgeable about the risks they may encounter online, many of them do not take preventative steps.

Other online risks

Hasebrink et al. (2009) reviewed 400 studies in 21 European countries and found that the common risks young people are more likely to be exposed to, in order of frequency,[4] are:

- giving out personal information: around half online teenagers (with national variations spanning 13 per cent–19 per cent)
- seeing pornography: around 4 in 10 across Europe

- seeing violent or hateful content
- being bullied/harassed/stalked: around 1 in 5 or 6
- receiving unwanted sexual comments: around 1 in 10 teenagers in Germany, Ireland, Portugal; around 1 in 3 or 4 in Iceland, Norway, Sweden and the UK
- meeting an online contact offline: around 9 per cent (1 in 11) online teenagers in most countries, rising to 1 in 5 in the Czech Republic, Poland and Sweden.'

(Livingstone 2009:163–64)

It is therefore quite common for teenagers to share personal information online with their online contacts even when amongst this list there are people that cannot strictly be considered friends. Many continue to add people they do not know to their SNSs and to make public personal information such as the school they go to, personal pictures and so on.

In the UK Ofcom's recent research exploring young people's (aged 16–24) online behaviour suggests that those in the younger age range (16–19) were much less aware of potential risks in accessing and entering personal information to websites than were the older age range in the sample:

> Young adults are less likely to make any kind of judgment about a website before entering personal details, less likely to have any concerns about entering personal details online – within the young adult population, it is the attitudes and behaviours of the youngest adults – those aged 16–19 – which are the most striking. These adults are the most likely to share information and download content from the internet, at the same time as being less likely to make any checks or judgments, and more likely to believe that the internet is regulated.
>
> (Ofcom 2009)

This suggests that older children are more likely to engage in risk-taking behaviour online and appear less likely to act on advice regarding internet safety. As argued by Davies et al. (2008), older learners seem quite knowledgeable about how to protect their own safety and identity online, but at the same time are less convincing as to whether they manage to act in such sensible ways when online. When asked the question 'what information do you include in the profile?' I found that the majority would include pictures of themselves posing alone or with friends. Many may include lyrics, films they like, what they are doing, where they go, what they are thinking. They would not include personal information such as their telephone number or address but would include pictures of themselves with their school uniform on (showing the logo of the school on their uniform).

One child told me:

> 'I include what I do, where I go. Particularly if I am excited I write "it is going to be so cool". I do this mainly because I am bored. But I am getting bored of Facebook' (Girl 13, Metropolitan Police Project)

As far as Facebook is concerned, most of the students have their profile public (42 per cent); some private (32 per cent); and some did not understand the difference (26 per cent).

Educational and informational measures directed at children, parents and the public

There have already been considerable efforts to increase online child protection, both nationally and internationally. Organisations such as the Virtual Global Taskforce (VGT) and the Internet Watch Foundation (IWF) are making some headway in attempting to protect children online. The VGT is an organisation that includes a number of law enforcement agencies[5] from around the world with the aim of building an international partnership to protect children from online abuse by providing awareness and support.

In the UK, public bodies such as CEOP, formed in 2006 proactively to combat online abuse of children, play a vital role in child protection. It launched a national campaign entitled 'Think you know' to provide children with advice and guidance on how to use the internet safely (CEOP 2006). This programme is now delivered to children throughout the UK. The programme seeks to impart internet safety advice to children and young people aged 5–16. The programme usually includes a presentation delivered in schools either by teachers or other trained dedicated people and a website with different sections for different age groups, parents, teachers and trainers. Safety advice is also provided on the website.

Other educational programmes have been developed by other charities such as ChildNet International, which has developed a comprehensive list of educational packages to help children to stay safe online. ChildNet's website provides general safety advice for parents, young people and teachers on important key issues such as how to protect privacy, be safe on SNSs, use mobile phones safely, ethical online behaviour and cyberbullying. Some of the key massages are illustrated below:

'1   Always explore the privacy settings of your SNS to protect your privacy and to protect yourself from strangers.
2   Get your friends and family to have a look at your SNS to check that you aren't giving out too much personal information or posting inappropriate photos/films because they might see something you've missed.
3   Keep your passwords to yourself.
4   Respect yourself and others online.
5   If you are unlucky enough to have a bad experience online report it to the service provider and tell an adult.
6   Think about who you give your number to – you don't know where it might end up.
7   If you receive a nasty text save it for evidence but don't reply to it; if you reply you are likely to get yourself into trouble too.

8   If you think you have downloaded a net nasty by mistake make sure you tell someone about it and report it.

9   Cyberbullying is NEVER acceptable. If you or someone you know is targeted by bullies online tell them

   a   to report the bully to the website/service operator

   b   to 'keep evidence of the bullying behaviour to resist the temptation to reply to nasty messages

   c   to tell an adult.'

(http://www.kidsmart.org.uk/)

Other countries around the world, including Italy (http://www.securityclick.it), the US (http://www.netsmartz.org), New Zealand (http://www.netsafe.org.nz) and Norway (the Norwegian Child Consent Initiative) have embarked upon very similar initiatives.

In Bahrain the Be-Free organisation has undertaken workshops on internet safety and offers advice to parents and children on its website.[6] The Be-Free organisation was set up to educate parents, children and teachers about child abuse. The organisations goals are to:

- build a smart, safe and strong child
- provide parents and caregivers with skills to build emotionally intelligent children
- empower children and adults victims of child abuse to regain strength and trust in self and others
- conduct specialised researches and studies
- increase society awareness on issues related to child abuse and neglect
- provide specialised consulting and training for professionals.'

(http://www.befreecenter.org/about-us.aspx)

In Europe and the US, educational programmes have also been created for parents, carers and the public. For example, the Internet Crime against Children (ICAC) Task Force in the US has initiated a program to help parents learn about the great resources the internet holds for their children but also how to be aware of, and to overcome, the dangers they may come across. The program has been developed by NetSmartz Workshop, an interactive educational safety resource from the National Center for Missing and Exploited Children (NCMEC) and the Boys and Girls Clubs of America (BGCA) that uses age-appropriate 3D activities to teach children and teens how to be safer when using the internet. NetSmartz has been implemented in more than 3000 BGCA Clubs nationally, serving more than 3.3 million young people (Davidson and Martellozzo 2008; http://www.netsmartz.org).

Parents share a great responsibility in educating their children on how to stay safe online and providing them with guidelines. As recommended by Davidson and Martellozzo (2004) in their evaluation of the Safer Surfing Programme (one of the first programmes created in the UK), it is vital that parents have direct conversations, particularly with teens, on a regular basis. In the real world, it is usual for parents to ask their children questions such as: 'Where are you going?'; 'Who are you going with?'; 'What time will you be home?' These three questions should be the bases for internet use also but formulated differently: 'What sites will you visit?'; 'Who will you talk to?'; 'For how long will you be online?'; 'Where will you be using the computer?'

However, asking these questions may not be sufficient. Parents need to be able to explore their children's answers and, in order to do so, they need to become involved in their children's use of the internet, including social networking and other user interactive services.

Furthermore, it is important for children to feel comfortable talking to their parents if they are involved in anything that made them feel scared, uncomfortable or confused. Often children are afraid to communicate bad experiences online for fear that their internet use will be taken away. If this happens, the children will be more reluctant to tell their parents of a problem because of fear of overreaction. Sometimes children get into situations that have escalated beyond their comfort level. Thus, trust should be created and maintained.

Balancing risks and opportunities is not an easy task. As argued by Livingstone: 'in regulating children's internet use, we risk two failures – the failure to take opportunities, and the failure to protect against dangers' (2002: 19). As research conducted to date suggests, parents' biggest fear is for their children to be groomed, abused, exposed to inappropriate material or bullied. It can be argued that this fear in part derives from the existence of a knowledge gap between young people and adults regarding the use of the internet and online safety (this gap was particularly pronounced in Bahrain). Where parents are aware of the risks they often do not know how to help their children to stay safe when navigating on line. This insecurity may result in children becoming fearful of, or not allowed to use SNSs, for example. This emphasises the need for both parents and teachers to communicate and educate children and young people about safe and appropriate use of the internet.

Young people's online behaviour and sex offending

It is important to note that the content posted online by young people may damage their reputation, now and in the future. While SNSs offer opportunities to young people to express themselves and to be creative, they are often unaware that their own photographs or text, although intended for a small audience, can quickly attract a far larger one and have a lasting impact on other people's perceptions of them:

'Once my friend was on Bebo and she was looking for random friends and she found a profile of a girl she had pictures of me on her Bebo. And she pretended to be and she was pretending her profile photos were me, and all her albums were pictures of me. That happens on Bebo sometimes. She pretended it was me, and then we saw her talking to boys and everything and my friends started saying why do you have pictures of me on your Bebo (Girl ID: 14, Evaluation of the ThinkUKnow project).

Ongoing research funded by the European Commission Safer Internet Programme (Webster et al. 2009) exploring online grooming behaviour in four European countries suggests that offenders may target socially isolated, vulnerable young people who respond well to attention received from online contacts. Abusers can use public online interactive spaces, including young people's Facebook profiles that are not set to 'private', to find and meet children and young people.

Conclusions

In this chapter I have argued that there is a concern that the capabilities of social networking services, combined with children's own risk behaviour, may increase the potential for sexual exploitation of children by adults. As will be discussed in the following chapters, technologies around SNSs allow relatively easy access to children by online groomers. Once the online groomer identifies a potential victim (or victims) he may use incentives to encourage the child's participation, towards the goal of sexual contact. Children and young people can be exploited online even when actual physical contact does not take place in the real world. This may happen by the exchange of indecent images and/or by persuading children and young people to send explicit images of themselves. Recent research conducted by Webster et al. (2009) with online groomers in four European countries suggests that the grooming approach can be prolonged, spanning months; alternatively, it can be over a very short time. An analysis of offender chat logs suggests that conversations with young people can become immediately sexualised and that offenders have many young people on their friends list, which they will work through in order to find a child who is willing to meet with them. As will be shown in the remaining chapters of this book, there have been a number of cases where adults have used SNSs as a means of contacting and grooming children and young people for sexual exploitation.

Notes

1 As part of my wider research, in 2010/2011 I was commissioned by the Metropolitan Police Paedophile Unit and High Technological Crime Unit to conduct an independent study to explore how young children from different cultural backgrounds behave online. I have based this study on qualitative research, which included 16 focus groups with 86 young people in schools in diverse areas of London. The study also included a small sample of five face-to-face interviews with head teachers, teachers and a school officer. Here I also include some data collected during the evaluation of the CEOP educational 'ThinkUKnow' programme in which I participated during 2009. This research aimed at understanding the impact that this particular educational programme had on young

people's online behaviour. The ThinkUKnow programme was designed by CEOP and distributed across UK schools to teach young people how to stay safe online.

2 In 2010, Julia Davidson and I conducted the first State of the Nation Review of Internet Safety in the Middle East. This review focused particularly on the Kingdom of Bahrain. A total of 816 participants completed an online survey, aged from 18 to 71. The results showed that the internet is part of everybody's life also in the East. The great majority of respondents (67.7 per cent) claimed that they spend more than four hours online per day, for a variety of reasons. The most common reason cited are to: send and receive email (91.4 per cent), look for information for work and homework (78.3 per cent), use SNSs (60.0 per cent) and to look for information on hobbies and interests (58.1 per cent) respectively. SNSs and games are very popular also amongst adults and offer a range of opportunities for development but also fun and learning. Interestingly, 100 per cent of respondents in Bahrain use social networking sites with the most popular being MySpace (96 per cent) and Facebook (69 per cent). These findings were validated by other research (Davidson et al. 2010), which shows that instant messaging and online games are the most popular online activities. This research was co-funded by the National Audit Office (NAO) and CEOP. The research included an online survey of 11 to 16-year-olds (n = 1808) and focus groups (n = 83) of young people.

3 A stranger may be defined as someone with whom the child may have spoken to online for some time, but has never met in person.

4 Cross-national differences in methodology for data collection should be taken into account when looking at these figures.

5 The VGT is formed by: the Australian Federal Police, the Child Exploitation and Online Protection Centre in the UK, the Italian Postal and Communication Police Service, the Royal Canadian Mounted Police, the US Department of Homeland Security and Interpol.

6 http://www.be-free.info/en/How_can_I_protect_myself_on_the_Internet.asp.

References

Banquil, K., Burce, C. A., Chua, N. A., Dianalan, S. D., Leaño, G. A., Matienzo, A. R., et al. (2009) *Social Networking Sites Affect One's Academic Performance Adversely*. Paper presented at the College of Nursing.

Biegler, S. and Boyd, D. (2010) *Risky Behaviours and Online Safety: A 2010 Literature Review*, Harvard University, Berkman Center for Inernet and Society.

Boeck, T., Fleming, J. and Kemshall, H. (2006) Young People and Social Capital; http://www.pcrrd.group.shef.ac.uk/reports/project_4.pdf. Accessed 5/10/08.

Boyd, D. and Ellison, N. (2007) Social Network Sites: Definition, History, and Scholarship [http://jcmc.indiana.edu/vol13/issue1/boyd.ellison.html]. *Journal of Computer-Mediated Communication*, 13(1).

British Office of Communications. (2 April 2008) *Social Networking. A Quantitative and Qualitative Research Report into Attitudes, Behaviours and Use*.

Bunting, M. (2001) From Socialism to Starbucks: the Decline of Politics and the Consumption of our Inner Self. *Renewal*, 9(2–3), 23–32; http://www.renewal.org.uk/issues/2001/summer/feature2003.asp.

Cavanagh, A. (2007) *Sociology in the Age of the Internet*, Berkshire, Open University Press.

CEOP. (2006) Thinkyouknow; www.thinkyouknow.co.uk.

Chibnall, S., Wallace, M., Leicht, C. and Lunghofer, L. (2006) *I-Safe evaluation; Final Report*, Washington, National Institute of Justice.

Child Online Protection Act 2000 (COPA) United States.

Clikymedia. (2011) UK Facebook Statistics for March 2011.

comScore World Metrix. (12/08/2008). Social Networking Explodes Worldwide as Sites Increase their Focus on Cultural Relevance; http://www.comscore.com/press/release. asp?press=2396, accessed 2/10/08.

Crombie, G. and Trinneer, A. (2003) *Children and Internet Safety: An Evaluation of the Missing Programme. A Report to the Research and Evaluation Section of the National Crime Prevention Centre of Justice Canada*, Ottawa, School of Psycology, University of Ottawa.

Davidson, J. and Martellozzo, E. (2004) *Educating Children about Sexual Abuse and Evaluating the Metropolitan Police Safer Surfing Programme*, London, University of Westminster and Metropolitan Police.

Davidson, J. and Martellozzo, E. (2008) Policing the Internet: Protecting Vulnerable Children From Sex Offenders In Cyberspace. *Police Investigations Police Practice and Research: An International Journal.*

Davidson, J. and Martellozzo, E. (2010) *State of the Nation Review of Internet Safety*, Kingdom of Bahrain.

Davidson, J., Lorenz, M. and Martellozzo, E. (2010) Evaluation of CEOP ThinkUKnow. Internet Safety Programme and Exploration of Young People's Internet Safety Knowledge. *Centre for Abuse and Trauma Studies.*

Davies et al. (2008) *The Learner and their Context – Benefits of ICT outside formal education*, Coventry, Becta.

De Gutzman, M. and Bosh, K. (2007) *High Risk Behaviour Amongst Youth*; http://www.ianrpubs.unl.edu/epublic/live/g1715/build/g1715.pdf. Accessed 30/06/11: University of Nebraska, US.

Department for Communities and Local Government. (2008) *Online Social Networks. Research Report.*

Douglas, A. C., Mills, E., Niang, M., Stepchenkova, S., Byun, S., Ruffini, C., et al. (2008) Internet addiction: Meta-synthesis of qualitative research for the decade 1996–2006. *Computers in Human Behaviour* (24), 3027–44.

Friedel, C. and Kraus, P. (2009) *Online Social Networks and Their Business Relevance.* Paper presented at the Information Management.

Garter Newsroom. (6 August 2008) Organizations Should Implement a Multilevel Approach to Policies for Effective Governance; http://www.gartner.com/it/page.jsp?id=737512.

Griffiths, M. (1998) Does Internet and Computer Addiction Exist? Some case study evidence. *CyberPsycology and Behaviour*, 3(2), 211–18.

Grohol, M. (2005) Internet addiction guide; http://www.psychcentral.com/netaddiction/.

Hasebrink, U., Livingstone, S., Haddon, L. and Olafsson, K. (2009) *Comparing children's online opportunities and risks across Europe: Cross-national comparisons for EU Kids Online*, London, LSE.

Home Office Task Force on Child Protection on the Internet. (2007) Good Practice Guidance for the Providers of Social Networking and Other User Interactive Services; http://www.homeoffice.gov.

http://www.be-free.info/en/How_can_I_protect_myself_on_the_Internet.asp.

http://www.befreecenter.org/about-us.aspx.

http://www.kidsmart.org.uk/.

http://www.netsmartz.org.

Livingstone, S. (2002) *Children's Use of the Internet: A Review of the Research Literature*, London, LSE.

Livingstone, S. (2009) *Children and the Internet*, London, Polity Books.

Livingstone, S. and Haddon, L. (2009) *EU Kids Online: final Report*, London, LSE.

Martellozzo, E. (2011) *Understanding Children Online Activities: Developing Research and Training for Covert Internet Investigators*, London Metropolitan Police.

Ofcom (2009) *Digital Lifestyles: Young adults aged 16–24*; http://www.ofcom.org.uk/advice/media_literacy/medlitpub/medlipubrss/digital_young/.

Shannon, D. (2007) *The Online Sexual Solicitation of Children by Adults in Sweden*, Stockhom; http://www.bra.se.

The Virtual Global Task Force; http://www.virtualglobaltaskforce.com.

Webster, S., Davidson, J., Bifulco, A., Pham, T. and Caretti, V. (2009) *European Online Grooming Project: Progress Report Covering Period: 1 June 2009–31 December 2009.*

Wellman, B. (1988). Structural Analysis: From Method and Metaphor to Theory and Substance. In Wellman, B. and Berkowitz, D. S. (eds.) *Social Structures: A Network Approach*, Cambridge, Cambridge University Press.

Wolak, J., Finkelhor, D., Mitchell, K. and Ybarra, M. (2008) Online 'Predators' and their Victims: Myths, Realities, and Implication for Prevention and Treatment. *American Psychologist*, 63(2), 111–28.

Wolak, J., Mitchell, K. and Finkelhor, D. (2006) Online Victimisation of Youth: Five Years Later. *National Centre for Missing and Exploited Children.* http://www.netsmartz.org

Yellowlees, P. and Marks, S. (2005) Problematic Internet Use or Internet Addiction? *Computers in Human Behaviour*, 23(2007), 1447–53.

Young, K. S. (1996) *Internet Addiction: The Emergence of a New Clinical Disorder.* Paper presented at the 104th Annual Meeting of the American Psycological Association.

Young, K. S. (1998) Internet Addiction: The Emergence of a New Clinical Disorder. *CyberPsycology and Behaviour*, 1(3), 237–44.

Chapter 4

The legal framework

Introduction

Recent academic debates on child sexual abuse, both online and offline, have been characterised by a notable disjunction between criminological contributions, informed by legal (eg Ost 2009) and socio-psychological (eg Quayle and Taylor 2005) approaches, and sociological research concerned with the political construction of the problem in the context of practices of neoliberal governmentality (eg Wacquant 2009). Debates in these strands of enquiry often seem to take place without mutual interpenetration. This chapter deals with the legal framing of sexual contact between adults and children online largely as a matter of descriptive context, in preparation for the empirical material to be explored in subsequent chapters. In doing so, I draw primarily on the legal and socio-psychological lines of enquiry. Nevertheless, it is important briefly to set my argument in its political context.

It must be acknowledged that legal constructions of sexuality and the protections and penalties they afford are never simply matters of practical expediency, being immersed instead in a variety of historically and locally specific moral discourses. Following extensive respective research in the sociology of sexualities over the past four decades (Foucault 1998; Laqueur 1990), this assertion is today largely unproblematic. From it follows the insight that social categories such as the paedophile or the child-as-victim are contingent upon and sustained by particular discursive framings and do not possess the sort of biological, psychological and social fixity that popular understanding often attributes to them.

These basic insights have allowed scholars such as Loïc Wacquant (2009) successfully to tie the legal pursuit of sex offenders to an overall political and cultural trend towards a punitive reconceptualisation of penal policy. Here the focus was primarily on 'warehousing' of populations regarded as undesirable by social elites in the context of neoliberal globalisation. Wacquant directly links this punitive turn to recent campaigns against 'sexual predators' in the US:

'Propelled by a vitriolic rhetoric that portrays the fight against crime as a moral battle to the death between good and evil – instead of an organizational matter of rights, responsibilities, and the rational allocation of penal and other means to prevent, mitigate, or suppress injurious deviance – the "sexual predator," typically portrayed in the colors of a "lowlife" social drifter, has acquired a central place in the country's expansive *public culture of vilification of criminals*. As the living embodiment of moral abjectness, he provides an urgent and perpetually refreshed motive for the full repudiation of the ideal of rehabilitation and the turn to fierce neutralization and vengeful retribution that has characterized US penal policy since the late 1970s' (Wacquant 2009: 214).

Similarly, Nancy Baym (2010) recently examined the disjunction between public perceptions and realities of sexual abuse online:

'These days, children are seen as likely to be exposed to (or, worse yet, exploited for) pornography and sexual encounters. The most prominent examples of this in the discourse around the internet concern sexual preda-tion. To hear much of the public representation of the internet is to imagine a world in which sexual crimes are reaching new heights as unwitting inno-cents are drawn into deceptive relationships that end in molestation, abduc-tion, and even death. Adult men do sometimes use the internet to lure girls into inappropriate relationships. This is surely awful, but it is very unusual. When adult men and underage girls do meet through the internet for sexual encounters, it is usually consensual and honest, if morally dubious (Baym 2010: 42).'

It does not seem far-fetched to argue that recent development in penal policy in the UK and related public debates have shown strong elements of the public culture of vilification Wacquant and Baym describe here. Campaigns by right-wing tabloids for the public disclosure of sex offenders' identity during the 2000s are a case in point, as is recent criticism by Home Secretary Theresa May of a Supreme Court ruling allowing individuals to seek to have their names removed from the sex offenders' register (BBC News 16 February 2011). It is beyond the scope of this book to analyse the social construction of the risk posed by sex offenders from such a political perspective. Instead, my research approaches the risk of online sex offending in terms of the on-the-ground pragmatics of policing operations. Questions about the ways in which such on-the-ground policing prac-tices might be informed by political context will be raised separately in the concluding chapter.

Defining online child sexual abuse

New digital media and other technological developments such as digital cameras, peer-to-peer (P2P) file-sharing technologies, social networking sites and web cameras (webcams) have encouraged many scholars and practitioners to think carefully about the definition of online child sexual abuse (CSA). Since the emergence of this serious problem, a number of definitions have been drafted, shaped and reshaped throughout the years.

In 2005, the Virtual Global Task Force (VGT) (www.virtualglobaltaskforce. com) defined online CSA as the sharing and downloading of images of children being physically and sexually abused and approaching children online with the aim of developing a sexual relationship in the 'real world', also known as 'grooming'. This definition highlights a number of rather serious risks that children may encounter when online: exposure to inappropriate conversation; unwittingly becoming the subject of sexual fantasy; being seduced by an adult posing as an adult or as a child; being sent indecent or obscene images; being asked to send naked images of themselves or their friends; being engaged in sexually explicit talk; or being encouraged to perform sexual explicit acts on themselves or their friends (so-called cybersex). All these activities and risks form the new reality of cyberspace, where every day a seriously significant number of children are approached for sexual abuse.

This critical situation has led to the emergence of national and international legislative frameworks to combat online child sexual abuse. Early laws prohibited the sexual abuse and exploitation of children and initial manifestations of online child sexual abuse in the form of 'child pornography'. More recent international legislative efforts have framed this problem as a form of 'cybercrime', a content-related offence associated with the production and circulation of illegal content in cyberspace.

Framing online CSA as a cybercrime has been and continues to be a challenging task. Child protection is a problem that has been dealt with at local level, as is the production of abuse images, grooming behaviour etc. In contrast, cybercrime is multijurisdictional. Therefore, the framing of online CSA as a form of cybercrime challenges existing police structures and requires the systematic harmonisation of policing and child protection practices, as well as underlying laws and policy frameworks. Likewise, the consistent allocation of resources at the translocal and transnational level amounts to a substantial challenge.

The convergence of these socio-legal challenges with technological developments has resulted in the emergence of the grooming offence, a distinct category of criminal behaviour with a requirement for bespoke and broad-based legal intervention. Socio-legal changes are often followed by law enforcement interventions. Here I present some case studies highlighting the UK policing response as an exemplar of how distinct policing specialisms have developed in response to recent grooming legislation and how policing practices have adapted to accommodate the provisions of these statutes. Finally, I identify new and emerging gaps and challenges in policing and child protection practice presented by the introduction of grooming legislation. These challenges are presented here and reinforced throughout this book.

The current legislative context: the Sexual Offences Act 2003

The Sexual Offences Act 2003 (SOA 2003), which came into force on 1 May 2004, has been created to close some significant loopholes that existed in the Sexual Offences Act 1956 and to reflect current, rather than Victorian, attitudes towards sex. It attempts to provide: a coherent definition of sexual offences with the aim to protect vulnerable individuals from exploitation and sexual abuse; important revisions to mental elements including questions of consent; and amendments to the laws governing the sex offender register (Home Office 2004). Furthermore, it re-enacts and extends the abuse of position of trust offences set out in the Sexual Offences (Amendment) Act 2000 and introduces new occupations to which the position of trust laws applies. These include roles such as: personal advisers appointed under relevant legislation (eg when young people leave local authority care); guardians as set out in the Children Act 1989, the Adoption Rules 1984 and the Family Proceedings Rules 1991; members of a Youth Offending Team and treatment provider etc (Home Office Communication Directorate 2004). Furthermore, the SOA 2003 applies to under 16s and the Sexual Offences (Amendment) Act (Position of Trust) 2000 applies to under 18s.

These strict measures have been set out to protect particularly young people aged 16 and 17 who, although they are over the legal age of consent, are vulnerable to exploitation by people they know and trust. In fact, the offences of those working in positions of trust are the same that apply to the general public. However, when the offence is committed by a person in a position of trust, the law applies where the young person is under 18 instead of under 16. These measures have been taken because research suggests that sex offenders often obtain employment or voluntary positions in which they have easy access to children (Gallagher 2000b; Miller 1997). This is what Gallagher (2000a) defines as 'institutional CSA':

> 'The sexual abuse of a child (under 18 years of age) by an adult who works with him or her. The perpetrator may be employed in a paid or voluntary capacity; in the public, voluntary or private sector; in a residential or non-residential setting; and may work either directly with children or being in an ancillary role' (Gallagher 2000a: 797).

Children under the age of consent or between the ages of 13 and 15 are protected by the general law of the Act.

The SOA 2003 merits close scrutiny and consideration, particularly of the new fundamental and extensive changes it offers. The first part of the Act examines sexual offences, creating new ones and widening the scope of existing ones. Its second part then focuses on children and child protection. Starting with the analysis of the first section of the SOA 2003, the primary non-consensual offences are at sections 1–4 and 5–8 of the Act. The offences are rape (section 1), assault by penetration (section 2), sexual assault (section 3) and causing a person to engage in sexual activity without consent (section 4). Sections 5–8 create the same four offences against child victims under 13 years of age.

Rape has always been understood as the most serious, the most feared and the most debated of all sexual offences (section 1) (Kelly 1988). Under the 1956 Act, rape was defined as penetration of the vagina or anus by penis without consent. This meant that other serious penetrative assaults, such as penetrative oral sex, were only treated as 'indecent assault'. However, the SOA 2003 has redefined the offence and classed oral penetration as rape. The new definition therefore requires the prosecution to prove three things – intentional penetration, absence of consent and absence of reasonable belief in consent. In terms of CSA, the Act defines rape as any sexual intercourse with a child under the age of 13. Other non-consensual offences against children under the age of 13 include sexual assault by penetration, sexual assault and causing or inciting a child to engage in any sexual activity. For those offences, it is unnecessary for the prosecution to prove the absence of consent. This defence applies to any defendant regardless of age and, as such, attracted some criticism for bringing the full weight of the criminal law to bear on cases where young people who are closer in age to each other are experimenting.

The SOA 2003 also reviews the offence of sexual assault (section 3). Under the Sexual Offences Act 1956 the term 'indecent assault' was used to encompass a wide range of activities, from kissing a child in a sexual manner to touching a child's genitals and enforced oral sex. However, as Ashworth (1999) points out, there is clearly a difference between the two categories of crime in terms of the impact that those might have on the victim. The effect of the 2003 Act is, among other things, to reconsider these categories, to define them accordingly and to reclassify forced oral sex as rape and penetration of the vagina or anus other than by the penis as assault by penetration. As a result, the new offence of sexual assault is redefined by its four elements: (i) the defendant (A) intentionally touches another person (B) (according to the Act 'touching includes touching with any part of the body, and with anything else, or through anything'); (ii) the touching must be sexual, as defined; (iii) 'B does not consent to the touching'; and (iv) 'A does not reasonably believe that B consents'.

Furthermore, in order to redress the balance in favour of the victim (without jeopardizing the defendant's rights to a fair trial), three new measures have been included on the issue of consent. These are:

- a person consents if he or she agrees by choice to the sexual activity and has the freedom and capacity to make that choice
- all the circumstances at the time of the offence will be looked at in determining whether the defendant acted reasonably in believing the complainant consented
- people will be considered most unlikely to have agreed to sexual activity if they were subject to threats or fear of serious harm, unconscious, drugged, abducted or unable to communicate because of a physical disability.

New offences are also stipulated in the Act to prevent children from being abused through prostitution and pornography. They cover a range of activities including: buying the sexual services of a child; causing or encouraging child prostitution or pornography; arranging or facilitating child prostitution or pornography; and controlling any of the activities of a child involved in prostitution or pornography. Furthermore, forms of non-contact offences have been included in the Act because they can cause embarrassment, distress or humiliation of the victim. These non-contact offences include exposure, that is, cases in which a man or a woman exposes their genitalia, and voyeurism (Sentencing Guidelines 2003). Those with mental disorders or unable to refuse because of lack of understanding are also protected under the new Act.

The 2003 Act created new offences in addition to redefining older ones. Crucially, the offence of grooming was introduced into the statute, which represents a truly desirable advance. For the first time, legislation has been designed to tackle sexual behaviour over the internet where a person has groomed a child for sexual purposes.

Indecent images

The collection and distribution of indecent images of children is often erroneously perceived to be a new trend, but in reality this phenomenon dates back to the 18th century (Lane 2001; Yar 2007). Research conducted by Quayle and Taylor (2005) suggests that the trade in indecent images of children already existed in Victorian times, where they constituted a substantial part of mainstream pornography. During those times, the medium seems to have been postcards, and evidence suggests that the ratio of child to adult pornography was five to one. However, the arrival of the internet has allowed the production and distribution of indecent images to take place on a much larger scale, more quickly and at almost no cost. Not until relatively recently has CSA also begun to take place in cyberspace, and the repercussions it has on children can be as serious as those in the real world (O'Connell 2003; Davidson and Martellozzo 2008; Yar 2007).

In the last few years, several debates have been put forward when discussing the most appropriate definition or terminology to adopt for 'child pornography' without minimising its seriousness and criminal nature. Max Taylor (2002) argues that the most central and important point that should be emphasised is that child pornography at its worst constitutes a visual representation of the commission of a sexual assault on a child (Taylor 2002). Indeed, 'child pornography' can be described as a picture of sexual assault or rape in progress. However, it is not simply a picture of a horrific act that can be physically destroyed or deleted with the click of a button. Its production is more serious than this. As Lanning correctly argues, it represents 'the permanent record of the sexual abuse or exploitation of an actual child' (Lanning 1984: 89), a record that cannot be traced or removed from cyberspace. Furthermore, not all images represent the sexual abuse of children involving adults or, in some cases, animals. Large quantities of images depict children posing in sexually provocative positions, either dressed, semi-naked or naked. How should these images be regarded? In answer to this question, we should ask ourselves: who is standing behind the camera? In 1993, Kelly and Scott (1993) argued that:

> '. . . [p]hotographs and films which include children in the frame involve adults outside who control the situation and children's behaviour within it: demanding of and/or instructing the children in what the photographer requires from them. This too is a form of sexual abuse' (Kelly and Scott 1993: 116).

All definitions explicitly stress the seriousness of the act of possessing, making, downloading or distributing pornographic pictures of children or young people. Some also criminalise the depiction of serious assault or rape which is used deliberately to gratify the user who is sexually attracted to children. With this in mind, is it still correct to talk about child pornography when what is produced and distributed is in reality images of abused children? Is it fair to define as 'kiddy porn' something that is 'a record of the systematic rape, abuse and torture of children on film, photograph and other electronic means'? (Edwards 2002: 1). To be able to answer these questions effectively, one may need to focus on the child depicted in the images. Joining the two terms 'child' and 'pornography' together is seriously erroneous, as it may lead to the objectification of the children depicted in the images. Evidence for this is readily available in chat rooms, where sex offenders refer to indecent images as a 'stamp' missing from their collection, whereby the child is not seen as a victim but as an object (Edwards 2002; Quayle and Taylor 2001; Davidson and Martellozzo 2008). This argument also supports Quayle et al.'s (2001) contention, who claim that, if the term 'child pornography' is used to describe indecent images of children, there is a risk of allowing a comparison with the depictions of consensual activity between adults that are so widely available from newsagents and video retailers. This view is endorsed by Commander Peter Spindler of the Metropolitan Police (2003), who believes that there is a risk that 'the term "child pornography" has become an acceptable passive term, which fails accurately to describe the reality of the sexual acts forced upon children'. Williams (2004) is more reserved, arguing that these statements give a distorted picture: 'certainly, at its worst, child pornography is proof of a serious crime. However, there are depictions of acts which would be caught by child pornography legislation but which do not record a crime being committed' (Williams 2004: 247).

Edwards (2002: 1–21) conducted the first national study of child pornography trials in the Crown Court in England and Wales. One of the key findings of the study was that the potential links between the possession of child pornography or the taking of indecent photographs of children and actual abuse are rarely acknowledged and, when they are, they are often downplayed. Edwards (ibid) demonstrated how in both magistrates' and Crown Courts a clear distinction is made between the taking of pornographic photographs of children and the abuse of children. Defendants charged with possession or distribution of child pornography were found successfully to minimise their actions in the eyes of the court, while judges failed to recognise the danger posed by defendants convicted of possession and distribution (http://www.dfes.gov.uk/acpc/docs/tcrureview.doc). This was reflected in the very short prison sentences often given to those found guilty, as if viewing or distributing indecent images of children was not a violation of the child's integrity and safety.

It can be argued that underestimating the seriousness of viewing child pornography can create further potential dangers. For instance, not only would we lose sight of the child depicted in the images, but also, perhaps unconsciously, we would end up distinguishing between offenders on the basis of a misperception of the seriousness of their offence: the bad offender who had physical contact with the victim, and the good offender, who merely viewed what the bad offender had done. This perception ought to be challenged, as viewing such material can increase demand and, as a result, the continuation of a cycle of victimisation. Indeed, Carr argues (2003): 'Possessors are simply active abusers by proxy. They could not possess or look at the images if someone else did not do the abusing for them. If they did not do what they do, fewer children would be abused' (Carr 2003: 15). As many practitioners that work in this area have repeatedly agreed, the term to use when referring to child pornography is 'indecent images' and this term will be adopted throughout this book. Finding an appropriate definition becomes even more complicated and contentious when the indecent images produced do not represent real children. Children may be depicted by non-photographic material such as *lolicon* or *shoracon hentai*[1] or young girls represented by avatar (the embodiment of a person or idea) engaging in sexual acts with adults in virtual environments such as in Second Life.[2] Technological innovations develop so quickly that it is challenging to keep up with all these changes, not only from the definitional point of view but also from the perspective of the legislation and law enforcement interventions. In 1985, Tyler and Stone defined child pornography as: 'pictorial depictions of children in sexually explicit poses or acts. Unlike sketches, drawings and statues, which may or may not have employed live child models, pictorial depictions require that a child must be exploited in order to produce the published product' (Tyler and Stone 1985: 314). Today, the sketches and drawings that Tyler and Stone are referring to have become animated realistic images representing children engaged in sexually explicit behaviour. As a result, the Council of the European Convention on Cybercrime (2001) includes in its definition of offences related to child pornography: 'realistic images representing a minor engaged in sexually explicit conduct' (ibid section 9.2.c). However, section 9.4 states that each party may reserve the right to opt out of applying this definition. A further definition was provided by the Council of Europe Convention on the Protection of Children against Sexual Exploitation and Sexual Abuse (2007). In Article 20 it claims that: 'the term "child pornography" shall mean any material that visually depicts a child engaged in real or simulated sexually explicit conduct or any depiction of a child's sexual organs for primarily sexual purposes'. Thus far, few countries have implemented this definition. As stated by Baines: 'Such imprecision is perhaps symptomatic of the current confusion and lack of consensus concerning computer generated child abuse imagery' (Baines 25–28 November 2008: 9).

Legislation on indecent images of children

The law to prosecute the production and distribution of indecent images of children is copious, clear and undergoes constant amendments. According to the Protection of Children Act 1978 (POCA 1978) it is illegal to permit to be taken, make, possess, show, distribute and advertise any image or pseudo-image[3] of children under the age of 18 (SOA 2003) that is considered to be indecent or abusive.

More amendments have also been made to clarify what constitutes the offence of 'taking', 'making' and 'distributing' indecent images of children. Section 1(1) of the POCA 1978, as amended by the Criminal Justice and Public Order Act 1994 (CJPOA 1994), states that it is an offence:

'a   to take, or permit to be taken, or to make any indecent photograph or pseudo-photograph of a child; or

b   to distribute or show such indecent photographs or pseudo-photographs; or

c   to pass such indecent photographs or pseudo-photographs, with a view to their being distributed or shown by himself or others; or

d   to publish or cause to be published any advertisement likely to be understood as conveying that the advertiser distributes or shows such indecent photographs or pseudo-photographs, or intends to do so.'

Smith and Jayson (2002) argue that the act of making or taking indecent or pseudo-photographs[4] must be a deliberate and intentional act, done with the knowledge that the image constitutes or is likely to constitute an indecent photograph or pseudo-photograph of a child. However, the word 'indecent' was not defined by the Act at the time. It was for the jury to determine whether the photographs or pseudo-photographs in question were indecent. In directing them on this point, the judge had to ask them to decide whether it would be considered indecent by right-minded people (Akdeniz 1997). The jury was entitled to take into consideration the age of the child when defining indecency. Thus, the jury had to consider whether the photograph of a 'child' was indecent, based on the motive of the person taking the photographs (Akdeniz 1997).

However, the SOA 2003 contains a large number of new or amended offences for which there is no sentencing case law. Since the Act came into force, for example, the Protection of Children Act 1978 (POCA 1978) and the Criminal Justice Act 1988 (CJA 1988) had to be further amended. As mentioned before, section 45 of the SOA 2003 increased the definition of 'child' from 16 to 18 years of age and, as a result, the age of the child depicted on indecent images also concerns children of 16 and 17 years of age. However, according to the Sentencing Guidelines Council 2007, the younger the victim, the harsher the sentence should be for offences involving the sexual exploitation of a child; the starting point for sentencing should be higher where the victim is younger than 13 and lower as the age gets closer to 16 and 17 years of age (Sentencing Guidelines Council 2007a).

To distinguish between abusive content and to facilitate the sentencing process, Combating Paedophile Information in Europe's (COPINE) typology of paedophile picture collections has been adapted in English law in the case of *R v (1) Oliver (2) Hartrey (3) BaLldwin* [2002] EWCA Crim 2766 and to signify sentencing guidelines (Taylor and Quayle 2003). These guidelines are based upon five categories of pictures that may be sexualised by an adult with a sexual interest in children. They range from level 1, where children pose as nude or semi-nude, through level 4, where penetrative sexual assault takes place, to level 5, where acts of sadism and bestiality are exercised (COPINE 2003). More precisely, the five point scale is:

'1   images depicting erotic posing with no sexual activity
2   non-penetrative sexual activity between children or solo masturbation by a child
3   non-penetrative sexual activity between adults and children
4   penetrative sexual activity involving a child or children or both children and adults
5   sadism or penetration of, or by, an animal.'

(Sentencing Guidelines Council 2007b: 10)

Although this levelling may contribute to the sanitation of indecent images, it represents an extremely important step towards recognising the seriousness of what images depict (Martellozzo and Taylor 2009). In 2002, the Sentencing Advisory Panel published guidelines on what factors should be taken into consideration when deciding the correct sentence for sex offenders who produce, make and distribute indecent images of children. The primary factors that determine the nature and the length of an offender's sentence are the seriousness of the indecent material collected rather than the quantity. In relation to the seriousness of the material, the Court of Appeal, promoted by the Sentencing Advisory Panel, decided that it would be helpful to classify images in terms of indecency and adapted the COPINE's index scale (Sheldon and Howitt 2007).

Online grooming

The process of grooming a child for sexual purposes is long-established and represents the main method through which children are abused (Beckett et al.1994; Erooga and Masson 2006; Finkelhor et al. 2000). However, with the advent of the internet, sex offenders do not need to lurk in parks or shopping centres; neither do they need to be family members or in a position of trust to attract potential victims

(Medaris and Girouard 2004). Instead, they groom children from the comfort of their homes, protected by the anonymity of cyberspace. 'Grooming' involves a process of communication and socialisation during which an offender seeks to interact with children or young people, possibly to share their interests and hobbies and to provide them with moral support and understanding in an attempt to gain trust in order to prepare them for sexual abuse (Davidson and Martellozzo 2008). John McCarthy and Nathan Gaunt (2005) share similar views and define the phenomenon of online grooming as a type of online behaviour designed to 'seduce' or lure children into sexual behaviour or conversations with or without children's knowledge. They claim that there are different ways of grooming a child online. These can be identified as *sexual harassment* (bullying or persistent unwanted contact by email, text or phone calls for sexual purposes), which can lead eventually to *sexual assault* (arranging meetings with children/young people through chat rooms) which later result in coerced sexual contact (McCarthy and Gaunt 2005).

According to the Sentencing Advisory Panel (2007), sexual grooming is a serious predatory offence that can be defined as a process of socialisation during which an offender interacts with a child in order to prepare him/her for sexual abuse (SOA 2003). The Sentencing Guidelines Council (SGC) points out that an offender can be caught for a grooming offence before he travels to meet the victim; in other words, during the process of 'socialisation'. Furthermore, the SGC states that the seriousness of the offence is based on the groomer's intention. Thus, when a person commits an offence the seriousness of the grooming is based on that offence. In this way, as Gillespie (2008) argues, it is recognised that 'the grooming was a separate preparatory act that led to the eventual contact' (Gillespie 2008: 117). It also recognises that grooming can be harmful in both ways.

Although there are different grooming techniques, in this book I seek to address only those who have been convicted of the offence of meeting a child following grooming contrary to section 15 of the SOA 2003. It is within the context of this landmark piece of legislation that the primary definitions of online child sexual abuse are established.

Legislation on online grooming

In 2003, the SOA in England and Wales recognised the offence of sexual grooming of children via the internet. Section 15 of the SOA 2003 makes 'meeting a child following sexual grooming' a serious offence, where a person arranges to meet a child who is under 18, having communicated with him/her on at least one previous occasion (in person, via the internet or via other technologies), with the intention of performing sexual activity with the child (Davidson and Martellozzo 2008). This applies to the internet, other technologies, such as mobile phones, and to the 'real world'. The concept of 'grooming' is also recognised in Scottish legislation (Davidson 2007). The Protection of Children and Prevention of Sexual Offences

(Scotland) Act 2005 includes 'meeting a child following certain preliminary contact' (section 1); the English equivalent of 'grooming' and the definition is the same. Sexual grooming has also recently been added to the Crimes Amendment Act 2005 in New Zealand. In the US it is an offence to transmit information electronically about a child aged 16 or under, for the purpose of committing a sexual offence (US Code Title 18, Part 1, Chapter 117, AS 2425). The Australian Criminal Code (section 218A) makes similar restrictions, as does the Canadian Criminal Code (section 172.1). The legislation in the UK differs in that the sexual grooming offence applies both to the internet and the 'real world', whereas legislation in other countries addresses only electronic grooming via the internet and mobile phones.

Child sexual abuse, technological change and the law: The case of Luke Sadowski

The case of Luke Sadowski (*R v Sadowski*) merits analysis, as it has been of paramount importance in helping to identify new offences and fill crucial gaps in UK legislation.

Luke Sadowski was an 18-year-old trainee school teacher completing the last year of his training. At the time of his arrest, he was within one month of commencing his first placement in a primary school with pupils from 5 to 11 years of age. The police operation was complex but successful and involved the collaboration of American and British authorities. In 2002, the US Law Enforcement Agencies had been working covertly on the internet to locate, arrest and prosecute predatory paedophiles who were using the internet to source children for sex. The US Law Enforcement Agency Immigration and Customs Enforcement Agency (ICE) had placed an advertisement on the web offering unique sex tours with children as young as 8 years. The aim of this advertisement was to entice predatory paedophiles into their site and identify them by entering into negotiation with them. Sadowski, who used the identity Ben Smith, responded to the advert and began email communication. His requests were straightforward: he wanted to be introduced to a 10-year-old girl for full sex. When it became clear that the advert was US-based, Sadowski stated that he was unable to travel to the US. The ICE then approached the US Embassy in London, which had close links with the Paedophile Unit based at New Scotland Yard (NSY). The Legal Attaché from the US Embassy was able to arrange for UK detectives to correspond with the US agents. It soon became clear that UK law enforcement agencies had yet to deal with or recognise such a crime and was unable to authorise and deploy a similar covert officer simply because they did not exist. The Paedophile Unit at NSY took the task on and used a covert officer[5] to facilitate their communication with Sadowski, and he was able to convince Sadowski that here in the UK it would be possible to source a child for sex (Sanderson 2007).

On 4 October 2002, Sadowski met with the covert officer and travelled to a London hotel, where he was arrested. However, in the UK, at this time, there was a lack of adequate legislation to allow proper and effective charges to be laid; there was also a lack of sentencing powers and control measures provided to courts. At the conclusion of his trial and during his sentencing Judge Gordon (2002 in BBC News 2003) made the following comment about the limitations of the law, as it existed at that time:

'I have to pass a sentence as the law permits to reflect your criminal behaviour. It is hoped urgent consideration will be given (as to) whether maximum in law gives remotely adequate powers to protect the young and vulnerable. If the circumstances of this offence give rise to very serious concerns about the danger you may pose to women. The internet in the wrong hands can be the feeding ground of fantasy and can also be the means of committing serious criminal offences' (Judge Gordon 2002 in BBC News 2003).

Sadowski was sentenced to three years' imprisonment but, owing to insufficient legislation, he was not placed on the sex offender register.

Some of the complications arising from Sadowski's case were addressed in the new Sex Offences Bill 2004, which made the procurement and sexual trafficking of children over the internet a criminal offence carrying a maximum penalty of 14 years' imprisonment (Sanderson 2007). Since this case, the problem of grooming, facilitated by the anonymous nature of cyberspace and its vague boundaries, has risen exponentially. As a result, UK law enforcement agencies have been taking serious steps and constantly adopting new methodologies to protect children against becoming new victims of online abuse.

The concept of sexual grooming is well documented in the literature on sex offenders (Marshall 1996; Quinsey et al. 1998; Wyre 1990) and extensively discussed and evaluated in the next chapter. This concept is now filtering into legislation, policy and crime detection and prevention initiatives.

International legislative framework

As I have argued above, the development of a harmonic international legal framework on online child sexual abuse constitutes a major advance, as well as a challenge. In an explanatory report, the Committee of Ministers of the Council of Europe argue:

'There are no statistics on the total amount of sexual abuse of children in Europe, but it is well known that there is a considerable discrepancy between the number of reported cases of sexual abuse of children to the police and social services and actual cases. It is also recognised that children usually experience extreme difficulties in telling anyone about being sexually abused, because very often they are violated by a person in their close social or family circle or because they are threatened. Thus, the available data shows that, in

Council of Europe countries, the majority of sexual abuse against children is committed within the family framework, by persons close to the child or by those in the child's social environment' (Council of Europe Convention on the Protection of Children against Sexual Exploitation and Sexual Abuse 2007).

It will never be possible to establish with certainty the total number of sexually abused children in any country in the world, as acts of abuse are often not reported and are committed in the private sphere of a child's life, which might be either the family environment or the child's social environment. But most importantly, what do we mean by social environment today? Traditionally, a social environment encompasses 'the physical surroundings, social relationships and cultural milieus within which defined groups of people function and interact' (Barnett and Casper 2001: 265). Components of the social environment of a child may include built infrastructures such as schools, playgrounds, religious institutions and, more recently, the internet. Thus, one of the key problems in policing online child abuse is dictated not only by the discrepancy between the number of reported cases of sexual abuse of children to the police and social services and actual cases, as stated by the Council of Europe, but also by the substantial differences in the law between the neighbouring countries in Europe and the rest of the world.

In the past 15 years in Europe vital progress has been made to combat the problem of sexual exploitation and sexual abuse of children. Since the second Summit of Heads of State and Governments, which took place in 1997 in Strasbourg, the Council of Europe has supported its Member States in creating the correct measures to protect children and innocent victims. Member States of the Council of Europe were asked to review national legislation and to ensure cooperation within the Council of Europe. The aim was to achieve common standards for the protection of children suffering from or at risk of inhuman treatment. This commitment was reaffirmed at the Third Summit in Warsaw in May 2005, where the protection of children against all forms of violence, including child pornography, became a top priority. Following this significant Summit, in July 2007, the Council of Europe adopted the Convention on the Protection of Children against Sexual Exploitation and Sexual Abuse, which was signed by the European Ministers. It can be argued that this represents the first instrument 'to establish the various forms of sexual abuse of children as criminal offences including such abuse committed in the home or the family' (Council of Europe 2007). The Convention also deals with grooming and sex tourism, which represents an attempt to fill the gaps in European legislation and harmonise the legal framework to fight against this serious and widespread problem. However, whilst it is clear that the equivalence in legislation across European Member States would improve the effectiveness of investigations in different jurisdictions, in practice this harmonisation is still in its infancy. For example, whilst the 2007 Convention on Child Protection strongly views the possession of child abuse material as a criminal act across all nations, viewing the same material without downloading is not necessarily a criminal offence in all countries (Baines 25–28 November 2008). The same is true for online grooming, as many nations do not recognise it as an offence and do not legislate against these activities. However, more countries such as New Zealand, Australia, the US and Norway have followed the UK example. In these countries the legislation against grooming is a form of 'preventative measure as it disrupts inappropriate online relationships before they have the opportunity to escalate and move offline' (Baines 25–28 November 2008: 10). Undeniably, more countries should welcome these legal changes and face the fact that the internet has changed dramatically and will continue to do so in the future. Furthermore, as the internet is changing, more and more people will change their way of socialising and will put themselves at risk of becoming more vulnerable unless there is an evolvement in the legislation. As argued by Victoria Baines (25–28 November 2008), not having a harmonised legislative framework will jeopardise the efforts of law enforcement agencies to prosecute perpetrators. Moreover, it will delay the efforts to access data for investigative purposes. Clearly, having equivalent legislation in all jurisdictions would improve the effectiveness of investigations across borders and 'offer enhanced protection to children worldwide' (Baines 25–28 November 2008: 8). However, for a strong legislation to work, it should be accompanied by a police force with adequate investigative skills, which is often absent in developing countries.

Some sex offenders travel abroad to abuse children and often select locations in which children are easily accessible and vulnerable. In some cases sex offenders may 'order' a child through some reliable networks of like-minded people, from the comfort of their own home, so when they arrive in the desired destination, they find everything already organised. Some may decide to visit a country where the age of consent is low and sex with children is tolerated. It is in these countries that the legislation is exceptionally weak and law enforcement agencies are poorly resourced. However, under section 114 of the SOA 2003, the police may apply for a foreign travel order to prevent offenders from travelling abroad to abuse children sexually outside the UK. Section 72 of the Criminal Justice and Immigration Act 2008 replaces the previous section 72 of the SOA 2003. The amendments have widened the circumstances in which a citizen or resident can be prosecuted in the UK for an offence committed in another jurisdiction. This is certainly an achievement for the UK, as sex offenders are no longer free to travel to countries where there is absence of adequate legislation to protect children. However, there are still many countries within Europe that do not recognise, for example, sexual crimes against children related to the internet and other media technologies. And at times, one does not have to travel too far to witness these types of problems.

Online exploitation of children in the Isle of Man: a case study of a British citizen

This case relates to attempting to engage in sexual activity in the presence of a child. Section 11 of the SOA 2003 makes it an offence for:

'a person (A) aged 18 or over intentionally to engage in sexual activity (as defined in section 78), in order to gain sexual gratification, when a child aged under 16 is present or in a place from which A can be observed' (Sexual Offences Act 2003 section 11).

The offence covers acts of exposure or masturbation in front of a child, or description of the act to the child where the child is covering his/her face, and via a webcam. In 2009 an individual called Adam contacted an undercover detective who was posing as a young girl, stating he was an English teacher. Over a short period of time the interaction continued, resulting in Adam chatting in a sexual manner to a person he believed was a 14-year-old girl via the internet and mobile phone. This behaviour continued and escalated to the point that Adam exposed and masturbated himself in front of the officer, via his web cam.

It was found that the officer was an English teacher working in a school on the Isle of Man. This proved to be the first hurdle of the operation in the sense that, although the offences outlined above are clearly covered by legislation within the UK, they are not covered by legislation in the Isle of Man. It was therefore the appropriate course of action to arrest Adam under section 72 of the Criminal Justice and Immigration Act 2008 (section 72 ('Offences outside the United Kingdom') of the SOA 2003).

He later appeared at a London Crown Court where he admitted two counts of attempting to engage in sexual activity in the presence of a child under 16 for the purpose of obtaining sexual gratification.

Conclusions

In this chapter I have argued that new information and communication technologies, particularly the internet, have created opportunities for perpetrators to find new avenues that anonymously fulfil their fantasies and satisfy their desires. These can include: the construction of sites to be used for the exchange of information, experiences and indecent images of children; the organisation of criminal activities that seek to use children for prostitution purposes and that produce indecent images of children at a professional level; and the organisation of criminal activities that promote sexual tourism (Davidson and Martellozzo 2008).

The production and distribution of indecent images of children is an industry that is becoming increasingly large and lucrative (Wyre 2003) and has been labelled a problem 'of international proportions' (UNESCO). However, there are greater dangers posed by cyberspace. Evidence suggests (McCarthy and Gaunt 2005; Sanderson 2007) that children can be approached and seduced online by adults with the aim of developing an intimate friendship which can turn into sexual abuse in the 'real world'.

To be able to protect children from victimisation or from further abuse, I argue that it is vital for law enforcement agencies to have the right tools to be able to carry out their work in an efficient manner; that is, to gather and analyse intelligence concerning online grooming of their citizens and to identify children in the immediate vicinity who may be at risk. However, the legislative differences amongst countries are so great that it is not possible for law enforcement agencies to act across borders.

As I will also explain in the forthcoming chapters, online grooming in the UK is generally cautiously investigated. Members of the public, for cases of online grooming, may report their alleged solicitation to the appropriate authorities such as the police and the CEOP, where online chats may be monitored. However, in most countries it is not mandatory for internet service providers to act as such and they have no legal obligation to store online data. This demonstrates again the need for the 2007 Council of Europe Convention of the Protection of Children's criminalisation of the solicitation of children for sexual purposes through information and communication technologies to be extended to jurisdictions beyond the European Union.

A further analysis of the online grooming process, the *modus operandi* of internet sex offenders and the police response constitute the key focal points of this research, which I will discuss in detail in the following chapters of this book.

Notes

1 It refers to a genre of *manga* and *anime* wherein pre-pubescent or pubescent young characters are depicted in a suggestive or erotic manner.
2 Second Life is an online virtual environment that enables its users or 'residents' to interact with each other through avatars. Residents can therefore create their own avatar and socialise, interact, participate in group activities etc. However, there are cases where child-like avatars are not just playing like children do but they also offer sex.
3 In the Criminal Justice and Public Order Act 1994 (CJPOA 1994) provisions were included to extend the ambit of the Criminal Justice Act 1988 (CJA 1988) and the POCA 1978 to prohibit the possession and distribution of 'pseudo-photographs', where an indecent image of a child is made up of a collage of images often modified by computer painting packages (Lloyd 2000). Under the POCA 1978, a crime has been committed: 'If the impression created by a pseudo-photograph is that the person shown is a child, the pseudo photograph shall be treated for all the purposes of this Act as showing a child and so shall a pseudo-photograph where the predominant image conveyed is that the person shown is a child notwithstanding that some of the physical characteristics shown are those of an adult' (s 7(7)).
4 Pseudo-photographs are indecent images of children made up of a collage of images modified by the use of computer packages. In the CJPOA 1994, provisions were included to extend the ambit of the CJA 1988 and the POCA 1978 to prohibit the possession or distribution of pseudo-photographs.
5 The principles of undercover investigations are defined, discussed and evaluated in Chapter 6.

References

Akdeniz, Y. (1997) The Regulation of Pornography and Child Pornography on the Internet. *Journal of Information, Law and Technology* (1).

Ashworth, A. (1999) *Principles of Criminal Law*, New York, Oxford University Press.

Baines, V. (25–28 November 2008) *Online Child Sexual Abuse: The Law Enforcement Response. A contribution of ECPAT International to the World Congress III against the Sexual Exploitation of Children and Adolescents*. Rio de Janeiro, Brazil; http://www.ecpat. net/worldcongressIII/PDF/Publications/ICT_Law/Thematic_Paper_ICTLAW_ENG.pdf.

Barnett, E. and Casper, M. (2001) A Definition of 'Social Environment'. *American Journal of Public Health*, 91(3).

Baym, N. K. (2010) *Personal Connections in the Digital Age: Digital Media and Society Series*, Cambridge, Polity Press.

BBC News (16 February 2011) Home Secretary Theresa May: Government is 'appalled' by sex offenders ruling.

Beckett, R., Beech, A., Fisher, D. and Fordham, A. S. (1994) *Community-based Treatment for Sex Offenders: an Evaluation of Seven Treatment Programmes*, London, Home Office Publications Unit.

Carr, J. (2003) *Child Abuse, Child Pornography and the Internet*, London, NCH.

Council of Europe (Budapest, 23.XI.2001) Convention on Cybercrime; http://conventions. coe.in/treaty/en/treaties/html/185.htm.

Council of Europe. (2007) http://www.coe.int/lportal/web/coe-portal/what-we-do/human-rights/sexual-exploitation-of-children.

Council of Europe Convention on the Protection of Children against Sexual Exploitation and Sexual Abuse. (2007) Explanatory Report; http://conventions.coe.int/Treaty/EN/ Reports/Html/201.htm.

Criminal Justice and Public Order Act 1994.

Davidson, J. (2007) *Current Practice and Research into Internet Sex Offending*, Risk Management Authority Research, London, Department of Social and Political Studies, University of Westminster.

Davidson, J. and Martellozzo, E. (2008) Policing the Internet: Protecting Vulnerable Children From Sex Offenders In Cyberspace. *Police Investigations Police Practice & Research: An International Journal*.

Edwards, S. (2002) Prosecuting Child Pornography possession and taking indecent photographs of children. *Journal of Social Welfare and Family Law* 22(1), 2000.

Erooga, M. and Masson, H. (2006) *Children who Sexually Abuse Others. Current Developments and Practice Responses* (2nd edn), London, Routledge.

Finkelhor, D., Kimberly, J. and Wolak, J. (2000) *On Line Victimisation: a report on the Nation's Youth*, Alexandria, Virginia.

Foucault, F. (1998) *The Will to Knowledge: The History of Sexuality Volume 1*, London, Penguin Books.

Gallagher, B. (2000a) The extent and nature of known cases of institutional child sexual abuse. *British Journal of Social Work*, 30, 795–817.

Gallagher, B. (2000b) Ritual, and child sexual abuse, but not ritual child sexual abuse. *Child Abuse Review*, 9, 321–7.

Gillespie, A. (2008) *Child Exploitation and Communication Technologies*, Dorset, Russell House Publishing.

Home Office Communication Directorate (2004).

http://www.dfes.gov.uk/acpc/docs/tcrureview.doc. Retrieved 30/07/07.

Kelly, L. (1988) *Surviving Sexual Violence*, Oxford, Polity Press.

Kelly, L. and Scott, S. (1993) The Current Literature about the Organised Abuse of Children. *Child Abuse Review*, 2, 281–7.

Lane, F. (2001) *Obscene Profits: The Entrepreneurs of Pornography in the Cyber Age*, London, Routledge.

Lanning, K. V. (1984) Collectors, in A. W. Burgess (ed), *Child Pornography and Sex Rings*, Lanham, Lexington Books.

Laqueur, T. (1990) *Making sex: body and gender from the Greeks to Freud*, Cambridge, MA, Harvard University Press.

Lloyd, I. (2000) *Information Technology Law* (3rd edn), London, Butterworths.

Marshall, W. L. (1996) Assessment Treatment and Theorizing About Sex Offenders: Developments over the Last Twenty Years and Future Directions. *Criminal Justice and Behavior*, 23, 162–99.

Martellozzo, E. and Taylor, H. (2009) Cycle of Abuse. *Index on Censorship*, 38(1), 117–22.

McCarthy, J. and Gaunt, N. (2005) *But I was only looking . . ..* Paper presented at the Responding effectively to on-line child pornography offenders.

Medaris, M. and Girouard, C. (2004) *The Impact of Viewing on Offending Behaviour*, Lyme Regis, Russell House Publishing.

Miller, K. (1997) Detection and Reporting of Child Sexual Abuse (Specifically Paedophilia): A Law Enforcement Perspective. *Paedophilia: Policy and Prevention*, 12, 32–8.

O'Connell, R. (2003) *Be Somebody Else but Be Yourself at all Times: Degrees of Identity Deception in Chatrooms*, University of Central Lancashire, http://www.once.uclan.ac.uk/print/deception_print.htm, Cyberspace Research Unit.

Ost, S. (2009) *Child Pornography and Sexual Grooming*, Cambridge, Cambridge University Press.

Protection of Children Act (POCA) 1978 (England and Wales).

Quayle, E. and Taylor, M. (2001) *Child Seduction and Self-Representation on the Internet Cyberpsychology and Behaviour*, 4, 597–607.

Quayle, E. and Taylor, M. (2005) *Viewing child pornography on the internet: Understanding the offence, managing the offender, helping the victims*, Lyme Regis, Russell House Publishing.

Quinsey, V. L., Harris, G. T., Rice, M. E. and Cormier, C. A. (1998) *Violent Offenders: Appraising and Managing Risk*, Washington, DC, American Psychological Association.

Sanderson, C. (2007) *The Seduction of Children. Empowering Parents and Teachers to Protect Children from Child Sexual Abuse*, London, Jessica Kingsley Publishers.

Sentencing Advisory Panel (2007), http:// www.cps.gov.uk (Legal Resources).

Sentencing Guidelines. (2003); http://www.sentencing-guidelines.gov.uk/docs/advice-sexual-offences.pdf.

Sentencing Guidelines Council (2007a).

Sentencing Guidelines Council (2007b) *Guidelines on Sexual Offences,* London, SGC.

Sheldon, K. and Howitt, D. (2007) *Sex Offenders and the Internet*, Chichester, UK; Hoboken, NJ: John Wiley & Sons.

Smith, G. and Jayson, M. (2002); http://www.chiark.greenend.org.uk.

Spindler, P. (2003) *Policing Paedophiles on the Internet*, The John Grieve Centre.

Taylor, M. (2002) The nature and dimensions of Child Pornography on the Internet: Perpetuating a cycle of abuse, in E. Quayle and M. Taylor, *Deviant Behavior* (2002) 23(4), 331–62; http://www.tandfonline.com/doi/abs/10.1080/01639620290086413 retrieved 7/11/05.

Taylor, M. and Quayle, E. (2003) *Child Pornography: An Internet Crime*, London, Routledge.

Tyler, R. P. and Stone, L. E. (1985) Child Pornography: Perpetuating the Sexual Victimisation of Children. *Child Abuse and Neglect*, 9, 313–18.

Wacquant, L. (2009) *Punishing the Poor: The Neoliberal Government of Social Insecurity*, Durham, NC, Duke University Press.

Williams, K. (2004) Child Pornography Law: Does it Protect Children? *Journal of Social Welfare and Family Law*, 26(3), 245–61.

Wyre, R. (1990) Sex Abuse 'Addictive'. *Social Work Today*, 9.

Wyre, R. (2003) No excuse for child porn. *Community Care* 14(89), 38–40.

Yar, M. (2007) *Cybercrime and Society*, London, Sage.

Chapter 5

Collaborative efforts to protect children from online child sexual abuse

'Police involvement in cases of child abuse stems from their primary responsibilities to protect the community and to bring offenders to justice. Their overriding consideration is the welfare of the child' (Paragraph 4.11 of 'Working together Under the Children Act 1989')

Introduction

The sexual abuse of children online is not a technological problem but a people's problem. Those who endanger children are people and not computers. As argued by Jones (2003), 'the most important issue surrounding "Child abuse and the Internet" is child protection' (Jones 2003: 41). Thus, law enforcement agencies will ultimately aim for solutions that involve the use of traditional policing methods in addition to computer technologies. However, the relationship between the police and technology is long-standing and complex:

'on the one hand, the police were created to deal with the social disorder caused by technologies of the industrial revolution. On the other hand their responsive and localised nature always meant that they feel behind in their access to, and use of, technology' (Wall 2007: 190).

In this chapter I explore the challenges that official agencies such as the police and charitable sectors face in promoting and enforcing the protection of children against online CSA. In the first part I seek to identify and evaluate how the government and the police have reacted to the exponentially growing problem of the production and distribution of indecent images of children and the problem of online grooming. I will therefore provide an historical overview of how online CSA spread, such as an epidemic, focusing particularly on some prominent police operations, including Operation Cathedral[1] and Operation ORE.[2] In the second part, I will look at the issue of grooming children online for the purpose of sexual abuse and the measures implemented to combat this solicitation.

Throughout the process of reviewing the literature, it has been found that there are considerable gaps in existing research, particularly around the issue of how the police and other agencies became involved in combating cyber crime and the question why certain operations, such as Operation ORE, were highly criticised and deemed unsuccessful. To an extent, the recent and fragmented nature of the existing literature will necessarily be reflected in the early section of this chapter. It is one of the key aims of this book to fill some of the extant knowledge gaps in order to provide a more holistic overview and analysis of the problem of online CSA, more specifically of grooming, policing and child protection.

Moreover, a good deal of the information provided in this review section does not come solely from academic sources but also from official policy documents, specialists conferences and primary empirical research I conducted in the area of child protection (Davidson and Martellozzo 2007; Taylor 2005; Livingstone 2009).

Government and police responses to CSA: indecent images

The production and distribution of child abuse images is a serious problem that takes place every second on the internet. Since the beginning of the internet age, this issue has been labelled as a crime of 'international proportion'. John Carr's recent contribution to a very informative debate which took place in the online newspaper *Huffpost UK*, is an excellent example of how this growing problem was perceived:

> 'They say when you walk along the streets of London you are never more than six feet away from a rat. Looking at some of the headlines carried by newspapers in the early days of the internet you could be forgiven for thinking every user was never more than two mouse clicks away from child pornography. In the public's consciousness the propagation of child pornography became one of the signature crimes of cyberspace.' (Carr 07/07/11)

There have been thousands of newspaper articles written on the first operations on online CSA. Every daily newspaper carried the headlines of the convictions and sentences issued by the Crown Court (BBC Panorama 2001). Unprecedented access was given to the BBC, which produced a Panorama television programme on Operation Cathedral. The documentary was subsequently shown in 18 different countries, which generated not only significant public support for the National Crime Squad but also public intolerance and anger towards child sex offenders. This is not to suggest that the National Crime Squad's Press Office launched this subject into the public arena unprofessionally, but rather that it did so forcibly. This 'fanned the media flames' (Cohen 1972) and allowed the public to ask the very significant question: How has it got to this?

The demand for child abuse images through, for example, the use of file-sharing technology has grown so rapidly that law enforcement agencies are now engaged in a global race to track down children who are being abused and considerable resources continue to be invested to eradicate this problem across the world. In 2006, the IWF processed 31,776 reports (IWF 2006). These figures are analysed and qualified so that intelligence and key information can be provided to law enforcement agencies and other bodies in their efforts to combat online images of children who are sexually abused. However, over 80 per cent of the websites are hosted outside the UK (many are hosted in the US and Russia) and are there-fore extremely difficult to police and control. Further, there is currently no international agreement on regulation of the internet in respect of online grooming and indecent child images.[3] The IWF 2008 Annual Report (2009) suggests a 10 per cent reduction in websites hosting indecent child images; however the report suggests 'a continuing trend in the severity and commerciali-sation of the images:

- 58 per cent of child sexual abuse domains traced contain graphic images involving penetration or torture (47 per cent of domains in 2007)
- 69 per cent of the children appear to be 10 years old or younger; 24 per cent six or under and four per cent two or under (80 per cent appeared to be 10 or under in 2007)
- 74 per cent of child sexual abuse domains traced are commercial operations, selling images (80 per cent commercial in 2007)
- it is still rare to trace child sexual abuse content to hosts in the UK (under one per cent).

A number of high profile police operations against those involved in the distribu-tion of indecent images via the internet have raised the public consciousness regarding child abuse online. These include, most notably, the very first inter-national police operation against paedophiles, Operation Starburst (1995), followed by substantially larger operations such as Operation Cathedral (1998) and Operation ORE (2001). This is not to say that the production and distribution of indecent images did not exist prior to Operation Starburst. On the contrary, as argued in Chapter 1, child abuse images have been in circulation since Victorian times (Quayle and Taylor 2005) and probably before.

Renold et al. (2003) argue that the first individuals possessing and distributing indecent images usually came to light in a reactive manner, that is after an arrest for CSA and the forensic analysis of the suspect's computer. One of the very first cases of internet abuse in Britain concerned a Roman Catholic priest who was arrested for the sexual abuse of four boys under the age of 14. He was found to be in possession of 9000 images (The Eros Foundation 2000), the largest collection of indecent images in the UK at the time (Renold et al. 2003) and a long list of explicit emails which he had exchanged with other paedophiles. It was found that his computer contained messages from newsgroups[4] in which a number of poten-tial sex offenders were communicating with one another and exchanging indecent images of children. His conviction related to the indecent assault offences, but what contributed to his sentence of six years was the use of the internet for distribution of these images (also involving pseudo-photographs) (Akdeniz 1997a).

Furthermore, when the West Midlands Commercial Vice Unit started to pay attention to the content of newsgroups, they soon realised that online CSA is not only limited to the closed doors of someone's presbytery or home, but that there is a strong, large and hierarchically structured internet community which shares the same interest in children. This is how Operation Sunburst commenced (Akdeniz 1997b). The analysis of one newsgroup led to the discovery of thousands of entangled webs that connect sex offenders all around the globe.

In 1996, law enforcement agencies increased their scrutiny of the production and distribution of indecent images and arrested individuals solely for these crimes (Renold et al. 2003). During Operation Starburst, nine British men and another 37 men (Akdeniz 1997a) were arrested worldwide. After the first person was arrested, the suspect posted two warning messages offering his expertise to Usenet, entitled 'UK users Security Alert' and 'UK Security Alert 2'. They alerted like-minded people as to police infiltration. In one of his postings, which during this research was available online, he informed others about police operations and provided advice:

> 'Do you suspect the UK police are monitoring certain Newsgroups? You are right they are. Are you concerned about the privacy of your e-mail? You should be. There is only one answer to achieving privacy and security on the net, the use of pgp.[5] If you would like to know where to get the program and to use it to full advantage just let me know. I don't have all the answers about pgp but I can get you using the basic functions in a short time.' (This quote was previously available at: http://www.google.co.uk/search?hl=en&q=%22 Operation+Starburst%22&btnG=Google+Search&meta.)

At his first trial, the judge warned him that he would get a custodial sentence if he ever reoffended.

Interestingly, during Operation W0nderland, another large police operation similar to Operation ORE (explored later in this chapter), the name of the same person reappeared. As a result, he was reconvicted at Lewes Crown Court for possession with intent to distribute. In his second conviction, where he is referred to as 'Smith', he argued that he did not 'make' the images when he opened the attachment. As argued in Chapter 1,[6] the Court of Appeal entirely accepted that 'a person was not guilty of an offence of "making" (or "being in possession" under s.160(1) of the Act) of an indecent pseudo-photograph contained in an email attachment if, before he opened the attachment, he was unaware that it contained or was likely to contain such an image'(Lord Justice Dyson et al.). However, this was not the case. The prosecution proved that Smith had deliberately sought images of a particular child, which he received as an attachment to an email (Lord Justice Dyson et al.).

This case highlights clearly the close links existing amongst sex offenders, as well as their fear that the police may block their means of communication and interfere with their cyber-community. Furthermore, it illustrates some of the challenges the British police faced for the first time: having to deal with potential 'hands-on' abusers living in the intangible and vast environment of cyberspace, and monitoring not only their illegal activities but also their disguised messages on legal and well-respected websites.

In the following sections I critically examine how, after Starburst, the most widely reported operation in the UK commenced and how this changed the landscape for dealing with such cases from both a governmental and law enforcement perspective. It will highlight how operations such as Cathedral and ORE helped the police to learn to identify potential sex offenders living in the anonymity of cyberspace and how the growth of internet use has required police forces, both nationally and internationally, to work together to be able to cope with the scale of the problem. It rapidly appeared that the aforementioned collection of 9000 indecent images was not the largest known collection of illegal material gathered electronically anymore. As the police became more aware of the problem and more experienced in the conduct of online child sexual abusers, a more transparent picture of individuals arrested and their social networks emerged (Renold et al. 2003).

Operation Cathedral

Operation Cathedral was the world's first large operation involving paedophilia on the internet that police embarked upon. In this operation, seven British sex offenders, who were members of the notorious 'W0nderland club', were convicted (Spindler 2003). According to Dowd (2003), the prosecutor in Operation Cathedral, the 'W0nderland club' was protected by powerful gate-keeping and encryption devices, including a computer program called Alice in addition to the letter 'o' in 'W0nderland' being replaced by the numeric '0'.[7] In order to become a member of the club, interested parties were asked to submit 10,000 indecent images after receiving an invite from an existing member. The images were distributed worldwide. However, what was even more disconcerting was that members of the club created a facility with which they could record real-time abuse and transmit it simultaneously to other members. These members could, in turn, have input and give instruction as the abuse took place (Dowd 2003: 89). Although not all members were hands-on abusers, the vast amount of indecent material available proved the seriousness of the matter being investigated.

The operation involved 12 other countries and was led by the National Crime Squad. It successfully seized nearly a million indecent images as well as around 1800 'computerised videos' depicting children suffering sexual abuse (Zdnet 2001). What was uncovered was defined as a vast 'lending library' of images of child abuse which attracted the world's largest internet paedophile gang (BBC News Online 2001). David Perry QC, the prosecutor of the seven British defendants, reported:

'All of the children involved were under the age of 16 and in one case the child was only three months [old]' (QC David Perry in BBC 2001).

Carman Dowd (2003), the CPS prosecutor in the Operation W0nderland case, was also shocked by the nature and the volume of the images:

'When I first embarked upon this case I had no idea of the nature of the images involved (actual abuse on children whose ages ranged from less than a year old to teenagers). Nor was I aware of the sheer volume of images the offenders possessed – there were an excess of 750,000 images recovered from the UK offenders alone. When I gave a presentation on the case in 1999, my observations were that the legislation did not take account of this type of offending and this was reflected in the fact that the maximum sentence for distribution was only three years at that time.' (Dowd 2003: 96)

Dowd's presentation had the desired impact. The operation was fully reported in the media and, soon after, Part II of the Criminal and Court Services Act 2000 came into force, which increased the maximum sentence for possession and distribution considerably. Prior to this operation, sentences for possession ranged from fines, through to probation, to six months' imprisonment for Gary Glitter in 1999 (BBC News Online 12 November 1999).

As a result of this particular operation, governments in many countries started to pay close attention to this growing and serious phenomenon. They felt the need to respond to the public concern fuelled by the extensive media coverage of sex offenders' activities (Soothill and Walby 1991; Greer 2003; Spindler 2003; Davidson 2008). As a result, the G8 ministers decided to place online CSA within the international political agenda. England and Wales set up a group of police officers representing the main law enforcement agencies.[8] Their task was to bring together expertise and ideas to find strategies to combat such problems and present them at the Association of Chief Police Officers' (ACPO) Crime Conference. According to Spindler (2003), 'this was the first real opportunity the various law enforcement agencies who had previously answered to separate ACPO leads – clubs and vice, child protection and high-tech crime, had been given to share their knowledge and experience in one group' (Spindler 2003: 35). Thus, it is apparent that the police, in recognition of the global nature of the problem, from the very beginning joined their forces together and cooperated internationally with other police forces.

In May 2001, former Home Secretary Jack Straw, in response to the concerns about possible risks that children may encounter online, announced the creation of the Home Office Task Force (HOTF) on Child Abuse and the Internet. The aim of the HOTF was to create a partnership amongst representatives from the internet industry, children's charities, the main opposition parties, governments departments, law enforcement agencies and others 'who share the aim of making the

United Kingdom the safest place in the world for children to use the internet' (Straw 2005: 4). Within the HOTF each group had a responsibility and a part to play. Furthermore, a number of subgroups were also created on issues around criminal law, law enforcement, training, child protection measures, education and awareness for children, parents and teachers.

The main remit for law enforcement agencies has always remained child protection and to make the internet a safe place for its users. As argued by Spindler (2003): 'while [. . .] this is a new business for policing [. . .] our investigations begin, not end, with the location of the computer and its users, as the internet has given us *the first opportunity* to identify those who have the propensity to abuse children' (Spindler 2003: 35; emphasis added).

As highlighted in previous chapters, the internet is a vital tool for accessing information and for communication, entertainment and education. It provides immediate access to a vast array of materials, as well as anonymity at an affordable price (Cooper et al. 2000; Robbins and Darlington 2003). However, with approximately two billion users in 2010 and with a massive increase of people having access to the internet at home (from 1.4 billion in 2009 to almost 1.6 billion in 2010) (International Telecommunication Union 19 October 2010), it is inevitable that offensive behaviour such as making, producing and distributing indecent images of children, as well as grooming, continue to take place. Therefore, the internet should not be viewed simply as a library or an exceptionally advanced encyclopaedia. It would be more appropriate to perceive the internet as a mirror image of our society in all its diversity and human expression, including deviance.

Operation ORE

Operation ORE[9] was the largest police operation to take place in the UK (Renold et al. 2003) and it has 'paradoxically accelerated and hampered the police's commitment to combating cybercrime' (Jewkes 2003b: 502). In April 1999, the US Postal Inspection Service in Texas received information concerning a website on the internet named Landslide Productions Inc., which was privately owned by an American couple. The purpose of Landslide Productions was to provide access either to images of adult pornography or children being subjected to sexual abuse. The company was acting as a brokerage business for hundreds of child abuse images and between 1997 and 1999 made an estimated profit of $9,275,900.[10] The website was very cleverly constructed, as it could not be found by chance and various screens provided warnings to prospective customers. Customers used credit card facilities to purchase periods of time on these sites, which contained images of children being abused.

On 17 May 1999, a federal Grand Jury in Texas indicted Thomas and Janice Reedy, who were sentenced to 1335 and 14 years respectively. As a result of this arrest INTERPOL was provided with the credit card and bank details of 250,000 subscribers to Landslide's website. One police respondent noted:

'. . . when a person pays for access to a website is creating demand for internet paedophilia and is guilty of the crime of inciting another to distribute indecent images of children. If they have also copied these images onto their computer they are guilty of making indecent images. However, the major concern for the police was that every single name on the LANDSLIDE list could have been an immediate risk to children' (Police Officer ID: 3).

It is argued that people who download these images assist in CSA. There is now a large volume of research that indicates that people who download and view these images 'increase the likelihood that children will be continued to be abused *in the service of providing pictures* for people to download' (Quayle 2003: 25 emphasis as in original; see also Carr 2003). It is important to note that anybody who downloads such images and views them is indirectly already taking part in the abuse. There is a huge number of legal images of children posing that are downloaded every second and supports the 'continuum of victimisation' (Quayle 2003). Carr and Hilton (2010) argue:

'Child abuse images are visual representations of a child being sexually abused. The abuse usually takes place in the offline world, although some forms of sexual abuse which involve the capture of images can take place remotely e.g. through the use of web cams. The internet facilitates the mass distribution of the images, often for profit. This, in turn, creates an incentive for abusers to harm yet more children in order to create new images for sale' (Carr and Hilton 2010: 52).

The examination of seized records belonging to Landslide Productions by the FBI revealed that over 7000 users were British (Carr 2003). The FBI handed over the names of suspects to the UK police, who disseminated these names throughout the country. The Metropolitan Police alone were dealing with approximately 1200 suspects and were under pressure to act rapidly.[11] Once investigations were conducted and the suspects identified, officers in possession of a warrant card had the power to enter and search suspects' premises and to confiscate their computers.

Because of the scale of Operation ORE and the publicity it received, the vast majority of the suspects who had downloaded images and accessed the sites were expecting the police to visit them sooner or later. As argued by a police respondent:

'When you go inside a house and show that you are executing a warrant under the Protection of Children Act 1978, you have just started to contribute to the destruction of this person's life. Up until now they thought they were safe in their environment downloading child abuse images; they thought it was acceptable for them to download indecent images into their computer; and you now are walking into their life to tell them that it is not and that they are paedophiles. We ruin their lives. If we find images, they get convictions and they go to the sex offender register. For a lot of these people the stress and the loss is far too much' (Police Officer ID: 6).

When a police officer walks into a person's home for CSA purposes, his[12] life is generally put on hold until the forensic examination confirms his innocence or guilt: he has to be separated from his children in one way or another and if his job involves working with children he is not allowed to return to work. Operation ORE also dragged some famous names into the spotlight. Alongside Gary Glitter, Pete Townshend, songwriter and guitarist for 'The Who', appeared to be on the police's long list of suspects. However, he claimed he joined the website 'for research purposes', but did not download any images to his computer. As a result he was only given a warning and put on the sex offender register. Undoubtedly, when conducting these operations it is important for the police to know about the suspect's occupation (in case he works with children), the suspect's location and whether there are children on the premises where he lives. These elements clearly prioritise police intervention. Assessing risk and identifying the victims is an extremely important task for the police.

A factor for the police to consider is the duty of care owed by the police to the public. The United Nations Convention on the Rights of the Child 1989, signed by the UK, aims to protect children's rights. Article 19 bestows upon all parties to take: 'all appropriate measures to protect the child from all forms of physical or mental violence, injury or abuse . . . including sexual abuse' (Article 19 in Fortin 2003: 57). This places a positive obligation on states to ensure children are protected, including an appropriate investigation when child safety is at risk.

It could therefore be argued that a failure to investigate people who are believed to have purchased indecent images of children or have paid to become members of illegal websites could be interpreted, in light of the duties and responsibilities mentioned above, as a breach of a failure to protect a child. Academic research indicates that those who purchase such material may present a threat to children (Quayle and Taylor 2001; Jewkes 2003a; Carr 2003; Bourke and Hernandez 2009). Indeed, indecent images of children have a specific role in Wolf's (1985) cycle of abuse: they fuel sex offenders' fantasy with the risk of becoming an addiction to the point of contact sexual offences (Wolf 1985; Finkelhor 1986; Sandberg and Marlatt 1989; Eldridge 1990; Sullivan and Beech 2003). Although it is not possible to calculate with accuracy the percentage of sex offenders who use indecent images of children to commit an offence (Wyre 1996; Itzin 1996), it is important to recognise the risk collectors may pose to children. Therefore, once the police force is in possession of the illegal and harmful material that identifies a potential person with a sexual interest in children, it has a duty to analyse each image in an attempt to trace the perpetrator and save further victimisation (Gillespie and Upton 2004). As argued by Sir Richard Mayne (1829), 'the primary object of an efficient police is the prevention of crime, the next that of detection and punishment of offenders if a crime is committed' (Sir Richard Mayne 1829 at http://www.met.police.uk/met/). These sentiments are adopted by modern-day policing with the implementation of the National Intelligence Model.[13] The combined theories of Finkelhor's 'inhibitors' and Sullivan's 'behavioural conditioning', as discussed in Chapter 2, are key to the positive search and arrest strategy. It should be noted that police activity and the criminal justice process acts both as an internal barrier (the fear of being caught) and an external barrier (imprisonment) (Carrabine et al. 2004). Thus, a positive search and arrest strategy will help reinforce such barriers, together with controlled press coverage, to assist in the prevention of such crime.

Working with various statutory authorities, the police identified individuals on Operation ORE's list who either worked with children or were known sex offenders (Carr 2003). However, what has been discussed so far does not highlight the complexities and the economic cost of one individual investigation. A senior police officer told me that:

> 'One individual job of the MET under Operation ORE comprised more than 10 computers seized, more than 2000 cd-roms, more than 500 floppy disks, 55 videos and 99 films' (Police Officer ID: 2).

It is clear that each arrest generates a vast amount of work for the police as every suspect has more than one computer, mobile phone, memory stick etc. Each item must be forensically analysed by experts. Publications on the scale of Operation ORE have highlighted both the difficulties and unique opportunities presented to modern policing. The difficulties lie in the competing policing priorities and the resources for the intense measures required in dealing with such investigations. It is both costly and time-consuming to amass electronic evidence from individual computers. Some UK police forces have waited over a year for forensic results and it may cost thousands of pounds to analyse each computer.

Clearly, the lack of funding and manpower has seriously undermined operations such as ORE. However, what also diluted the operation from the very beginning was the lack of both specialists within the police force and of decision-making capabilities. As argued by a number of undercover police officers at the HTCU, which at the time of ORE did not exist, 'when the list provided by the US authorities landed on the UK authorities' desks, not much was done for a long time' (Police Officer ID: 4). Therefore, by the time the problem was acknowledged, decisions were made, resources and funding were allocated, new units were created and trained, and two years had passed before any form of police intervention took place. Thus, many of the alleged suspects appearing on the list, most likely terrorised by the media portrayal of CSA online as the moral panic of our age (Jewkes 2003b), destroyed their old computers containing the evidence and bought new ones, resulting in charges being dropped owing to a lack of evidence.

Police tactics were widely criticised during Operation ORE and from the ensuing debate many lessons were learnt for future operations. First of all, it was argued that the UK police invested far too many resources and funding to try to arrest people who were presumably guilty of downloading child abuse images. By doing this, they overlooked other more serious problems related to child protection or cyber crime in general.

Furthermore, a common allegation that was raised during ORE is that the police failed to establish if the suspects reported by the US authorities were the real users of the credit cards to purchase indecent images, or if they had really purchased indecent images, considering that Landslide contained both legal and illegal material. These flaws have not been documented within the academic arena but are present in a series of controversial articles published by investigative journalist Duncan Campbell (19/04/2007).

According to Campbell, an expert witness in defence cases, some of the people that purchased indecent images from the American base site were using stolen credit cards; others used their credit cards to purchase legal material only and the people who allegedly signed up to visit the sites never logged in on the site (Campbell 19/04/2007). In a letter to the House of Lords, which is available online,[14] Campbell sympathises with the defendants who 'continued to be prosecuted and to face jail sentences, loss of family career and the stigma of a sex offender register entry, *solely on the basis of* their credit card data and personal information having being used by third parties for fanatical gains in 1998 and 1999' (Campbell 2007: 2; emphasis added). In the same letter, he openly accuses the police of misconduct for failing to understand the nature of the internet and for the inappropriate use of resources 'that should have been deployed against internet financial crime and internet organised terrorism' (Campbell 2007: 2).

However, Campbell's beliefs and accusations contain notable flaws. When Jim Gamble, the former Chief Executive of the Child Exploitation and Online Protection Centre (CEOP) was asked whether the prevalence of credit card fraud raised any problem in the conduct of online CSA investigations, his response was as follows: 'we never prosecute someone simply on the basis of their credit card being used. You are going to look at *all of the circumstantial evidence* which when taken together provides overwhelming evidence' (Gamble 01/06/2007; emphasis added).

In a letter to Lord Broers in response to Campbell's accusations, Gamble provides some interesting statistics with regards to ORE. He claims:

> '. . . more than 2450 individuals have been successfully held to account. This figure presently shows a ninety three per cent rate of guilty pleas and includes more than 700 people admitting their guilt upon receiving a formal caution. In almost 2300 cases, child abuse images were discovered' (Gamble 01/06/2007: 2).

Furthermore, he also claims that a stolen credit card number does not provide as much information on an individual as does a subscription to a website offering child abuse. It in fact may provide:

- name
- postal address

- email address
- a personal password
- credit card details.

In addition, the IP address of the subscriber, which can provide information indicating the address or location of the subscriber, may be captured by the system. As a result, this information is analysed by the local police who then start with the identification of the subscriber. The enquiries may include:

- offending history
- verification of the postal address
- whether the credit card was reported as lost or stolen
- whether the suspect works with children.

(Gamble 01/06/2007: 3)

It is certainly fair to claim that Operation ORE has presented the police with enormous challenges in terms of effectively investigating and accumulating evidence. However, what should also be taken into account is that the internet is technologically sophisticated and difficult to monitor, as it constitutes a highly fluid and changeable environment (Shannon 2007). Furthermore, as previously stated, Operation ORE has also provided the police with unique opportunities, namely to be proactive against those who may present a threat to children. When people download or simply view indecent images of children, they create a demand for more children to be abused. If there was no market for downloaded images fewer children would be abused in order to supply it. Indecent images of children give a view into the previously impenetrable hidden world of child exploitation, which is primarily domestic in nature. Therefore, the importance of the operations mentioned above can be perceived as a 'wake up call' not only for law enforcement agencies but also for the government and other organisations such as the CEOP and the Internet Watch Foundation (IWF), which have been established as a result of the identification of such serious problems.

The IWF employs a dedicated team to track and monitor commercial child abuse websites. Its work faces a number of challenges. For example, in 2006 it found that some of the most prolific websites selling child abuse images avoided detection by changing servers. In other words, they changed their websites' domicile to change police jurisdiction so as to avoid prosecution and their sites being closed down (IWF 2006: 9). According to the IWF annual report, one site had been reported to the IWF 224 times since 2002; another 54 times since 2000 (and in that time it had been found on seven different servers in different countries). Some of the most prolific of these commercial child abuse websites have remained 'live' for long periods of time, despite the IWF's concerted efforts to the contrary (IWF 2006: 9). As stated in a report by the NSPCC, 'children suffer in the knowledge that there is a permanent record of their sexual abuse, which can subsequently prevent, delay or exacerbate the fear of disclosure' (Renold et al. 2003: 3). The words of a 16-year-old child summarise this fear:

'I never escape the fact that pictures of my abuse are out there forever. Everything possible should be done to stop people looking at pictures of child abuse. Each time someone looks at pictures of me, it's like abusing me again' (IWF 2006: 9).

Research and governmental responses to online grooming

As outlined in Chapter 2, online child abuse comprises the act of 'online grooming', which involves the process of socialisation during which an offender interacts with a child in order to prepare him/her for sexual abuse (Sexual Offences Act 2003).[15] This emergent online offence, facilitated by the anonymous nature of cyberspace and its vague boundaries, has grown exponentially during the past four years and the government, the police and other agencies such as the IWF and CEOP have been training and developing new tactics and awareness programmes to protect children from sexual abuse.

Like the production of child abuse images, the process of grooming is not a new phenomenon. It dates back to when CSA was first identified and defined (Conte et al. 1989) and it takes place offline as much as it does online (Gillespie 2004). However, there has been little systematic research on the process whereby adults identify, recruit and maintain the compliance of child victims (Conte et al. 1989).

Studies have generally focused on the victims' or offenders' characteristics and the type and frequency of deviant sexual acts (Groth et al. 1982; Abel et al. 1987; Stermac et al. 1989), despite the significance of offenders engaging in repetitive patterns of behaviour (Groth 1978), carefully planning their offences (Herman 1981; Laws 1989; Salter 1995) and repeating these patterns with multiple victims (Abel et al. 1987).

Research examining the grooming process in the real world (Lang and Frenzel 1988) revealed remarkable similarities. They identify that offenders utilise strategies that are part of the positive aspects in normal, non-abusive adult-child relationships. Most offenders acted alone with individual children. Groth (1985) also found that 95 per cent of offenders had no co-perpetrators; offenders preferred their own children or those who were pretty, young, small, passive, quiet, trusting, lonely, lacking in confidence, physically alone or from broken homes. They rarely abused a child unknown to them, although 34 per cent of the perpetrators in Elliott et al.'s (1995) study had assaulted strangers. The offenders generally had a preference regarding the gender of their victims, with 58 per cent targeting girls, 14 per cent preferring boys and 28 per cent targeting both boys and girls (Elliott et al. 1995). Also, as reported by Berliner and Conte (1990), sex offenders believe they possess a special 'skill' for identifying vulnerable children.

Offenders who found child victims outside their immediate families frequented places where children were likely to go such as schools, shopping centres, arcades, amusement parks and playgrounds.

In Conte et al.'s (1989) study, the offenders were asked to produce a strategy manual on how to abuse a child. The response included: use of pornography; invasion of privacy; sympathy; compliments; accidental touches; targeting damaged children with family problems; being friendly; confiding and providing extra attention; befriending parents; deceiving the child as to choice; promoting fear and convincing the child that nothing is wrong. Risk assessment was another crucial factor which determined whether or not to abuse a specific child. Offenders describe a process by which they manufacture a situation enabling them to become interpersonally engaged with the child, thus laying the foundations within which the abuse would take place (Conte et al. 1989).

Interestingly, children who are victimised in the realm of the cyber show characteristics similar to those abused in the real world. The IWF found that 80 per cent of the child victims in all the uniform resource locators (URL) since 2003 are female. Of these, 91 per cent appear to be 12 years of age or under (IWF 2006: 9) and are lonely, trusting and vulnerable (Wolak et al. 2003).

As argued in previous chapters, the main difference between the real world and cyberspace is anonymity. Although it can be exciting and fun for children to go online and form new friendships, what should not be underestimated is that the internet allows people to be whoever they want to be, at any time and in any place (Davidson and Martellozzo 2007). In a small number of cases, young people thought they had met someone special who they could trust implicitly but, in reality, they had been talking to an adult who had a sexual interest (O'Connell et al. 2004).

These adults target children and young people with the intention of making the child feel loved and comfortable enough eventually to meet so they can take advantage of them. The Home Office Task Force (2007), together with practitioners and consultants, put together a list of techniques that they believe sex offenders could use to make contact and establish relationships with children or young people. These are:

- gathering personal details, such as name, address, mobile number, name of school and photographs
- offering opportunities for modelling, particularly to young girls
- promising meetings with pop idols or celebrities or offers of merchandise
- offering cheap ticket to sporting or music events
- offering material gifts including electronic games, music or software
- offering virtual gifts, such as rewards, passwords and gaming cheats
- suggesting quick and easy ways to make money
- paying young people to appear naked and perform sexual acts via webcams

- gaining a child's confidence by offering positive attention and encouraging him or her to share any difficulties or problems he or she may have at home and providing a sympathetic and supportive response
- bullying or intimidating behaviour, such as threatening to expose the child by contacting his or her parents to inform them of their child's communications or postings on a social networking site and/or saying they know where the child lives or goes to school
- using webcams to spy and take photographs and movies of victims
- asking sexually themed questions, such as 'Do you have a boyfriend?' or 'Are you a virgin?'
- asking children or young people to meet offline
- sending sexually themed images to a child, depicting adult content or the abuse of other children
- masquerading as a minor or assuming a false identity to deceive a child
- using schools or hobby sites to gather information about a child's interest, likes and dislikes.

(*Source:* Home Office Task Force on Child
Protection on the Internet 2007: 15)

During the four years spent with undercover officers, I came across hundreds of cases such as this where individuals engaging with children adopted a number of different approaches with the same objective. Scholars such as Young also examined the emergent phenomenon of virtual sex offending but from a clinical perspective. Specifically, she looks at the role of online addiction in the development of virtual sex offending. Interestingly, based on the analysis of 22 forensic interviews with virtual sex offenders, Young's (2008) research on internet addiction found that all her clients met the basic criteria of internet addiction. She claimed that: 'similar to an alcoholic who consumes greater levels of alcohol in order to achieve satisfaction, clients routinely spent significant amounts of time online' (Young 2008: 301). She used a model which follows five stages of developing internet addiction: discovery; exploration; escalation; compulsion; and hopelessness or regret (Young 2008: 301). Unlike classic sex offenders who go through cycles of abusive behaviour by their distorted thinking (denial, blaming, omitting and believing the child enjoys and wants to be sexually active), Young's offenders were first-time offenders, with no previous history of sexual activity towards children (however, the research was based on a small sample and the results may not be typical). Furthermore, the offences committed by Young's sample were not entirely confined to the realm of cyberspace. That is to say, offenders went beyond the fantasy and discovery stages and committed some serious offences in the real world. They detached themselves from the internet and travelled with the intention of sexually abusing a child.

In the following chapters, I will provide a more detailed and comprehensive overview of these particular characteristics and compare them with the case studies selected for this study.

Measures to combat the grooming of children via the internet

After the case of Luke Sadowski,[16] whom the police described as 'a real and significant threat to children' (BBC News Online 20 August 2003) and the introduction of section 15 of the SOA 2003 (grooming), the police began to consult previous research, in order to learn and employ new undercover tactics effectively to combat the problem of online grooming. Findings from previous research helped the police to set up online children's profiles to track down sex offenders and to understand their modus operandi.[17]

Research suggests that the primary means of establishing sexual contact were reported as accidental touches and children's games which became increasingly sexual. A combination of different grooming techniques such as: establishing trust through friendship; showing the victims adult pornographic material slowly to desensitise the child into sexual activities; rewards and bribes; threats; and physical force (Finkelhor et al. 2000) are well rehearsed in the literature. In a study of children's victimisation by 84 male offenders, Briggs and Hawkins (1996: 230) found that the most brutal and sadistic offenders were religious figures, fathers and men of high social status in 'paedophile rings'. These findings are also shared by research conducted in Italy by Prometeo, a leading charity that works towards the fight against the problem of CSA (Frassi 2011). Furthermore, compliance, cooperation and maintenance of the child's silence were achieved by not disclosing the 'special secret' and by portraying the abuse as education or as a game. The police, in setting up undercover police operations, carefully took into account these important elements of offending behaviour.

Clearly, internet abuse has presented and continues to present law enforcement agencies with some unique challenges. However, despite the difficulties involved in controlling the crime problem, the police recognised that they have an important role to play And, in order to maximise their contribution, police departments needed to:

- acquire technical knowledge and expertise in internet child abuse
- establish links with other agencies and jurisdictions
- establish links with ISPs
- prioritise their efforts.

(adopted from Wortley and Smallbone 2006: 42)

From the very beginning, the NHTCU had a remit to counter national and transnational computer-enabled criminality that impacted on the UK. A number of objectives were set out but the most significant factor for tackling online grooming was to run proactive network investigations to identify and disrupt CSA.

Other objectives of the training included the development of a coordinated police response to hi-tech crime across all criminal jurisdictions in England and

Wales (Taylor 2005). Police training enabled officers to carry out proactive operations on the internet where they could locate, trace, identify and ultimately arrest individuals or organisations who were abusing children online. They started to monitor the web where people traded the images, such as user groups, chat rooms, file-sharing programs and 'pay per view' websites.

Conclusions

In this chapter I have sought to provide an historical overview of how online CSA has developed and to explore the challenges that official agencies – including the criminal justice and charitable sectors – face in promoting and enforcing the protection of children against this horrific crime.

Reports from a number of leading agencies such as the police, the Home Office Task Force, the CEOP, the IWF, the Virtual Global Task Force (VGT) and international scientific academic research have shown that adult male sexual interest in children is more extensive than previously thought. The internet has clearly provided new pathways for sex offenders to express their attraction towards children. Its anonymity has motivated them and given them confidence to search for images of abused children in order to satisfy their imagination and eventually to help their deviance take form.

Policy-makers and law enforcement agencies have had to understand and learn how to tackle this 'old crime in a new technology' (Martellozzo 2006). As highlighted in the first part of the chapter, the police's initial response to online CSA has been deemed as reticent, belated and uneven (Gallagher et al. 2006). This inefficiency was mainly owing to a lack of experience and appreciation of the seriousness of the problem. Furthermore, the massive scale of the operations previously discussed, together with the lack of resources and expertise, did not contribute to a fast and efficient response.

There is no doubt that operations such as Cathedral and ORE have been the benchmark for the investigation of online CSA. These operations have highlighted the need for law enforcement agencies to enhance their knowledge and skills in this arena. Individual governments have been encouraged to review their legislation and, in many cases, to change their sentencing guidelines and procedures. In the UK, for example, the sentencing for possession of indecent images of children has been increased from six months' to five years' imprisonment and for the distribution of images it has been increased from three to 10 years. Those convicted will also be added to the sex offender register.

Since the completion of Operation ORE and the implementation of the new Sexual Offences Act 2003 in which the 'grooming' offence was incorporated, the police have embarked upon an increasingly robust response to the problem and have been investing more resources in training, undercover operations and thorough investigations. However, this is not to say that the problem has been resolved.

The world of cyberspace is in a constant state of flux and the police, the government and supporting agencies need to continue to build upon previous improvements, particularly in terms of 'resources, prioritisation and commitment' (Gallagher et al. 2006: 125) and to learn from past experiences and mistakes. However, for a crime to be prioritised and for it to receive the necessary financial support, it needs to be documented with statistical data.

If a crime statistic is created based on the reporting of a crime, then law enforcement agencies and senior management teams can deliberate its importance, establish the risk and act upon it. Unfortunately, online CSA does not get reported and, as a result, it does not appear in the statistics (Taylor 2005).

Indeed, online child abuse can be reduced by sharing responsibilities. Law enforcement agencies need to continue to focus on the policing aspects, carers on the educational efforts aimed at protecting children and the IT industry on improving child-safety technologies in the online environment (Carr 2003).

In the remaining part of this book, I will concentrate on the policing aspect of online CSA. Primarily, I will look at the problem of online grooming with the hope of filling the gaps present in the theoretical-methodological-empirical literature that has been reviewed in previous chapters.

Notes

1 Operation Cathedral was an international police operation which started in October 1997 with the arrest of Ian Baldock, by Sussex Police. His computer was seized and a large library of indecent images was found. Further forensic analysis showed that the suspected offender was a member of a large group called 'W0nderland'.

2 Operation ORE was an international police operation which started in 1999 following information from the US law enforcement agencies which reported thousands of worldwide internet users featuring indecent images of children.

3 A breakdown of countries where websites containing child abuse images appear to have been hosted during the period 1996–2006 is provided by the IWF: US 51 per cent; Russia 20 per cent; Japan five per cent; Spain seven per cent and the UK 1.6 per cent (IWF 2006).

4 A newsgroup is a discussion group on the internet about a particular subject consisting of notes written to a central internet site and redistributed through Usenet (or user Network), a worldwide network of news discussion groups. Usenet uses the Network News Transfer Protocol (NNTP) Techencyclopedia (http://www.techweb.com/encyclopedia/defineterm.jhtml?term–ewsgroup). Many of these newsgroups, such as alt.pedophilia.com, have now been closed down.

5 Although some of the material was encrypted (with PGP as stated by the sex offender), there was plenty of unencrypted material available on which to base a prosecution and conviction in one particular case. There was no trace of encryption in the other criminal prosecutions following Operation Starburst. In this context, see Akdeniz, Y. (1997b); http://www.isoc.org/inet99/proceedings/3g/3g_3.htm, accessed on 25/09/08.

6 See also Chapter 4 for an in-depth analysis of the legal framework.

7 This is also defined as 'elite spelling', whereby letters are replaced by numbers.

8 These included: the Greater Manchester Police Indecent Images Unit; West Midlands Paedophile Squad, Metropolitan Police Clubs and Vice Unit; Scotland Yard's Paedophile Unit joined with the National Criminal Intelligence Service (NCIS) Serious Sex Offenders Unit and the National High-Tec Crime Unit (NHTCU). This project was under the chair of Detective Peter Spindler, who also provided me with complete access to the HTCU and Paedophile Unit at the London Metropolitan Police.

9   Operation ORE in the UK was a consequence of a massive undercover operation in the US in 2002, Operation Avalanche.
10 Approximately 85 per cent of this was attributable to the scale of websites depicting child abuse images.
11 Police officers of the Metropolitan Police took action against a number of these customers and prosecuted where indecent images were found. They were charged with 'making an indecent photograph of a child contrary to section 1(1) a of the Protection of Children Act 978 and/or possession of an indecent photograph of a child contrary to section 160 of the Criminal Justice Act 1998'. In cases where no images were found, consideration was given to charging 'incitement to distribute indecent photographs of children contrary to section 1(1) a of the Protection of Children Act 1978 subject to the rules of incitement'.
12 The majority of individuals investigated during ORE were males (99.9 per cent), ranging from 25 to 65 years of age. Although 95 per cent of these did not have any previous conviction for CSA, 46 per cent were abusing children when investigated (Sanderson 2007).
13 The National Intelligence Model (NIM) provides a model for policing. In April 2004, all forces in England and Wales were officially required to adopt the model to a set of agreed minimum standards. Codes of Practice came into effect on 12 January 2005.
14 http://www.publications.parliament.uk/pa/ld200607/ldselect/ldsctech/165/165we01.htm.
15 See Chapter 1 for the definition of grooming and of the evaluation of the Sexual Offences Act 2003.
16 See Chapter 4 for a full analysis of the case.
17 A full analysis of online undercover police operations, including the evaluation of the profiles designed to attract sex offenders and their modus operandi will be provided in the remaining chapters of this book.

References

Abel, G., Becker, G., Mittelman, J. V., Cunningham-Rathner, J., Rouleau, J. L. and Murphy, W. D. (1987) Self-reported sex crimes of non-incarcerated paraphiliacs. *Journal of Interpersonal Violence*, 2, 3–25.

Akdeniz, Y. (1997a) The Regulation of Pornography and Child Pornography on the Internet. *Journal of Information, Law and Technology*, 1.

Akdeniz, Y. (1997b) Whisper Who Dares: Encryption, Privacy Rights, and the New World Disorder; http://www.isoc.org/inet99/proceedings/3g/3g_3.htm, accessed on 25/09/08.

BBC (2001) Paedophiles vast 'lending library', London; http://news.bbc.co.uk/2/low/uk_news/1166643.stm, accessed on 06/06/07.

BBC News Online (12 November 1999) *UK Glitter Over Child Porn*, accessed on 23/08/08, http://news.bbc.co.uk/1/hi/uk/517604.stm.

BBC News Online (20 August 2003) Sex Threat Teacher Escaped Ban, accessed on 8/4/07, http://news.bbc.co.uk/1/hi/england/kent/3168475.stm.

BBC Panorama (2001) W0nderland Club.

Berliner, L. and Conte, J. (1990) The Process of Victimisation: The Victims's Perspective. *Child Abuse and Neglect*, 14, 29–45.

Bourke, M. L. and Hernandez, A. E. (2009) The 'Butner Study' redux: A report of the incidence of hands-on child victimization by child pornography offenders. *Journal of Family Violence*, 24, 183–91.

Briggs, F. and Hawkins, R. M. F. (1996) A Comparison of the Childhood Experiences of Convicted Male Child Molesters and Men who were Sexually Abused in Childhood and Claimed to be Non-Offenders. *Child Abuse and Neglect*, 20, 221–233.

Campbell, D. (18/04/2007) Personal Internet Security; http://www.publications.parliament.uk/pa/ld200607/ldselect/ldsctech/165/165we01.htm.

Campbell, D. (19/04/2007) Operation Ore flawed by Fraud. *Guardian*, accessed on 19/06/08.

Carr, J. (07/07/11) Microsoft Attacks Online Child Pornography *Huffpost UK*; http://www.huffingtonpost.co.uk/john-carr/microsoft-attacks-online-child-porn_b_890098.html?ir=Technology. London.

Carr, J. (2003) *Child Abuse, Child Pronography and the Internet*, London, NCH.

Carr, J. and Hilton, Z. (2010) Protecting children online, in J. Davidson and P. Gottschalk (eds), *Internet Child Abuse: Current Research & Practice*, London, Routledge.

Carrabine, E., Iganski, P., Lee, M., Plummer, K. and South, N. (2004) *Criminology. A Sociological Introduction*, London, Routledge.

CEOP (2006) Thinkyouknow online; http://www.thinkyouknow.co.uk.

Cohen, S. (1972) *Folks Devils and Moral Panics*, London, MacGibbon and Kee.

Conte, M., Wolf, S. and Smith, T. (1989) What Sexual Offenders Tell Us About Prevention Strategies. *Child Abuse and Neglect*, 13, 293–301.

Cooper, A., Mclaughlin, I. P. and Campbell, K. M. (2000) Sexuality in Cyberspace: Update for the 21st Century. *Cyber Psychology and Behaviour*, 3, 521–36.

Davidson, J. (2008) *Child Sexual Abuse: Media Representations and Government Reactions*, London, Routledge.

Davidson, J. and Martellozzo, E. (2007) Child Security Online: A Shared Responsibility *IPES. Urbanization & Security*, Dubai. 8–12 April Unpublished Conference Paper.

Dowd, C. (2003) A Case for the Prosecution: Operation Cathedral Prosecutors Perspective in A. MacVean & P. Spindler (eds), *Policing Paedophiles on the Internet*, Estbourne, East Sussex, The New Police Bookshop on behalf of The John Grieve Centre.

Elliot, M., Browne, K. and Kilcoyne, J. (1995) Child Sexual Abuse Perversion: What Offenders Tell Us. *Child Abuse and Neglect*, 19, 579–94.

Finkelhor, D., Kimberly, J. and Wolak, J. (2000) *Online Victimisation: a report on the Nation's Youth*, Alexandria, Virginia, National Centre for Missing and Exploited Children.

Fortin, J. (2003) *Children's Rights and the Developing Law*, London, Lexis Nexis, Butterworths.

Frassi, M. (2011) *Il Libro Nero dell Pedofilia*, Palermo, La Zisa.

Gallagher, B., Fraser, C., Christmann, K. and Hodgson, B. (2006) International and Internet Child Sexual Abuse and Exploitation. Research report. Huddersfield, Centre for Applied Childhood Studies. University of Huddersfield.

Gamble, J. (01/06/2007) http://www.publications.parliament.uk/pa/ld200607/ldselect/ldsctech/165/165i.pdf.

Gillespie, A. and Upton, A. (2004) Child pornography: duty to look? *Childright*, 211, 10–11.

Gillespie, A. A. (2004) Tackling Grooming. *The Police Journal*, 77, 239.

Greer, C. (2003) *Sex Crime and the Media. Sex Offending and the Press in a Divided Society*, London, Willan Publishing.

Groth, A. N. (1978) Patterns of Sexual Assault Against Children and Adolescents, in A. W. Burgess, A. N. Groth, L. L. Holmstrom and S. M. Sgroi (eds), *Sexual Assault of Children and Adolescents*, Lexington, MA, Lexington Books.

Groth, A. N. (ed.) (1982) *The Incest Offender*, Lexington, MA, Lexington Books.

Groth, A. N. (1985) *Men Who Rape: The Psychology of the Offender*, New York, Plenum.

Herman, J. L. (1981) *Father-Daughter Incest*, Cambridge, MA, Harvard University.

Home Office Task Force On Child Protection on the Internet (2007) Good Practice Guidance for the Providers of Social Networking and Other User Interactive Services; http://www.homeoffice.gov.

International Telecommunication Union (19 October 2010) The World in 2010: ICT facts and figures Geneva; http://www.itu.int/net/pressoffice/press_releases/2010/39.aspx.

Itzin, C. (1996) Pornography and the Organisation of Intrafamilial and Extrafamilial Child Sexual Abuse: Developing a Conceptual Model. *Child Abuse Review*, 6, 94–106.

IWF (2006) 2006 Annual and Charity Report. London, Internet Watch Foundation.

IWF (2009) http://www.iwf.org.uk/media/news.archive-2009.258.htm.

Jewkes, Y. (2003a) *Dot.cons: Crime, Deviance and Identity on the Internet*, Cullompton, Willian.

Jewkes, Y. (2003b) Policing Cybercrime, in T. Newburn (ed), *Handbook of Policing*, Collompton, Willan.

Jones, T. (2003) Child Abuse or Computer Crime? The Proactive Approach, in A. MacVean and P. Spindler (eds), *Policing Paedophile on The Internet*, Estbourne, East Sussex, The New Police Bookshop on behalf of The John Grieve Centre.

Lang, R. A. and Frenzel, R. R. (1988) How Sex Offenders Lure Children. *Annals of Sex Research*, 1, 303–17.

Laws, D. R. (1989) *Relapse Prevention with Sex Offenders*, New York, Guilford.

Livingstone, S. (2009) *Children and the Internet*, London, Polity.

Lord Justice Dyson, Mr Justice Johnson and Judge Rhys-Davies QC *R v Smith and R v Jayson* [2002] EWCA Crim 683; http://www.geocities.com/pca_1978/reference/smithJayson2003.html, accessed on 29/08/09.

Martellozzo, E. (2006) Policing Child Sexual Abuse on the Internet: An Old problem, a New Technology. *Sex in the Criminal Justice*. Stirling. 28–30 March, University of Stirling. Unpublished Conference Paper.

O'Connell, R., Price, J. and Barrow, C. (2004) Cyber Stalking, Abusive Cyber Sex and Online Grooming: A programme of Education for Teenagers. Lancashire; http://www.FKBKO.net, University of Central Lancashire.

Quayle, E. (2003) The Impact of Viewing Offending Behaviour, in M. Calder (ed), *Child Sexual Abuse and the Internet: Tackling the New Frontier*, Dorset, Russell House Publishing.

Quayle, E. and Taylor, M. (2001) Child Seduction and Self-Representation on the Internet. *Cyberpsychology and Behaviour*, 4, 597–607.

Quayle, E. and Taylor, M. (2005) *Viewing Child Pornography on the Internet*, Lyme Regis, Russell House Publishing.

Renold, E., Creighton, S., Atkinson, C. and Carr, J. (2003) *Images of Abuse. A review of the evidence on Child Pornography*, NSPCC.

Robbins, P. and Darlington, R. (2003) The Role Industry and the internet Watch foundation, in A. MacVean, and P. Spindler (eds), *Policing Paedophiles on the Internet*, Estbourne, East Sussex, The New Police Bookshop on behalf of The John Grieve Centre.

Salter, A. C. (1995) *Transforming Trauma*, Newbury Park, Ca, Sage.

Shannon, D. (2007) *The Online Sexual Solicitation of Children by Adults in Sweden*, Stockholm, Brå.

Sir Richard Mayne (1829) Crime Prevention; http://cms.met.police.uk/met/, accessed on 23/09/08.

Soothill, K. and Walby, S. (1991) *Sex Crime in the News*, London, Routledge.

Spindler, P. (2003) *Policing Paedophiles on the Internet*, The John Grieve Centre.

Stermac, L. E., Hall, K. and Henskens, M. (1989) Violence Among Child Molesters. *Journal of Sexual Research*, 26, 450–459.

Straw, J. (2005) *Home Office Task Force on Child Protection on the Internet*, London Home Office.

Taylor, J. (2005) Just an Epidemic or Another Crime? *Criminology Lecture*. University of Westminster 24/10/08.

Techencyclopedia; http://www.techweb.com/encyclopedia/defineterm.jhtml?term–ewsgroup.

The Eros Foundation (2000) *Hypocritesitese. Evidence and Statistics on Child Sexual Abuse Amongst Church Clergy, 1990–2000*, The Eros Foundation.

http://www.unicef.org/crc/ (the United Convention on the Rights of the Child) 1989.

Wall, D. (2007) Policing Cybercrimes: Situating the Public Police in Networks of Security within Cyberspace. *Police Practice and Research: An International Journal*, 8, 183–205.

Wolak, J., Mitchell, K. J. and Finkelhor, D. (2003) Escaping or Connecting. Characteristics of Youth Who Form Close Online Relationships. *Journal of Adolescence*, 105–19.

Wortley, R. and Smallbone, S. (2006) Child Pornography on the Internet. *Problem-Oriented Guides for Police*; http://www.cops.usdoj.gov, 3–92.

http://www.google.co.uk/search?hl=en&q=%22operation+starburst%22&btng=google+s earch&meta.

Wyre, R. (1996) The Mind of the Paedophile, in P. Bibby (ed.), *Organised Abuse: the Current Debate*, Ashgate, Hants.

Young, K. (2008) Understanding Sexually Deviant Online Behaviour from an Addiction Perspective. *International Journal of Cyber Criminology*, 2, 298–307.

Zdnet (2001) http://www.news.zdnet.co.uk/internet/0,1000000097,2083614,00.htm, accessed on 06/06/07.

Chapter 6

Observing sex offenders' online interaction and assessing risk

An empirical overview

Introduction

In the chapters that follow I present and evaluate data collected over a four-year period, from 2005 to 2009, at the Metropolitan Police High Technological Crime Unit (HTCU) and Paedophile Unit. The findings were obtained through the analysis of observational notes, recorded live-online communications between offenders and undercover police officers, and face-to-face semi-structured interviews that I conducted with 21 police officers. For example:

> 'You have been told to go grubbing in the library, thereby accumulating a mass of notes and a liberal coating of grime. You have been told to choose problems wherever you can find musty stacks of routine records based on trivial schedules prepared by tired bureaucrats and filled out by reluctant applicants for aid or fussy do-gooders or indifferent clerks. This is called 'getting your hands dirty in real research'. Those who thus counsel you are wise and honourable; the reasons they offer are of great value. But one thing is more needful; first-hand observation. Go and sit in the lounges of the luxury hotels and on the doorsteps of the flophouses; sit on the Gold Coast settees and on the slum shakedowns; sit in Orchestra Hall and in the Star and in the Garter Burlesk. In short, gentlemen, go get the seats of your pants dirty in REAL research' (Park in Bulmer 1984: 97).

The use of qualitative methods has allowed me to get my 'hands dirty in real research'. As a result, I observed live interactions between officers and suspects; I became involved in discussions around effectiveness of existing techniques and the development of new ones; I interviewed police officers on the processes and practices of policing CSA online and sex offenders' online behaviour and to analyse case studies. The fundamental issue that led me to follow the methodological blueprint first laid down in sociology by the Chicago School's director and founder Robert E. Park (Park and Burgess 1969) is the sensitive nature of CSA. Farberow (1963) equates sensitive topics with those areas of social life surrounded by taboo (see also Orfanelli and Tiberio 2005). CSA is one such sensitive topic, surrounded by some of the most impenetrable taboos in contemporary society. The new millennium, the internet and the hyper-mediatisation of contemporary social life have increased the public visibility of previously hidden social problems (Greer 2008). Many of the taboos that prevented public discussion around CSA have been broken down. Whilst many people still have great difficulty discussing intra-familiar CSA because it is laden with emotion and inspires feelings of disgust and revulsion (Greer 2003; Kitzinger 2004), it is undeniable that sexual offending against children is more a matter for public debate today that it was, for example, two decades ago (Greer 2003). Thus, the definition that Farberow (1963) provides is too narrow and does not allow for the possibility that the research may have a sensitive character for cultural or situational reasons.

For these reasons, Lee has given sensitive topics a wider interpretation as: 'Research which potentially poses a substantial threat to those who are or have been involved in it' (1993: 4).

Lee widens this definition and describes three different types of 'threats' that intervene in the research process, namely potential intrusion into private or confidential domains of participants' social lives, political threats and threats of sanction (Punch 1994). The first of these is related directly to my study. Much of this research did encroach upon the private, secretive sphere of the police and explored police tactics and their interaction with online sex offenders. Of course, given the covert nature of the police's targeting of online child sex abusers, it was neither possible nor desirable to seek research permission from potential child sex offenders, since this would have fundamentally jeopardised the integrity of police operations. Permission was, however, formally sought wherever possible. In particular, this included: observing covert police interaction with suspected online child sex offenders; and accessing case files and other documentation relating to convicted sex offenders. Furthermore, as this is a new area of policing, I was exposed to new exploratory police methodologies which were tested and implemented for the first time throughout this research. Lee warns that research may be seen as a threat because of the repercussions it might have in the research setting; 'it disrupts operational routines, there are fears of exploitation or it may result in damaging disclosures' (1992: 56). In order to attempt to overcome this 'threat of intrusion', all those who participated were reassured that complete anonymity and confidentiality would be respected at all times. Moreover, my research underwent a rigorous ethical approval process at the academic institutions at which I was employed during my fieldwork.

When reviewing qualitative data the objective is always to establish the 'main story' (Strauss and Corbin 1990). In this case the 'main story', which is supported by the theoretical framework, established in Chapter 2 of this book, is to explore how sex offenders perpetrate online child sexual abuse and how law enforcement deals with this phenomenon. The way sex offenders use the internet in order to fulfil their desires and create their cyber community is well documented (Jewkes

2003a; Gillespie 2004; Quayle and Taylor 2001; Davidson and Martellozzo 2008b; Jewkes 2003b; Carr 2003a; NSPCC 2007; Brennan 2006; O'Connell et al. 2004; Home Office Task Force on Child Protection on the Internet 2007; Spindler 2003; Taylor 2005; Davidson 2008; Martellozzo 2007; Sanderson 2007; Yar 2007; Davidson and Gottshcalk 2010). In combating this crime, the police enjoy the support of the majority of the public and the media.

In this chapter I aim to contribute to a better understanding of how the policing of online grooming occurs and how the police assess risk and prioritise suspects. Here I focus on policing CSA online and on police officers' daily activities. I structured as follows: in the first part I discuss the context in which undercover policing takes place; more specifically, the complex principles involved in covert investigations, such as the use of police officers as *agents provocateurs*, the regulation of surveillance and risk-management models. The second part focuses on the online grooming process, the police's risk assessment strategies and the corresponding prioritisation of policing interventions. I present research evidence in the form of verbatim quotes and transcripts of online interactions between sex offenders and undercover police officers acting either like children or adults with a sexual interest in children.

Police conduct

For the police to be able to intervene effectively, obtain evidence for their investigations and reduce this online 'epidemic', they employ a variety of both reactive and proactive tactics. The fact that the police are covertly accessing the internet in their efforts to capture those engaging in sexual offences against children is widely known and it is recognised as a legitimate tool. As argued by Noorlander (1999), 'modern policing no longer relies solely on detection, confession and the hope that witnesses will come forward. Increasingly, law enforcement agencies in the United Kingdom and in other countries are turning to pro-active, intelligence-led methods such as the use of surveillance devices, informants and undercover officers' (Noorlander 1999: 49). However, while these are regarded as effective policing methods, there are a number of fundamental principles of covert investigation that the police need to respect in order not to interfere with the human rights of those 'under surveillance'.

Principles of covert investigation

According to Harfield and Harfield (2005), one of the most fundamental principles of covert investigation is that all cover human intelligence sources (CHIS),[1] whether they are participating informants or undercover investigators, should never incite the commission of a crime. Choo and Mellors (1995) argue that executive guidelines do exist and are contained in the Home Office Consolidated Circular to the Police on Crime and Kindred Matters (reprinted 1986) (Home Office Circular 35/1986). The guidelines suggest that:

'a. No member of a police force and no public informant should counsel, incite or procure the commission of a crime.

b. Where an informant gives the police information about the intention of others to commit a crime in which they intend that he shall play a part, his participation should be allowed to continue only where –

   i.   he does not actively engage in planning and committing the crime;
   ii. he is intended to play only a minor role; and
   iii. his participation is essential to enable the police to frustrate the principal criminals and to arrest them (albeit for lesser offences such as attempt or conspiracy to commit the crime or carrying offensive weapons) before injury is done to any person or serious damage to property.'

(Source: Choo and Mellors 1995: 2)

During undercover investigations, both informants and police officers must take into account that they cannot incite or procure the commission of a crime. That is to say, if they are acting as participating informants, they may only take part in an offence that has already been planned and, even then, their role should be minor. If this principle is not respected because police officers or informants have incited the commission of an offence that would not otherwise been committed, then the court would hold that the investigators have been acting as *agent provocateurs*.

An *agent provocateur* is defined in *R v Mealey and Sheridan* (1974) 60 Cr App R 59 at 61, as 'a person who entices another to commit an express breach of the law which he would not otherwise have committed and then he proceeds or informs against him in respect of such offence' (The Royal Commission on Police Powers 1974: 614). This behaviour would be deemed to be unacceptable in policing. However, in defining what is acceptable behaviour, Harfield and Harfield (2005) underline the importance of showing interest and excitement for the proposed criminality when conducting undercover work (either as an undercover investigator or as a participating informant), so as to maintain efficiency.

Covert investigation in practice

Whilst the principles of covert investigations are widely available, it is only through in-depth interviews and ethnographic observations of police officers that we can begin to understand how these legal and operational principles are translated into everyday practice. For example, *agent provocateur* is an extremely important principle, which is applied to policing CSA and particularly to grooming online, where officers need to play different roles depending on the operation. Whilst keeping the issue of *agent provocateur* in mind, CIIs need to be fully immersed in the identity of the person they chose to be. For example, if they are assuming the identity of a child, officers have to learn children's language and they have to learn about pop music, children's TV programmes, computer games, fashion etc. They also need to know the differences in tastes, language etc that exist amongst girls under the age of 13. Some of the difficulties for undercover police officers dealing with grooming techniques were described by one of the officers interviewed in the context of this study:

> 'I was running a profile of a 12-year-old girl. [Before starting the operation] I researched what year she was in at school and her interests, what her particular pop band was. But then I come up against a teacher who took an interest in the girl sexually. He took an interest in her education and in particular maths. So then he went on to try and help the girl with her maths homework. I was sitting there thinking: 'I don't know what you're talking about'. So if something like this happens we have to research further. Well, someone else researched for me immediately whilst I was on line, so I'd have an idea of what a 12-year-old was learning in maths, and we got away with it' (Police Officer ID: 6).

When, on the other hand, officers are posing as an adult with sexual interests in children, they need to show enthusiasm, interest and commitment to the proposed criminality without committing any offence. For example, in the conversation presented in the table below, CII 'Dave' interacts with an adult that I call 'Suspect'. The CII 'Dave' met 'Suspect' in a 'child lover's forum' where, before it was

---

Table 6.1 Conversation between CII (Dave) and suspect in 2007

Suspect	hiya mate how are you today?
Dave	come on you Villa . . . . .
Suspect	piss off lol
Dave	what a come back
Suspect	well it had to happen they would have got lynched if they lost lol
Suspect	but i think we should shoot robbinson
Dave	yh him and James . . .
Suspect	the mans a liability
Dave	neither should be England Keeper
Suspect	i actualy agree with you there but the thing is we as a nation are short on top class keepers
Suspect	do you like this girl? *suspect sends pink20.jpg*
Dave	she is lovely
Dave	who is she
Suspect	im not sure of her name i just kow that she is a ex ls model and she has a beautifull pussy wanna see?
Dave	u got a pic
Suspect	ive got a set or two of her in the nude *suspect sends PTHC Childlover P006.jpg*
Suspect	ive got some pics of her when she younger as well
Dave	Yeah lovely
Dave	how many you got

Suspect	about a hundred or so pics of her I think
	suspect sends lsm04–01–053.jpg
Suspect	she has a lovely little arse
	suspect sends pink10.jpg
Suspect	here she is in her younger days
	suspect sends ln–157–46.jpg
	suspect sends ln–157–47.jpg
Suspect	which do you prefer?
Suspect	Younger or older?
Suspect	ar you still there mate?
	suspect sends f0370.jpg
Dave	yh sorry abit busy . . .
Dave	lovely pics
Suspect	so what sort of pics have you got then?
Dave	is that last one you . . . lol
Suspect	no i wish lol
Dave	cute pic . . .
Suspect	ive got some nice vids as well mate
Dave	have you got time . . .
Suspect	yeah ive got the day off work and im all alone at the mo so its not a problem

closed down, people used to meet to discuss their love for children, their fantasies and desires. The aim of this site was to create a global community of adults with a sexual interest in children. However, to keep this site the legal boundaries had to be respected. Thus, the originator had to set up precise and strict rules including:

- no frontal nudity
- no male interaction in any picture or video
- no trading of images
- no offensive language towards the children (referred to by the participants as 'models').

If links to pornography or nudity were posted, the person was banned from the 'realm' immediately and permanently. Therefore, if members of the forum wanted to exchange indecent images and openly discuss fantasies, they moved on to a more private site such as MSN.

The CII or 'Dave' succeeded in becoming a member of the forum by proving to have similar interests through posting topics or pictures in the relevant rooms. There is a crucial issue here relating to morality and law regarding posting online images of children in order to gain credibility within internet forums and advance the goals of child protection. This debate is developed fully in Chapter 7. For present purposes it is sufficient to note that all images posted by police officers in the course of policing online child sex abuse are entirely decent, as decency is defined in law. In the case discussed above, there were rooms for any topic; there were rooms, for example, for girls in red skirts, riding bikes, in school uniforms etc. And in each room members were expressing their ideas and feelings and often justifying their behaviour. One user, for example, stated:

'Yes mate, I am a perv just like every other man alive. It's a perfectly natural trait in order to continue the existence of the human race. All men like young girls. Don't think any differently. Some like them younger than others though and of course, some are gay. I am not sexually attracted to preteens but I like to gaze upon their beauty. Does this make me a bad person? I don't think so really' (Suspect ID: 2).

The dedicated CII focused on establishing trust with other members of this site to be able to move on a more private online space, such as MSN. Through MSN, the CII could then obtain more information on the suspects, such as their IP addresses, and risk-assess them. The chat-log in Table 6.1 shows how the suspect is clearly interested in child abuse images. In fact, after a short general conversation about a football game he immediately starts distributing images of a particular victim; '[I have] about a hundred or so pics of her I think'. The CII in the meantime continues to show interest, appreciate the photos ('lovely pics') and accept more indecent material ('ive got some nice vids as well mate') which will be saved and used as evidence in court.

CIIs are not allowed to distribute indecent images as a means of securing legitimacy with online perpetrators, as the distribution of indecent images systematically promotes the abuse of children. It can be noted from the chat log that, when cautious offender asks the CII 'so what sort of pics have you got then?' the CII ignores the question and asks something else – 'is that last one you . . . lol'.

The mutual exchange of indecent images is not necessarily the key means of establishing trust. Undercover operations generally involve adopting a profile of a suspected online abuser or creating a brand new profile in the guise of, for example, a young child or an adult offender. The aim is to engage in dialogue with suspected offenders. Generating a new profile is a demanding task. Police officers need, first of all, to obtain a picture of a child, generally online, and camouflage it with the aid of technology, so as to protect the identity of the child. In selecting the picture, what they need to consider is the age factor. As this officer explains:

'I believe, and probably the rest of the team believe, that a child under 13 will add more weight at court when it comes to sentencing because a child they think they're going to abuse is aged under 13. But if I'm targeting a particular individual then I will create a profile as near to what I think that person's sexual interest is' (Police Officer ID: 3).

The age factor depends on the offender's sexual interests. If, for example, a suspected offender is attracted to teenage girls, then the profile the police create will correspond to this preference. Interestingly, it was found that the age of the victim has an overall impact on the sentence the offender receives, that is to say, the younger the victim the harsher the sentence. However, the validity of this data can be questioned on the basis that this issue could not be thoroughly substantiated with statistical evidence. Generally, the discussions about sentencing revealed an enormous need for additional information and research. Why is there a decrease in custodial sentences in comparison to when the problem became visible with Operation ORE? How are the courts dealing with online abuse today? How seriously are they treating this crime? The internet is a rapidly changing environment and there is much that is still not clear and that needs to be explored further.

Principles of surveillance

Surveillance is a crucial and necessary element of any covert investigation. Like the wider practice of covert investigation, surveillance is underpinned by certain key principles, which are outlined in the Investigatory Powers Act 2000 (Regulation of Investigatory Powers Act (RIPA)) and the Human Rights Act 1998.

During online undercover operation, the use of surveillance is common practice. Surveillance is defined in section 48(2) of the RIPA and includes:

a   monitoring, observing or listening to persons, their movements, their conversations or their other activities or communications
b   recording anything monitored, observed or listened to in the course of the surveillance and
c   surveillance by or with the assistance of a surveillance device.

There are two types of surveillance: directed and intrusive surveillance. Directed surveillance is defined in section 26(2) of the RIPA. It requires a directed surveillance authority if:

- it comprises covert observation or monitoring by whatever means
- it is for the purpose of a specific investigation or specific operation
- it will or is likely to obtain private information about any person, not just the subject of the operation (this is the key element that engages also with Article 8 of the ECHR) but
- it does not include observations conducted in an immediate response to spontaneous events.

The last point refers to a scenario where on patrol, police officers notice someone acting suspiciously near a house. Because this is an immediate event or circumstance, authority for surveillance is not required (Harfield and Harfield 2005: 31). Therefore, directed surveillance includes instances where the police or other authorised public authorities follow an individual in the public, monitor and record their movements (The Crown Prosecution Service 07/07/08).

Intrusive surveillance is defined in section 26 (http://www.bishop-accountability.org/reports/2004_02_27_JohnJay/LitReview/1_3_JJ_TheoriesAnd.pdf) of the RIPA and it comprises:

- covert surveillance
- carried out in any residential premises or in any private vehicle and which involves
- the presence of an individual on the premises or in the vehicle or
- the use of a surveillance device.

During their online CSA abuse investigations, the Metropolitan Police Paedophile Unit strictly use directed surveillance. There is a long checklist that the officers need to address and follow before they carry out directed surveillance. For example, they need to demonstrate to their superintendent that the surveillance activity is proportionate. The principle of proportionality aims to ensure that the surveillance methods used achieve the intended objective, but do not exceed the necessary minimum requirements for achieving that objective. In other words, the surveillance must be balanced against the seriousness of the offence (Regulation of Investigatory Powers Act (RIPA)) 2000). In many undercover police investigations, the use of directed surveillance and CII methodology are deemed proportionate. They are crucial to the gathering of evidence in relation to online activities of individuals, such as grooming children for sexual exploitation.

Furthermore, the use of directed surveillance is necessary to allow the CII to monitor the activity of the subjects whilst they are in the chatrooms. The Paedophile Unit for example requires directed surveillance authority to be able to monitor the movements of the subjects where intelligence dictates a need to disrupt their activities. The evidence obtained during surveillance is valuable for ensuring that the suspects are arrested and their activities disrupted.

Surveillance in practice

During undercover operations, not all suspects are put under surveillance. Other avenues of investigations are usually considered. These are the execution of search warrants or the arrest of the subjects followed by the seizure and examination of the material found in their computers and premises. These methods are often discounted, as the evidence likely to be gained would not be of sufficient value to the investigation as that to be obtained through CII.

Whilst the previous sections have dealt with the regulatory constraints and justifications for the use of directed surveillance in undercover operations, the following sections describe and evaluate the operation itself. More specifically, they look at how individuals communicate with undercover investigators purporting to be young girls and the police response to this interaction.

Policing online CSA

The principles and practices of covert investigations and surveillance are brought to bear in the everyday policing of online child sexual abuse and in particular the policing of online grooming. The online profile created by sex offenders plays a significant part of online abuse and the grooming process. It can be argued that the online profile represents the beginning of such a process. Figure 6.1 below highlights how sexual offences are committed and how the London Metropolitan Police respond to the problem.

As discussed in the previous section, the profile 'opens the door to a chat', which may or may not lead to a relationship. The profile may contain a limited amount of information to determine if the person hidden behind it poses a risk to children. That is to say, the profile represents the visual attraction to children, which leads to an online 'chat'. It is during the 'chatting' process that the offender overcomes his internal inhibition against carrying out the offence. Whilst in the real world the offender would cautiously need to set up a situation in which the offence can occur and overcome any external obstacles that may come up, in cyberspace this effort is not required.

Figure 6.1 shows that the offender may commit the offences of:

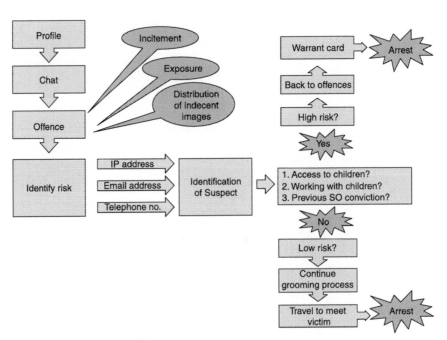

Figure 6.1 Policing online CSA.

a   exposing and masturbating on the webcam or
b   inciting a child or
c   distributing indecent images of children or
d   a combination of these.

When any of these offences are committed, the police carry out an open source research to identify the offender. The majority of suspects are researched in the same manner. The identification process may take as long as two to three weeks. Therefore 'the police would artificially delay the grooming process' (Police Office ID: 3). During this time, the CII continues to communicate with the suspect while 'the researchers interrogate the internet to find out any information about the suspect' (Police Officer ID: 3).

> 'Once we had a suspect who was keen to travel. He was into vintage cars and told the CII about his customised plate number. Through his plate number we obviously identified him very rapidly, but it is not always so quick' (Police Officer ID: 3).

The police prioritise operations in order to allocate their limited resources to deal with those online offenders who are perceived to pose the greatest risk in the physical world. Informed prioritisation is a process that requires undercover officers entering the world of the online offenders and interacting over time to develop an understanding of their intentions. Undercover officers need to obtain personal information on the suspects to be able to risk assess them. As Figure 6.1 shows, this can be done via online interaction whereby the undercover officer can trace the offender's IP address, email address or telephone number. This demonstrates that detection would not be feasible without the aid of undercover work. As soon as a suspect is identified, findings indicate that, depending on the offences committed, the police need to take into account a number of risk factors. They need to ascertain if the suspect has direct contact with children, if he has access to children, through his work for example, or if the suspect has any previous sexual convictions. If the answer to any of these questions is positive, then the individual would fall into the 'high risk' bracket and the arrest would take place immediately. If the answer is no, he would represent a 'low risk' to children. Therefore, the police would allow the online interaction to continue to the point that he may travel to meet the 'child'. However, it is imperative to note that the risk factor is constantly examined, even when the offender represents a low risk.

If, however, the offender expresses the intent to travel to meet a child for sexual purposes (see Figure 6.2), the police categorise him as a high risk suspect and employ resources to identify the suspect and risk assess him. Furthermore, if the suspect travels to meet the child who he believes to be under 16 (with whom he has communicated on at least two earlier occasions), he commits a grooming offence contrary to section 15 of the Sexual Offences Act 2003. As a result, officers of the Paedophile Unit would carry out the arrest at the meeting point. However, if the suspect expresses the desire to meet but cancels or fails to attend the meeting, the police would produce a warrant card and arrest him at his home address.

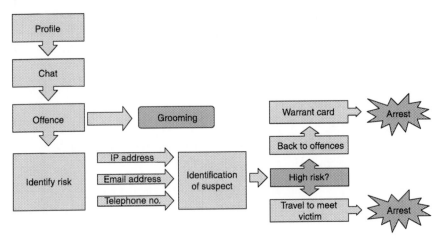

Figure 6.2 Policing online grooming

Clearly, as rehearsed in previous chapters, the Sexual Offences Act 2003 is designed to tackle behaviour where a person has groomed a child for sexual purposes and intends to meet that child In other words, 'rather than criminalise the grooming process, i.e. the befriending, the offence instead hangs the criminal liability on the concept of meeting a child' (Gillespie 2008).

Some of the techniques used during the grooming process can be identified in the short conversation presented below:

Table 6.2 Conversation between CII and suspect on 01 September 2006	
CII	hi Amy here
Suspect	hi how are you sweetie?
CII	kwl
Suspect	I used to play hockey in my younger days by the way
CII	how old r u now
CII	yeh
Suspect	lol. not too old I hope. good at sex anyway lol
CII	i dont play now
Suspect	discovered boys and sex huh
CII	aint dun sex yet
Suspect	interested though?
CII	corse
Suspect	I'd love to be your first
CII	yeh rite
Suspect	lol

CII	im only 12
Suspect	I would though – I'm good at it. did you read my hi5 profile?
Suspect	doesn't matter to me – if you want to that's all that counts
CII	hav anothr look in mo
CII	where r u im in London
Suspect	south london
CII	serious
Suspect	of course. I don't lie hun. and if you wanted to visit I'd love that
CII	im in oval
Suspect	really? only 20 minutes from me – I'm in croydon
CII	wow so kwl
Suspect	so maybe we can have some fun together sometime. if you wanted to hehe
CII	u jokin me rite

The table above presents the first conversation between the suspect and the CII. They first met on a social networking site (Hi5), and then he invited her to move to MSN,[2] an instant messaging service. The suspect is a 34-year-old man with no previous convictions who approaches the CII because he wants to become her friend and get to know her better. He is a confident type. He introduces himself with his real name but seems to be reserved about his age. When the CII asks him about his age he replies: 'not too old I hope' and immediately moves on to what O'Connell (2003) defines as the 'sexual phase': 'good at sex anyway lol'. He feels confident that the CII will want an older boyfriend.

O'Connell (2003: 44) identifies five different phases of the grooming process. These are:

- friendship-forming phase
- relationship-forming phase
- risk assessment phase
- exclusivity phase
- sexual phase.

During each stage, a deep sense of mutual trust is established before the final stage (the sexual phase) is reached. However, many undercover police investigations, which involved many cases such the one described above, do not reflect O'Connell's findings. First of all, it appears that the suspect is aware of Amy's age, but he does not seem to be concerned whether Amy is at home with somebody and he does not question Amy's identity. On the contrary, when the girl reveals her age ('im only 12') he promptly asks 'I would [like to be your first] though – I'm good at it'. He then moves further and suggest they should meet 'so maybe we can have some fun together sometime. if you wanted to hehe'. It is evident that the risk factor is completely overlooked.

Furthermore, in less than three minutes the suspect moves directly to the sexual phase and asks: '[have you] discovered boys and sex huh' and 'I'd love to be your first [lover]'. It appears that often, online groomers do not invest much time in forming a relationship with a child and do not assess risk. It has been estimated that it takes approximately eight minutes for an offender to introduce a sexual topic into their conversations.[3] Along these lines, the suspect mentioned sex during the very first conversation. These findings are supported by the recent literature. According to Gottschalk (2011), internet grooming is often different from 'real world' grooming. This is so because some offenders spend less time chatting in order to come straight to the point, sometimes within a few minutes. This would suggest that the internet might act to remove inhibitions that might be heavily present in face-to-face contact. This may be explained by the disconnected nature of personal communication on the internet. However, research suggests that some sex offenders spend a long time online identifying the right victim to groom and eventually abuse (Davidson and Martellozzo 2004; O'Connell 2003; O'Connell et al. 2004). Arguably, those offenders who spend more time grooming young people online pose a more serious risk to children. Spending a prolonged amount of time online trying to identify vulnerable victims, communicate with them and learn about their life is a sign of determination and interest. Secondly, from the young person's perspective, research suggests (Davidson and Martellozzo 2008a; Martellozzo 2011; Davidson et al. 2010) that young people, after a period of online interaction, have the tendency to consider an online friend a real friend; someone they can interact with and trust.

As this officer argues:

'You tend to get the impression quite quickly of who is serious about meeting a child or not. Say he just wants to incite you to commit an offence or put the camera on and masturbate then that would happen in the first 10, 15 lines of a chat. It would be quite in your face: 'Are you a virgin? Have you ever seen a cock before? Do you want to see one?' And they're off and running. To me that's not grooming; that's just someone who wants to commit that offence. Whereas someone who might talk to me, show an interest in me: 'Oh do you like doing that? Oh wow! What sports do you like?' And then they'll interject with a little bit of flattery: 'Oh you have a nice picture; you're a really pretty girl'. And they might pull it open a little bit. Next time they speak to you they would ask: 'How's school today?' Yeah fine. 'It would be nice to take you for coffee one day.' These may be the most dangerous. You tend to find it's the ones that don't rush you are the ones who are probably going to want to meet. Not every occasion is the same however' (Police Officer ID: 7).

There are a number of benefits that online groomers gain from the internet. One of the of the most obvious is that of 'universality' (Gottschalk 2011), in the sense that they are able to contact anyone, anywhere, anytime. Furthermore, cyberspace provides the offender with an inflated sense of security and the achievement of immediate personal rewards via exposure and the use of pornography, which may be used for personal gratification (eg masturbation).

Sex offenders often use a number of tools to groom children. This may involve developing a friendship with the child, using bribes of affection and gifts, adult pornography or indecent images, either for personal sexual stimulation or to entrap and blackmail children. These tools are used both in the real world and, increasingly, in cyberspace. However, the 'time' factor seems to be different in the two worlds. As argued by Gottschalk (2011) time is central in online victimisation of children. When children do not desire to receive gifts or messages or when they are offline, the groomer can continue to send messages or can leave gifts to view next time children are online.

Identifying risk

A great amount of research has been undertaken to identify and evaluate the risks posed by those who target and groom children (Carich and Calder 2003; Calder 1999; Davidson 2007). Generally it was found that offenders convicted for indecent images-related offences who may be assessed as 'low risk' under current risk-assessment tools may constitute a higher risk in terms of their propensity for contact offences. For example, an individual with indecent images may not have direct and routine contact with children, in the sense that he is not a parent and does not work with children on a daily basis. In accordance with current intelligence-gathering practices, he may be categorised by police as a lower risk and thus a lesser priority than an individual who possesses indecent images *and* has direct and routine contact with children. Access to children, however, does not need to be direct, and individuals may gain contact through networks of family, friends or neighbours. Thus, as Davidson suggests, 'any attempt to assess internet sex offenders must also take into account the diversity of this offending group and the potential for contact abuse' (Davidson 2007: 4).

The risk of identifying risk – police priorities around contact and non-contact offences

Contact and non-contact online sex offences

As previously argued, the internet facilitates serious offences against children that could not be carried out with such ease, speed and anonymity in the real world (Cooper et al. 2000b; Davidson and Martellozzo 2005).[4] However, it is important to distinguish between different types of online offending. Through ethnographic observations and interviews with police officers, it became clear that the police perceive two broad categories of online CSA. These can be identified as contact and non-contact offending.

Non-contact offending can be defined as those types of online sexual offence which involve no real-time, live interaction between the victim and the offender. This category primarily involves the downloading and distribution of indecent images. As the social networking capabilities of the internet become more widespread and technologically advanced, the types of online CSA that can be carried out become more varied and potentially severe. Social networking sites such as MySpace, Bebo and Facebook enable real-time live interaction and have facilitated the perpetration of new kinds of online abuse, here termed 'virtual contact offences'. This category of offences includes live online communications, for example an offender encouraging a child to perform sexual acts, or himself masturbating into a webcam in full visibility of the victim. The broad distinction between contact and non-contact offences has important implications for the assessment or risk and subsequent police prioritisation and activities. Whilst this distinction has been acknowledged by a number of scholars (see, for example, Sanderson 2007; Cawson et al. 2000; Carr 2003b), it has yet to be explored in any great detail.

The nature of internet offending against children has become more diverse and serious in the past 10 years. Changes in the nature of online CSA have, in turn, resulted in changes to police tactical planning and risk assessment practices. In particular, there has been a shift in the stratification of offence seriousness and risk assessment.

Police officers, broadly speaking, argue that there are three types of offending: contact offending, non-contact offending and virtual contact abuse. Whilst virtual contact abuse comprises only a few sentences within the voluminous current legislation on sex offending in the UK, its legal acknowledgement has been fundamental in shaping the everyday policing of online CSA. Indeed, the daily operations within the Metropolitan Police's HTCU are, to a significant degree, structured around policing virtual offending.

There seems to be a strong relationship between contact offending and virtual offending. As argued by this officer: '[Whilst] the link between non-contact offending and virtual offending is accepted, as it deals with those offenders who download, view and distribute indecent images of children using the internet, I believe there is also a strong link between virtual offending and contact offending. We focus a lot of our work on this' (Police Officer ID: 8).

Contact offending accounts for a relatively small and constant proportion of the total offences, not because such offences are uncommon but because they seldom come to the attention of law enforcement agencies and are thus not officially recorded, for the reasons highlighted in Chapter 1. Since CSA – both online and offline – remains a 'hidden crime', it is difficult for the police to address the problem proactively. However, dedicated operations aimed at tackling online CSA can shed light on this hidden figure, constituting the vast majority of online child sex offences. Operations Cathedral in 1998 and ORE in 2001 revealed that the number of people purchasing, collecting and distributing indecent images of children – non-contact offences – was much higher than even the most conservative estimates at that time.

It has been argued throughout this book that online child abuse does not only include the production and the distribution of indecent images of children (non-contact offences), but also that of 'online grooming' and other virtual (contact) offences. As explained previously, virtual offences were introduced and defined for the first time in 2003 with the creation of the Sexual Offences Act 2003. Since Operation Cathedral in 1998, the introduction of the Sexual Offences Act, which has led to the implementation of proactive policing strategies, has proved to be fundamental for law enforcement agencies to combat online CSA.

The Sexual Offences Act 2003 has established a number of new sex offences against children. It is significant to note that, in line with the increasingly interactive nature of the online environment, each of these new offences relates (or leads) to contact abuse. These new offences are:

a   to cause or incite a child to engage in a sexual activity
b   to expose in front of a child via a webcam
c   to cause a child to look at an image of a person engaging in sexual activity
d   to cause a child to look at an indecent image, which is a common part of the grooming process (Taylor and Quayle 2003)
e   to suggest to a child to meet and arrange a meeting.

The police HTCU and Paedophile Units view these offences as virtual contact offences and it is on these offences that they focus to implement proactive strategies to combat online CSA. The great majority of undercover officers support the contention that if someone commits a virtual offence, he may pose as serious a risk to children as someone committing a contact offence in the physical world. As this officer argues:

'Of course the actual contact between the child and the adult does not take place on the internet. However, if an adult exposed himself in front of a child in a corner of a dark alleyway, this would immediately be denounced as a serious contact offence, even if there has been no physical contact between the child and the adult' (Police Officer ID: 21).

This principle is applied to cyberspace, where the act of exposure, masturbation or incitement has taken place via a web camera. Indeed, the Sexual Offences Act 2003 (see http://www.opsi.gov.uk/acts/acts2003-sections 14 and 15) takes virtual contact offences very seriously.

However, as previously argued, the most serious offence is committed when a person travels to meet a child with the intention of sexually abusing the child. The offence is the most serious, punishable by a maximum sentence of 10 years' imprisonment (section 15(4)) and is a sexual offence for the purpose of sentencing (Gillespie 2008).

For this reason, some police officers distinguish between offenders committing virtual contact offences and those who travel, and argue that resources should be invested in those who travel and not on those people that may become travellers:

'. . . they (travellers) may well have come down the route of downloading images, many of them haven't, as far as we can tell, cos they haven't all got indecent images on their computers. But the truth of it is they are a far more serious and dangerous offenders. Whilst taking any people that are masturbating at home might prevent them from becoming travellers in the future, there are so many people that are prepared to travel already and it is on these that we should focus' (Police Officer ID: 6).

Undoubtedly, assessing risk is a complex task that needs to be done with accuracy and at all levels of risks. One of the most difficult tasks that the police have to deal with on a day-to-day basis is to assess which of the suspects interacting online with CII officers and distributing images is most likely to pose a risk to children. They ask themselves one simple question: Is this groomer merely fantasising and playing games, or is he a contact sex offender whose hands-on behaviour involving children has gone undetected? In principle, all virtual offences are included in the high risk category. However, some of the officers do not think this is the correct approach. As this officer argues,

'We've come across a number of people that they come on line they say "Hi how are you? How old are you?" They say they are 18, 19 or whatever. Then they just want to expose themselves or masturbate on line, that sort of stuff. I wouldn't consider them as paedophiles. I would consider these people as sex pests who use the internet to get some cheap thrills. They are probably sat at home; maybe they haven't got a girlfriend or haven't got a very good sex life, so they want to have a chat on line to somebody whilst they sit at home and masturbate' (Police Officer ID: 5).

These types of 'sex pests' often would not arrange to meet a child. Nevertheless, the police have the responsibility to check that the person behind the screen does not pose a danger to children. And this process takes time:

'The whole process is that we have to review the chat logs; put that on an intel sheet so someone researches that person. Then we carry out some enquiries that need to be done to identify somebody who may never chat to us again. If they live in London we go and arrest that person, bring him into the police station and we interview him and send his computers off. And it's so much work for really not the right type of person that we should be after. That's the difficulty with the internet work, because you don't know whether or not they're going to be dangerous targets or not' (Police Officer ID: 5).

It was possible to sense an element of frustration in the voices of officers discussing this issue. The majority of the officers interviewed of course want to focus on the right targets: the most dangerous subjects; targets that travel to meet children; targets that are hands-on abusers. However, the nature of cyberspace does not always permit the police to focus solely on the right targets or the most dangerous ones straight away without having tested the territory first. It should not be over-looked that cyberspace allows people to be whoever they want to be, anytime, anywhere. Thus, only with the aid of undercover policing tactics can the most dangerous groomers be tracked down (Carr 2006).

As soon as a virtual offence is committed, practitioners need to take into account a number of risk factors. They need to determine: Does he live with chil-dren? Does he have any access to children? Does he have any previous sexual offence convictions? Does he work with children? If the answer to any of these questions is positive, then the individual would fall into the 'high risk' bracket and the arrest would immediately take place. If the answer is no, he would be classi-fied as a 'low risk' to children. Therefore, the police would allow the grooming process to continue to the point that he would travel to meet the 'child', which is considered to be the most serious virtual offence. However, if the offender does not attend the meeting or changes his mind at the last minute, the police may request a search warrant in order to arrest the suspect at home. This indicates that risk assessment is a constant and ongoing process and includes evaluating all potential offenders, from those perceived as presenting the highest immediate risk to children, to those perceived as presenting very little risk. The point is that the spectrum of perceived risk varies enormously, but that everyone who is perceived as posing any risk at all to children must be evaluated accordingly with the limited resources available.

Virtual offending

At the beginning of an undercover police investigation, offenders' propensity to abuse and the risk they may pose to children are unknown. It is only through the police operating proactively undercover online that risk can be assessed. It is imperative for practitioners to target those suspects who clearly pose the greatest risk to children, for example those who commit virtual contact offences and travel to abuse a child sexually. Resources are invested on someone posing an imme-diate risk to a child by, for example, causing or inciting a child to engage in a sexual activity. This police officer explains:

'Their propensity to abuse is not known to us and there is no time between suspects to demonstrate the risk between having images and abusing a child. There are obviously some clear indications that they would pose a risk to children but there is no definable discernable risk. I can't say 90 per cent are contact offenders, that's not the case. I don't know. So I have a pot of say of 100 people who I know share images and then I have one who wants to meet up with a child for sex. That person would take priority. When that person has been dealt with then we look at those who want to share images. We would look to identify them and find out what individual risk they pose to children. So as soon as we found one who is a teacher for example, they would be higher risk and would be prioritised' (Police Officer ID: 1).

The officer stresses that often neither time nor resources are available for focusing on suspects caught with, for example, a few indecent images of children. Therefore, priority is always given to the offender who expresses the desire to meet the child and travels to do so (Krone 2004).

Although research in this area is still underdeveloped, some scholars have suggested that people who download indecent images of children are likely to become contact offenders. For example, the COPINE project (Taylor and Quayle 2003) found that among 23 interviewed men convicted for downloading indecent images, 20 had traded indecent images of children, three were producers and 11 had committed contact offences with children during the period they were downloading and viewing these images (Taylor and Quayle 2003). Furthermore, an investigation by the US Postal Service in 2000 found that around 35 per cent of people who look at child abuse images are also abusers in the real world (in Carr 2003a). In this study I also found that the nine offenders arrested for travelling to meet a child for abuse were all found to be in possession of indecent images of children. Although these findings may not be sufficient to assist the police in identifying the level of risk that online abusers may pose to children in the real world, they are very significant, as they help to advance understanding of online CSA with respect to the grooming process and other virtual contact offences.

What needs to be stressed about risk assessment is that, had it not been for virtual crimes, online perpetrators may have escaped detection by the police and prosecution. One officer claims:

'I think the internet has made it easier to detect these people. I think a lot of these people live in the shadows and it was difficult to infiltrate their groups. Often they work alone and take enormous strides to cover up their activities. But on the internet they feel that they have that anonymity and they're wrong. This has made our job a lot easier and it's just revealed the scale, so it's now there for all to see, whereas before we didn't know just how big it was. I have dealt with other types of crime: drugs, robbery, burglary. Most of the times you are dealing with repeat offenders, with previous convictions. Whereas in this field it is so not the case. That, as a policeman, tells me there is a massive undisclosed problem in this area' (Police Officer ID: 6).

This leads to the conclusion that the internet has not created a new type of sex offender but a new type of offending: virtual contact offending. Furthermore, the internet has not fundamentally changed human nature; it has provided a fresh opportunity to people with a sexual attraction to children to explore it. Therefore, online sex offenders may be undetected hands-on abusers, and the use of the internet may be seen as 'an adjunctive behavioural manifestation of their pre-existing paraphilic orientation' (Hernandez 2009: 5).

Conclusions

As I argued in previous chapters, over the past 10 years online CSA has brought some innovative changes in the legislative context and particularly in policing. The advent of the internet allowed paedophiles to seek out like-minded people with whom to exchange indecent material. When internet abuse was first detected, police forces focused on the viewing, possessing and distribution of indecent images. However, sex offenders did not stop there. They found ways to groom victims to abuse sexually by using the internet. Since the Sexual Offences Act 2003, the concept of 'grooming' has been recognised in the UK and several other countries are beginning to follow the UK lead and criminalise grooming behaviour (Davidson and Gottschalk 2011) and police forces have been able to train officers proactively to police the internet.

Online CSA, however, is not an easy problem to police as the internet is constantly developing and new social networking groups attract more children. As shown in Chapter 4, social networking sites such as Facebook are very popular amongst adults and teenagers. The more children are connected to a network, the more attractive the network is to groomers.

Social networking sites by definition are designed to let people meet new people online. These sites encourage and enable people to exchange information about themselves, share pictures and videos and use blogs and private messaging to communicate with friends and share interests, either with individual contacts or all site users. This indicates that both the public and law enforcement agencies need to maintain a level of awareness concerning the possible pitfalls that come with online social networking sites. The majority of practitioners who took part in this research spoke of a share of responsibility to address virtual offences and evidenced a strong willingness to take steps better to police CSA online. A starting point for the police is to be able to identify, at an early stage, the risk factors that some individuals may pose to children whilst online.

Notes

1 Covert Human Intelligence Sources (CHIS) is defined under the RIPA as: 'A person who establishes or maintains a personal or other relationship with a person for the purpose of facilitating the doing of anything that (a) covertly uses such a relationship to obtain information or to provide access to information to another person; or (b) covertly discloses information obtained by the use of such a relationship, or as a consequence of the existence of such a relationship. Surveillance is covert if, and only if, it is carried out in a manner that is calculated to ensure that persons who are subject to the surveillance are unaware that it is or may be taking place.'

2 MSN is an instant messaging service within the Microsoft Network. MSN allows people to chat privately and securely.

3 It is important to emphasise that this research sample is relatively small and may not be typical of the whole internet community.
4 These findings relate to a paper presented at and published by Oxford University. The paper presented findings from an earlier study. The study was a project funded by the Metropolitan Police Authority and Crimestoppers, which sought to explore child safety on the internet and the role of the police in raising awareness amongst children about sexual abuse.

References

Brennan, M. (2006) Understanding Online Social Network Services and Risks to Youth. London, Child Exploitation and Online Protection Centre; http://www.ceop.gov.uk, accessed 1/10/08.

Bulmer, M. (1984) *The Chicago School of Sociology. Institutionalization, Diversity and the Rise of Sociological Research*, Chicago, University of Chicago Press.

Calder, M. (2005) *Children and Young People who Sexually Abuse. New Theory, Research and Practice Developments*, Lyme Regis, Russell House Publishing.

Carich, M. S. and Calder, M. (2003) *Contemporary Treatment of Adult Make Sex Offenders*, Dorset, Russell House Publishing.

Carr, J. (2003a) *Child Abuse, Child Pornography and the Internet*, London, NCH.

Carr, J. (2003b) *Child Sex Abuse and the Internet*, London, NCH.

Carr, J. (2006) *Out of Sight, Out of Mind. Tackling Child Sex Abuse Images on the Internet: a Global Challenge*, London, NCH.

Cawson, P., Wattam, C., Brooker, S. and Kelly, G. (2000) *Child Maltreatment in the United Kingdom: a Study of the Prevalence of Child Abuse and Neglect*, London, NSPCC.

Choo, L. T. and Mellors, A. (1995) Undercover Police Operations and what the Suspect Said (or didn't say). *Web Journal of Current Legal Issues*, http://www.ncl.ac.uk/~nlawww/articles2/choo2.html.

Cooper, A., McLaughlin, I. P. and Campell, K. M. (2000b) Sexuality in Cyberspace: Update for the 21st Century. *Cyber Psychology and Behaviour*, 3, 521–36.

Davidson, J. (2007) Risk Management Authority Briefing. Current Practice and Research into Internet Sex offending, Glasgow, Risk Management Authority: http://www.rma-scotland.gov.uk/ViewFile.aspx?id=235, accessed 10/06/08.

Davidson, J. and Gottshcalk, P. (2010) *Online Groomers: Profiling, Policing and Prevention*, London, Russell House Publishing.

Davidson, J. and Gottschalk, P. (2011) *Internet Child Abuse: Current Research and Practice*, London, Routledge.

Davidson, J. and Martellozzo, E. (2004) *Educating Children about Sexual Abuse and Evaluating the Metropolitan Police Safer Surfing Programme*, London, University of Westminster and Metropolitan Police.

Davidson, J. and Martellozzo, E. (2005) 'Policing the Internet and Protecting Children from Sex Offenders on Line: When Strangers Become Virtual Friends'; http://www.oii.ox.ac.uk/research/cybersafety/extensions/pdfs/papers.

Davidson, J. and Martellozzo, E. (2008a) Policing the Internet: Protecting Vulnerable Children From Sex Offenders In Cyberspace. *Police Investigations Police Practice & Research: An International Journal*.

Davidson, J. and Martellozzo, E. (2008b) Protecting Children in Cyberspace, in G. Letherby, P. Birch, M. Cain and K. Williams (eds), *Sex Crime*, Cullompton, Willan Publishers.

Davidson, J., Lorenz, M. and Martellozzo, E. (2010) Evaluation of CEOP ThinkUKnow. Internet Safety Programme and Exploration of Young People's Internet Safety Knowledge. Centre for Abuse and Trauma Studies.

Davidson, J. C. (2008) *Child Sexual Abuse: Media Representations and Government Reactions*, London, Routledge-Cavendish.

Farberow, N. (1963) *Introduction. Taboo Topics*, New York, Athernon Press.

Gillespie, A. (2008) *Child Exploitation and Communication Technologies*, Dorset, Russell House Publishing.

Gillespie, A. A. (2004) Internet grooming: the new law. *Childright*, 204, 10–11.

Gottschalk, P. (2011) Stage Model for Online grooming, in J. Davidson and P. Gottschalk (eds), *Internet Child Abuse: Current Research and Policy*, London, Routledge.

Greer, C. (2003) *Sex Crime and the Media. Sex Offending and the Press in a Divided Society*, London, Willan Publishing.

Greer, C. (2008) *Crime and Media. A Reader*, London, Routledge.

Harfield, C. and Harfield, K. (2005) *Covert Investigation*, Oxford, OUP.

Hernandez, A. E. (2009) Psychological and Behavioural Characteristics of Child Pornography Offenders in Treatment. Global Symposium: Examining the Relationship between Online and Offline Offences and Preventing the Sexual Exploitation of Children The Injury Prevention Research Centre The University of North Carolina, Chapel Hill.

Home Office Task Force on Child protection on the Internet (2007) Good Practice Guidance for the Providers of Social Networking and Other User Interactive Services; http://www.homeoffice.gov.

http://www.bishop-accountability.org/reports/2004_02_27_johnjay/litreview/1_3_jj_theorie-sand.pdf.

Jewkes, Y. (2003a) *Dot.cons: Crime, Deviance and Identity on the Internet*, Cullompton, Willian.

Jewkes, Y. (2003b) Policing Cybercrime, in T. Newburn (ed), *Handbook of Policing*, Collompton, Devon, Willan.

Kitzinger, J. (2004) *Framing abuse: media influence and public understanding of sexual violence against children*, London, Pluto.

Krone, T. (2004) A typology of online child pornography offending. *Trends and Issues in Crime and Criminal Justice*, 279.

Lee, R. M. (1992) *Researching Sensitive Topics*, Newbury Park, Sage.

Lee, R. M. (1993) *Doing Research on Sensitive Topics*, London, Sage.

Martellozzo, E. (2007) Policing Child Sexual Abuse On Line: Understanding Grooming in the 21st Century. *Crime, crime prevention and communities in Europe*, September 26–29 Bologna, Italy.

Martellozzo, E. (2011) *Understanding Children Online Activities: Developing Research and Training for Covert Internet Investigators*, London, Metropolitan Police.

Noorlander, P. (1999) The Impact of the Human Rights Act 1998 on Covert Policing: Principles and Practice *The International Journal of Human Rights*, 3, 49–66.

NSPCC (2007) *Sexual Abuse*.

O'Connell, R. (2003) From Fixed to Mobile Internet: The Morphing of Criminal Activity On-Line, in M. Calder (ed.), *Child Sexual Abuse and the Internet: Tackling the New Frontier*, Lyme Regis, Dorset, Russell House Publishing.

O'Connell, R., Price, J. and Barrow, C. (2004) Cyber Stalking, Abusive Cyber Sex and Online Grooming: A programme of Education for Teenagers. Lancashire; http://www.FKBKO.net, University of Central Lancashire.

Orfanelli, G. and Tiberio, A. (2005) *L'Infanzia Violata*, Milano, Franco Angeli.

Park, R. E. and Burgess, E. W. (1969) *Introduction to the science of sociology, including the original index to basic sociological concepts*, Chicago, University of Chicago Press.

Punch, M. (1994) Politics and Ethics in Qualitative Research, in N. K. Denzin and Y. S. Lincoln (eds.), *Handbook of Qualitative Research*, Thousand Oaks.

Quayle, E. and Taylor, M. (2001) Child Seduction and Self-Representation on the Internet. *Cyberpsychology and Behaviour*, 4, 597–607.

Regulation of Investigatory Power Act 2000 http://www.opsi.gov.uk/acts/acts2000/uk, accessed on 14/10/08.

Sanderson, C. (2007) *The Seduction of Children. Empowering Parents and Teachers to Protect Children from Child Sexual Abuse*, London, Jessica Kingsley Publishers.

Spindler, P. (2003) *Policing Paedophiles on the Internet*, The John Grieve Centre.

Strauss, A. and Corbin, J. (1990) *Basic of Qualitative Research*, London, Sage.

Taylor, J. (2005) Just an Epidemic or Another Crime? *Criminology Lecture*. University of Westminster 24/10/08.

Taylor, M. and Quayle, E. (2003) *Child Pornography: An Internet Crime*, London, Routledge.

Taylor, M. (09/03/07) Flying Squad Officer Jailed for Child Sex Offence on Internet. *The Guardian Online*, accessed on 3/10/08.

The Crown Prosecution Service (07/07/08) http://www.cps.gov.uk/legal/a_to_c/covert_surveillance/, accessed 14/10/08.

The Royal Commission on Police Powers (1974), *R v Mealey and Sheridan* 60 Cr App R 59 at 61.

http://www.opsi.gov.uk/acts/acts2003, accessed 20/08/09.

Yar, M. (2007) *Cybercrime and Society*, London, Sage.

Chapter 7

Police challenges and sex offenders' activities online

An empirical overview

Introduction

In this chapter, I turn my attention to practitioners' views about policing child sexual abuse (CSA) and sex offenders' *modus operandi*. In the first part I focus on covert policing; more specifically, I evaluate how the police operationalise a profile and how they interact with potential sex offenders. I then explore sex offenders' online behaviour. Whilst the occurrence of online sexual grooming has been demonstrated (Davidson and Martellozzo 2008a; Davidson and Martellozzo 2009; Gillespie 2008; Sanderson 2007), there is no substantial body of research to show how it is committed. It is my intention to ensure a better understanding of how online grooming takes place and how policing the internet has developed and is perhaps beginning to make a significant difference.

The process of online grooming as observed in the context of a police undercover operation emerges from the interaction between groomers and police officers posing as children. This interaction, in turn, is informed by the understandings that officers and groomers bring to their encounters, as well as by the organisational framework of undercover online police operations. Within these contexts, this chapter relies strongly on the accounts of police officers to examine grooming. In doing so, I do not wish to argue that these officers' accounts can or should simply be taken at face value as sources of factual information. While there is a baseline of 'facts' about the policing of online CSA, the officers' experiences are obviously coloured by the particular features of police cultures, as well as matters of gender, class, ethnicity, age and so forth. The following discussion shows how, through these necessarily 'coloured' standpoints, experiences and practices of online policing emerge. In this sense, qualifying these narratives in terms of traditional notions of validity and reliability is not my focus here. Rather, I seek to unpack them in order to arrive at a better understanding of the social construction of online policing.

Police activities and challenges: creating a profile

Exploring how the police create a profile and how they interact undercover with potential sex offenders helps the analysis of sex offenders' online *modus operandi*. Furthermore, it provides a deeper understanding of the socio-cultural and technological context in which virtual offences occur and of how online grooming takes place. Online grooming is a much more extensive, complex and challenging problem than has been thought hitherto and 'one in need of a much wider-ranging, co-ordinated and concerted policy and practice response' (Gallagher et al. 2006: 14). The findings have a wider application given that other police forces worldwide – those of America, Australia, New Zealand, Canada and Sweden – have adopted a similar model.

There is an incredible amount of preparation that an undercover police officer needs to do prior to any communication with potential online groomers. First of all, it is important that consistency is maintained in the narration of the young person's life: who she is, where she is coming from, what her interests are, where she lives etc. However, as argued by the police officer below, it is not feasible to prepare all possible answers to the questions that might be raised during a CII investigation:

> 'You're never going to be able to research everything you get asked. You get the basics: what's the name of the school and what pop group you like, but you're still going to be asked questions that you haven't considered that you're going to be asked' (Police Officer ID: 6).

Sex offenders are usually very good at obtaining cooperation and gaining control of the child through well-planned grooming techniques. For example, they may show to the child that they are interested in what the child does and are willing to listen, show support and understanding. The profiles created are those of children who are simply looking for new friends; children with a difficult family situation; children who are vulnerable and are often on their own because they come from a single parent family or because both parents are at work. Arguably, any child is vulnerable to seduction by any adult, 'but troubled children from dysfunctional families targeted by adults who are authority figures seem to be at even greater risk of being seduced' (Lanning 2005: 57). This research has proved that sex offenders are well aware of this. Stanley (2001 in Calder 2004: 14) argues that sexual offenders target children with particular characteristics, such as children with a strong respect for adult status and children from single parent families. Furthermore, troubled children from dysfunctional families are targeted by authoritative adults who exploit these children's greater risk of being victimised (Lanning 2005; Platt 1969).

One of the profiles used by an undercover police officer was that of 13-year-old Lucy, who had never had a boyfriend or kissed anyone. However, like the majority of teenagers, she was very curious about sex. She liked older people, as she found boys of her age too young and immature. Her curiosity to meet new and older people clearly transpired from her online conversations. At the time of grooming, Lucy had been living in London for four months, but because she did not have many friends and her mum was always at work, she was often on her own and spent a long time online. It is not surprising that children spend long hours on the internet unsupervised (Davidson and Martellozzo 2008a; Livingstone and Bober 2005). It appears in fact that children increasingly spend more time online than watching television (Franko Aas 2006) independently from their social class. Coming from a less privileged background does not seem to affect children's or offenders' use of the internet, as it used to when the internet started to expand (Davidson, Grove-Hills et al. 2009). This reflects Tony Blair's initiative in 2000 called UK Online, which set out a number of measures to boost internet use in the UK. The UK Online initiative set up training measures such as:

- 600 online centres to give hi-tech access to poorer communities
- piloting internet access in post offices
- offering discounts of 80 per cent to all adults for online courses, reducing a £200 course down to £40.

(*Source:* BBC News Online, 11 September 2000)

Some police officers recognised that Blair's initiative has certainly had an impact both on people's use of the internet and on who uses the internet:

'I've seen lorry drivers [being arrested]. The social class has changed, the economy has changed, the education level has changed. Tony Blair wanted everyone to have a computer and so we're moving towards that, aren't we? It seems a disadvantage not to have one so yes you're seeing the difference between now and then' (Police Officer ID: 1).

Since computers are very affordable and internet connections are practically free, it can be argued that users' social status may become more and more irrelevant.

Police constraints

There are a number of major problems on the horizon for policing CSA online, including the lack of obtaining pictures of children to use to create new profiles. Many police officers openly expressed concerns such as this:

'[When we create a profile] we go for the fact that most of these males are white males looking for females. So predominately set them [the profile] up as a young female and depending on what the availability of pictures are and that's our big job, the images, that's our big, big job that is the lack of images that we can supply to a suspect' (Police Officer ID: 16).

It is not easy for undercover officers to obtain credibility. Their success depends on the credibility of the profile, which in turn depends on the legend created, which in turn relies on the availability of images. Answering or making phone calls is another problem faced by most police forces, which is clearly a limitation. Very few forces hold devices to camouflage officers' voices. A police officer outlines his concern regarding the relationship – or lack of – between technology and policing:

> 'As technology progresses, our job is going to becoming incredibly harder because the expectation of the bad guy, the suspect is that we would have access to all the facilities that would allay their fears. Things like being on the webcam, having a mobile phone, being contactable. These things that we have to now use our initiative to negate, phone calls, covert messages that we do to get through this I think it will get to a stage where between the publicity that we give ourselves and the technological advances you have to be thick to get caught by us. I give it a couple more years. I think the average internet top proper paedophile will not waste time' (Police Officer ID: 7).

Thus, communication with the most cautious offenders, who wanted to speak to the victim before even establishing an online relationship, is hardly possible.

> 'The hyper cautious [sex offender] wants more. He wants a face picture; generally what they'll ask for is either a phone call or he'll ask for the distribution of a picture. Generally he won't even ask for the distribution of an indecent picture, he'll just say I want a phone picture now. Obviously if you send him a phone picture the date is in the picture. Or he would ask you to put on your webcam. 2 out of 3 defeat us on day 1, 99per cent of the time 3 out of 3 will defeat us on day 1' (Police Officer ID: 16).

What was found was that some offenders wanted to be able to see their victims via webcam to verify they were really speaking to young girls. As this officer commented, this proved to be another major obstacle:

> 'We need help; we need help because our methods of investigations are now known and this creates challenges everyday. I don't think we can necessarily get away with not having webcams for example on our computers for that much longer' (Police Officer ID: 20).

During undercover investigations, webcams are required to verify the identity of the girl to be used for sexual activities. When undercover operations were in their infancy, not all computers had integrated webcams. Now, however, through the availability of webcams, the reason as to why undercover officers do not use them may be questioned by the most suspicious sex offenders.

However, as argued by this practitioner, some sex offenders are so strongly driven by sexual desire that they continue the interaction, hoping that this may develop into an online sexual relationship:

'If they're thinking about it they'll do it, whether we can be on a webcam or not. What they see on the TV (TV programmes on undercover operations) is not going to stop them having the feelings that they're having overnight. Like the guy for example that I've lost the other day; the fact is that he wanted to have sex with a 13 year old girl will not go away. Just because he stopped speaking to me, as a 13 year old, doesn't mean that his urges have stopped. In fact he came back to me few days later' (Police officer ID: 18).

Today, social networking sites (SNSs) assist sex offenders even further. Children often publish on their website their blog or a weblog of their day. Current research (Davidson, Lorenz and Martellozzo 2009) highlights that children, in their profile, include pictures of themselves posing or with friends. Children are extremely open in sharing personal information on their online social networking profiles. They often include pictures of themselves wearing their school uniforms, which show the name of the school they attend. Many include lyrics and films they like, their hobbies etc, thus giving sex offenders a vast amount of information which may be used for grooming purposes (see Chapter 3 for a full discussion). As far as Facebook and MSN are concerned, most of the young people who took part in Davidson et al.'s study (2010) keep their profile public. Few students make it private and many do not understand the difference between a public profile and private profile. Thus, because of the amount of information that children post on their SNS profile the offender does not need to communicate with the child to understand whether she is happy or sad; whether she went to school or she is sick at home. He may simply carry out some online research to detect the most needy and vulnerable.

Indeed, the dynamics and interaction of an online relationship between victims and offenders is extremely complex. With this in mind, in the following section I evaluate the different profiles used by online sex offenders, their behaviour during the grooming process and the way in which law enforcement agencies respond.

Creating a profile

When sex offenders set up their profiles, they do so through the requirements of standardised electronic membership forms (name, sex and age) of social networking and similar websites and go through the verification processes of service providers. The data they insert is checked electronically and not physically by a real person. Therefore, offenders can make any desired claim about their identity, including the use of any profile picture. These profiles are designed, directly or indirectly, to attract either children or like-minded people. Thus, the visual element (such as pictures, lists of friends, links to favourite sports, pop singers etc) is essential, as it draws undercover officers' interest and may help them decide whether to add the new 'virtual friend' to their contact (cf. Martellozzo 2010). However, it is very challenging for a CII to assess risk on the basis of a person's online profile. Often, very little information is posted publicly. Offenders who are very reserved and cautious about their personal details may be more dangerous than perpetrators who openly post their photographs or other types of images, listings of hobbies, interests in children, their location, their age or their sex (Martellozzo 2010). Some of the online profiles analysed during the course of this research were relatively bland and gave no inclination of the subject's sexual preferences. Other profiles were open about their sexual preferences.

As this officer claimed:

> 'I've arrested people who have given us so many details on line, everything about them and shown to be true. I've dealt with people who were completely suspicious, really sort of testing the water before they go any further' (Police Officer ID: 9).

It can therefore be argued that whilst there is no such thing as a typical online groomer using a typical profile, it is possible to identify a distinctive grooming behaviour. Here, I seek to understand grooming behaviour – as feminists have sought to understand male violence (Kelly 1988) – as existing across a spectrum of confidence. The spectrum of openness illustrated in Figure 7.1 has purposively avoided using a positivistic approach underpinned by the often pseudo-scientific classification of people or objects into discrete typologies with rigid boundaries. Positivistic typologies would not have worked in this context; they would have placed online sex offenders' profiles into boxes, categorised them and reinforced a stereotypical notion overlooking the nuance and fluidity of human characteristics and behaviours.

Figure 7.1 shows that sex offenders who target young children form a diverse group that cannot be 'accurately characterised with one-dimensional labels'

Hyper-confident   Hyper-cautious
Open Profile   Hidden Profile
Indecent Profile   Decent Profile
                              Suspicious

Figure 7.1 A spectrum of openness from most confident to hyper-cautious

(Wolak et al. 2009: 1). It can be noted that, at one end of the spectrum of open-ness, some groomers are hyper-confident and will declare their sexual intentions to children from the outset. The hyper-confident individual is usually open about his identity; in his profile he posts a picture and details of himself (all offenders in the sample were male) and often he posts pornographic pictures in his profile. It was found, however, that most of the online groomers lied about their age. As this police officer explains:

'It is difficult because when the trust starts to develop and they say I'm not really 21, I'm 31, and then a couple of weeks later I'm not really 31, I'm 41. Before you know it they're up to about 51 and then they show you a picture of a horrible old man. And they ask: do you like me? I mean would a 13 year old say no I don't like you. So it's difficult to actually keep talking thinking your profile (that of a child) would like an older man' (Police Officer ID: 18).

Hyper-confident groomers

Hyper-confident groomers may create a decent or indecent profile. They would create a decent profile, for example, by posting a photo of themselves, to make the child feel comfortable, but at the same time curious about the person depicted in the profile. Once the hyper-confident-decent groomer contacts the child and inter-acts once or twice, the undercover officer adds him to his list of friends. Friendships normally develop thereafter, in some instances leading to the confident-decent groomer travelling to meet the child for abuse.

Hyper-confident-indecent groomers would choose their profile to be indecent, for example by posting a picture of their penises, probably hoping that the child would be curious and inquisitive about the profile and accept a virtual friendship. Furthermore, the profile may explicitly state the sexual interest of the person. For example, a groomer in one of the profiles examined in this study posted: 'I am a nice, decent, very loving caring guy with a pervy side – daddy/daughter, incest etc'. Some had listed their interests under categories such as 'incest', 'cherry popping Daddies' and 'dreamer of teens'. One suspect's profile contained a picture of a young female performing oral sex on him and a link to a 'paedo paradise' website. In these cases the subjects are ignoring any element of risk, drawing attention to themselves by making their interest in children extremely explicit.

As one officer stated:

'These types of offenders are also the most familiar with the internet. From their behaviour it is clear they have experience in chatting with a lot of people. Newer ones to the "game" are more cautious and may explore the risk further' (Police Officer ID: 3).

Hyper-cautious groomers

At the other end of the spectrum, hyper-cautious groomers will not post any abusive images or declare any sexual interest in children until interaction takes place. Hyper-cautious groomers post cartoons or toys as their pictures and spend time establishing that individuals are genuine. It can be argued that they do so because they are concerned that someone in society may report their inappropriate behaviour or that they are wasting time with perverts who fantasise about being young girls. In this way they play a passive role in the sense that they require the child to make the majority of approaches. For example, if they were speaking to an adult they would ask for indecent images of children, believing that law enforcement agencies would not post them based 'on legal and moral ground' (Gallagher 2007: 112). It emerged, however, that when they communicate with someone they believe to be a young girl, they would not ask for indecent images of children.

The hyper-cautious groomer is one 'who could possibly be the most dangerous, who are not easy to identify and lie from start to finish' (Police Officer ID: 2). Hyper-cautious groomers are so concerned about being caught that they are not willing to furnish details about themselves until they are completely sure it is safe to do so. This type of offender may insist on viewing the potential victim on webcam, hearing her voice over the phone and receiving more photographs. Eventually, when they feel they are chatting to someone real, they start grooming the child. However, this is not always the case. If they do not feel comfortable in establishing a closer relationship, because of a lack of credentials, they may decide to move on to the next victim. This contention was supported by the majority of the police officers working in the field:

> 'Hyper-cautious online groomers are the ones that we don't know how dangerous they are, we don't know if they're paedophiles, we don't know anything about them because we don't have the tactics or technology to go up against them. We're not able to prove at a very early stage that we are an authentic child and they switch off and go elsewhere and quite possibly go elsewhere to real children' (Police Officer ID: 20).

This spectrum should be interpreted as fluid, as a wide range of grooming behaviours exists at every stage in between. That said, despite the fluidity of grooming behaviours, it is possible to discern certain characteristics that are common to all groomers explored in this study, regardless of levels of confidence. The key common characteristic across the spectrum is suspiciousness.

Understanding online offenders

By using the internet, individuals have the opportunity to explore the dark side of their sexuality by pretending to be whoever they feel like being and by disclosing as much or as little about themselves as they wish to others (Cooper et al. 2000). A man can be younger or older, a woman, a child or a cartoon character. Moreover, by hiding behind their fictitious profiles, they explore any opportunity cyberspace may offer, including that of sexually abusing children.

During the police operation I studied, more than 3000 individuals visited fictitious Lucy's online profile. Of these, more than 450 individuals with adult male profiles initiated contact with Lucy and 80 became virtual friends and prolonged their relationship. Experience with covert internet investigators suggests that the vast majority of male adults contacting Lucy would do so for sexual purposes. Some were simply interested in having sexual conversations with the girl. Young (2001: 300) defines these individuals as 'fantasy users' and distinguishes those who utilise online chat rooms and instant messaging for the express purpose of role-playing in online fantasy sex chat.

However, many suspects went beyond the fantasy stage; they distributed indecent images, exposed themselves and travelled to meet potential victims. Research and experience have repeatedly shown that sex offenders cannot be easily 'picked out' of a crowd (Grubin 1998; Stanko 1990). There is no consistent model or typology into which they can accurately be placed for the purpose of identification and isolation – and public denunciation. In other words, 'it is not possible to describe the "typical" child molester' (Grubin 1998: 14). This contention can also be applied to online forms of CSA. All the practitioners interviewed for this study – particularly those operating as undercover officers – maintained that, although media portrayals often imply that child sex offenders are somehow different, this is not necessarily the case in reality. Furthermore, they all shared the opinion that online child sex offenders cannot be classified under any categories:

> 'I couldn't describe to you necessarily a person who I would say he is, or she is a typical groomer but I can describe to you, in my experience, what typical grooming is. The gain and the trust being the big friend and doing things for that child beyond the cause of duty. So, there's certainly a typical grooming methodology but I certainly couldn't sit here and if there's 100 people there point to one and say he's a groomer, unless I've interacted with that person on line' (Police Officer ID: 17).

Online police investigations have shown that online groomers come from diverse backgrounds and are a heterogeneous group.

The subjects in this particular operation, for example, were all males between the ages of 36 and 69 years old; the most common age range was 36 to 45. All the suspects were white, except for one who was of mixed ethnicity. A police officer commented:

> 'I just think that our sort of the demographics of our offenders are normally 21 years old to 75 years old. White men who are either single, because they

are typically sad individuals who live at home; have poor social circles; have the inability to form relationships with people . . . Or there's the person who is a professional vicar, a teacher, policeman, magistrate who has a respectable veneer. But I haven't dealt with anybody from Asian origin, I haven't dealt with any Chinese people, I haven't dealt with any black people' (Police Officer ID: 5).

Apart from their ethnicity, the subjects had diverse lifestyles, spanning a wide range of backgrounds and occupations. Of the 23, 21 subjects were employed at the time of their arrest, one was long-term unemployed and another had retired. Occupations were varied, ranging from executive management positions to driving, security and manual labour. This officer claims:

'What I haven't seen many of is your normal Joe public bloke; the bloke who builds your house, the bloke who fixes your plumbing, I can't think of too many of them type of people. In a funny kind of way, its either someone whose got a professional occupation or kind of no occupation or like a dead end job, but I couldn't tell you the last time I arrested a mechanic' (Police Officer ID: 7).

Three individuals arrested during this operation worked in high-ranking IT-related positions. It could be expected that expertise in this area may help a person cover his 'traces' when offending online and escape detection. Despite the subjects' extensive knowledge of computers, this was not the case. Those who worked in IT were found to have large collections of child abuse images and movies on their computers. All three could be described as compulsive collectors of child abuse images and pornography in general. It can be argued that working with computers made it easier for them to research for images and collect them.

It appears as if collecting these images was a compulsive habit so important to the subjects that it far outweighed any risk of getting caught. One male was arrested in possession of a DVD he had compiled, containing 1206 images of child abuse and bestiality, which he brought to the meeting to show Lucy. Another male had already spent time in prison for being in possession of over 20,000 images but was yet found to have hundreds of images on his computer when arrested.

Several of the subjects had jobs that meant that they would have been in contact with children on a regular basis. Two of the offenders were teachers and another had applied for a Criminal Record Bureau (CRB) check with the intention of assisting his wife as a classroom supervisor. The dataset also included a police officer and a paramedic; both jobs have a high level of responsibility and would have brought the suspects in close contact with children.

Box 7.1 Exploring what the internet represents for sex offenders

These data derive primarily from one-to-one in-depth interviews conducted by police officers with sex offenders following their arrest. Although 23[1] suspects had been arrested and prosecuted during a police operation,[2] only 12 in-depth interviews[3] were available for analysis. Of the 23 offenders arrested, one committed suicide and 10 did not make any comment during the interview. However, analysis of the perpetrators' online behaviour, which is likely to provide a more accurate assessment of their motivation than anything they say in interview (Sullivan 2008), had already taken place in the observational stage of this research.

The analysis of the sex offenders' interview accounts and police officers' narratives showed that the majority of sex offenders differentiate the real world from cyberspace. As the quotes below illustrate, some feel that their behaviour is acceptable because, to them, anything available on cyberspace is neither real nor tangible:

S (2):   '. . . it seemed (masturbating on the webcam) fun at the time, I won't say innocent fun but innocent fun on my part, almost in that I'm in my room and it just seemed like fun at the time.'

Q: 'Ok, what would the difference be if that girl had been sat in the room with you, what's the difference between that and doing it over the webcam?'

S (2):   'There is no difference at all but I don't, I wouldn't do that in front of a real girl I don't think.'

It is interesting to note that this offender makes a clear distinction between masturbating in front of a 'real' girl and a webcam. This issue emerged in other interviews:

S (7):   'Honest, it is hard to explain but when I am sitting there I am not talking to anyone real it's just a box on the screen and there's no one on the other end it's just a TV screen thing.'

Other sex offenders recognise their wrongdoings but continue offending against children, hoping not to be caught. This may be related to the fact that the internet provides anonymity, a sense of protection and security (Cooper et al. 2000). The majority of sex offenders perceived the internet as a safe place, like their own community, where they are allowed to be whoever they wish to be and behave in a way that they would not find so easy in the real world. The brief letter below, written by a convicted sex offender to his wife, highlights this sense of security:

'This is the hardest letter I have ever written. I am in a dark and lonely place, without you. . . . The truth is that I shall never see you again! For I simply can't bear the shame of my horrible actions. You deserve a full and frank explanation so here it is. I've always found young girls sexually attractive, especially pubescent girls of about 11–14. I obviously never acted on my perverted desires except when masturbating, where I would fantasise about having sex with one. Well along came the internet and I was able to look at your girls in what I thought was anonymity. I should have known better but I thought the precautions I was taking were good enough. . . . I've used it [my email] to trade pictures of underage girls . . . As is the case with normal adult porn, things have a habit of getting stronger and stronger and it was not different with lasting. I went from being satisfied with school uniforms/bikini/underwear pictures, to where I am now. I now want to actually rape and kill young girls. I have been trading the worst kind of pictures and videos – young girls being raped, tortured and forced into having sex. . . . I just was unable to separate myself from the dark side' (SO ID: 5 Letter to his wife).

However, not all suspects keep their fantasies within the boundaries of cyberspace. What could have happened if SO7 was not stopped in time? Would his fantasy and desire have escalated to real-life abuse?

Suspect 2, for example, brought his fantasy into real life and travelled to meet Lucy. Moreover, upon further forensic examination of the suspect's laptop and home computer, other conversations were retrieved from his chat file. It appeared that he was talking with another 20 like-minded people about fantasising of having sex with young children. During his conversations, the suspect stated his preference for girls between 7 and 11 years of age. He was asked by several people whether he had a sexual interest in his daughter, but he stated that she was too young and that he was waiting until she was older. He also stated that he had a fantasy to kidnap a young girl of about 9 years.

S (2) 'Mine [fantasy] is to kidnap a yng girl, say 9yo, with 1 or 2 guys, then have her in the back of a van 4 a day or 2.'

Others see the internet as just a tool that can help them to escape boredom, and to fulfil their fantasies. Furthermore, what helps sex offenders to justify their behaviour is the great availability of images and the existence of supportive communities of like-minded people. In this case, they use the internet as an excuse: 'because others do it, they also do it'. This is highlighted clearly below:

'I know what's wrong and I know what's right and I look at these things [inde-cent images] like legal laws and you know the age of consent in this country and the age of consent in other countries and all that kind of stuff. I see it as a social acceptance, so I know that what I've done is outside of that and is wrong, so I know that, but when you are talking to somebody in the virtual world those boundaries aren't there' (Sex Offender ID: 11).

As argued by Young (2008), conventional messages about sexual behaviour that would be respected in the real world are completely ignored in the virtual world. All of a sudden, the virtual world appears to be without any social, moral or legal bound-aries. Overall, it emerged in all interviews that internet users feel free to explore anything with no inhibition or fears, including paedophilic themes.

Previous convictions

Of the 23 suspects examined, only one had a previous conviction for sexual offences. Interestingly, 15 of them had no criminal records at all before their arrest. A further two had committed minor offences in the 1970s and had not come to the notice of the police since. One individual had a conviction for handling stolen goods in 1993 but nothing after that. Two individuals had substantial criminal records before their most recent arrests and one had been charged with six offences between 1989 and 2003. Most of the offences appeared to relate to drinking excessively and becoming physically but not sexually violent. The one subject with a previous sexual offence was a registered sex offender, who had convictions for possessing over 20,000 images in 2002. These findings could be generalised to other operations conducted. As argued by this officer:

'Interestingly the vast majority of people that we deal with whether it be through the pro-active internet operations or through search warrants, most of them have very few previous convictions and certainly no sexual offences. Very, very few of them are registered sex offenders' (Police Officer ID: 6).

Similarly, Smallbone and Wortley's (2001) research on offenders' characteristics and *modus operandi* also found that a large majority of offenders (82.2 per cent of a sample size of 182 respondents) with previous convictions were first convicted of a non-sexual offence.

Overall it would appear that those convicted of grooming are not particularly criminally inclined when compared with the general population. Research has indicated that 33 per cent of all males in the UK have at least one conviction by the age of 46 (Prime et al. 2001). The proportion of groomers analysed in this research with prior convictions is slightly lower than that of the general population at 28 per cent. Admittedly the dataset is small, but this points to an interesting area for further research. These findings back up those of the National Juvenile Online Victimization Study (Wolak et al. 2005), which found that in general those arrested for possessing child abuse images do not tend to have extensive criminal records. Furthermore, studies such as Abel et al. (1987) and, more recently, Hernandez's (2009) work indicate that sex offenders often have an extensive offending history but few criminal convictions, given the hidden nature of the offending.

Intelligence showed that three of the subjects were known to police databases for domestic incidents with their wives or girlfriends. For two of the subjects who had no prior criminal records, there were indications of some signs of sexual abnormality. One subject had been seen by neighbours on several occasions naked in front of his window and taking his dogs for walks naked in the garden. Another suspect had come to the notice of police as early as 1990 for enquiring about child abuse images.

The role of technology in policing online CSA

Since Operation ORE, the police in Britain, particularly the Metropolitan Police, have made massive progress in their computer literacy and technological expertise (Jewkes 2003a). As argued by this officer:

'Operation Ore forced a lot of police forces to suddenly change. They had all this work they had to deal with but did not have any infrastructure in place. In many cases they had to buy a kit, they had to train people, they had to set aside offices, they had to get policies, they had to get procedures for dealing with child abuse material coming from a high technological side' (Police Officer ID:17).

As demonstrated in this chapter, the police force has accepted that technology plays a fundamental part in child protection, in removing children from abuse and in policing perpetrators. They have realised that a covert investigation unit specialising in child protection is paramount. The majority of the police officers agreed that covert internet investigations are the way forward in relation to the Paedophile Unit, which has developed and still is developing rapidly:

'The main thing that we've done around child protection and the most positive move that the police have done are the pro active side of it. When I first joined the unit we weren't proactive, we were reactive and I feel as though this unit can double the size because we're not even scratching the surface' (Police Officer ID: 19).

A police officer outlines some of the changes:

'When I first started there was 2 of us working on the internet and I think I had something like 6.3 gigabyte computer and 128 kilobytes of ram or something like that, I don't want to start going down technical lines and now we're dealing with your everyday computer now is sort of like 500 gigabyte' (Police Officer ID: 17).

It can be argued that, today, the business of investigating CSA online is still a new area of police work and officers, forensic examiners and analysts need to be provided with the resources necessary to investigate suspects and scrutinise their computers. However, it is clearly not just about possessing the technological capabilities, but also to be provided with relevant training to learn how to utilise them (Wall 2007). The HTCU and Paedophile Unit provide CII training for all the detectives and forensic examiners in the unit so they can work undercover and identify subjects who want to abuse children via the internet. Furthermore, they can act on intelligence and produce search warrants to seize suspects' computers so they can work backwards and trace who they have been talking to. Or, as this chapter has highlighted, they can use a more proactive approach and create profiles of children (or of adults) to see who responds and who arrange a meeting with the child or want to develop conversations for fantasy purposes.

Overall, all the police officers that participated in this research supported the contention that the quality of policing CSA over the years has improved greatly. As this officer argues:

'I think we've responded as a necessity to the internet and I think we are in the stage at the moment of pushing boundaries as far as we can. It is our responsibility to save and protect children from abuse and we are committed to succeed' (Police Officer ID: 4).

Since the completion of Operation ORE and the implementation of the Sexual Offences Act 2003, in which the 'grooming' offence was incorporated into the legislation for the first time, the police have embarked upon an increasingly robust response to the problem and have been investing more resources in training, undercover operations and thorough investigations.

Whilst all the officers agreed that there has been a clear development in policing online CSA, some of the officers interviewed believed that the police are not always targeting the most dangerous people. In Goodman's (1997) terms, at times, they aim for the 'low-hanging fruit'. In other words, they focus on those criminals who commit 'ordinary' crimes, which require fewer resources and less complicated investigations to secure an arrest and a conviction.

For a crime to be prioritised and receive sustained police attention, it needs to be statistically and politically significant (Taylor 2005). Police priorities are pressurised by government-set performance targets 'which are themselves frequently a reaction to public anxiety following high-profile criminal cases' (Jewkes 2003: 517). Because of Operation ORE, for example, governments felt the need to respond to the public concern fuelled by the extensive media coverage of sex offenders' activities (Davidson 2008; Greer 2003; Soothill and Walby 1991; Spindler 2003). As a result, the G8 ministers decided to place online CSA within the international political agenda. As argued by Jewkes (2003b), specialists units, including the Metropolitan Police, are most concerned with obtaining evidence and carrying out arrests.

Whilst it is vital that governments pay close attention to the growing and serious phenomenon of online CSA, it can be argued that the police feel under pressure to produce results and figures. This problem was addressed by half of the officers interviewed. Officers feel that the police should focus on the most dangerous offenders, that is, those who travel across the country to meet a child for abuse:

'I think we're going for easy catches at the moment, people who aren't paedophiles. We've got people that go on line and make pictures of kids because its there because it's available. It is too easy to band people as paedophiles, and a lot of police officers don't know the definition of a paedophile. And as soon as they commit an offence and they should be punished for it but I think they're too easy to catch. I think as a unit that we're just going for figures, for numbers rather than quality, because that's the only way the government think. They go for quantity rather than quality (Police Officer ID: 12).

As argued by the police officer above, this pressure leads officers to focus on low-hanging fruit which yields quick but not always the best results:

'For me there's a big difference between people that sit at home in front of a computer screen masturbating to an indecent image of a child and some-body that then leaves his home, travels across the country and pitches up hoping to meet a child and to abuse a child. They are poles apart for me' (Police Officer ID: 6).

Whilst those who download and collect indecent images take part in the exploita-tion of children, as reflected in the definitions provided in Chapter 1, there are people who are prepared to move a step further: to travel to meet a child for sexual abuse. According to the majority of the police officers, travellers are the most dangerous individuals and should be police priorities.

Conclusions

On the basis of the evidence presented in this chapter, a number of proposals can be advanced about undercover policing CSA online and sex offenders' *modus operandi*.

First, the case studies analysed in this chapter illustrate some key issues in the study of online CSA and in particular of online grooming. It is clear that the internet is more than just a medium of communication. There is overwhelming evidence presented here to suggest that the internet constitutes a complex virtual reality with its own roles and language. For example, to be able to interact success-fully undercover, police officers need to learn the appropriate computer language (Davidson and Martellozzo 2004) and they need to learn about children's educa-tional development at school, music groups etc. Furthermore, the internet provides the supportive context within which the child abuser is no longer a lonely figure, but forms part of a larger community that shares the same interests (Davidson and Martellozzo 2008b).

Secondly, the internet provides offenders with the opportunity to hide their real identity, as in the aforementioned case of the hyper-cautious offender. This makes the job of undercover officers extremely challenging. As explained in Chapter 6, undercover officers in most cases need to obtain personal information on the suspects to be able to risk-assess them. The majority of practitioners interviewed in this study acknowledged that it is not possible to identify a typical online groomer using a typical profile. Online behaviour and the risk that a suspect may pose for a child can only be understood and analysed through online interaction and not only on the basis of the information provided in online profiles. However, all practitioners supported the notion that, regardless of levels of confidence and despite the fluidity of grooming behaviours, it is possible to distinguish certain characteristics that are common to all groomers explored in this study.

Thirdly, practitioners expressed the view that hyper-cautious sex offenders are aware that the internet can be explored by anyone, and that, as a result, they request increasingly more evidence to ascertain that the child they are talking to is a real child and not a male adult. Practitioners find this aspect of policing both challenging and frustrating. Whilst the police force has accepted that technology plays a fundamental part in child protection and that covert internet investigations are the way forward, the majority of police officers feel they should be pushing the boundaries further. For example, they should be able to respond to the demands of the most hyper-cautious sex offender by keeping up with technology.

Finally, practitioners expressed different views about the success of undercover work. Whilst the majority of the officers who participated in the study support online undercover policing and believe that policing of CSA has clearly improved in the past few years, they feel that the pressure that comes from the government and management to obtain more and quicker results undermines the qualitative value of this type of work, which requires patience, time, training and, ever increasingly, new resources.

Notes

1 As online grooming is a relatively new type of offence, the data sample used in this study is small. However, this analysis represents a valuable starting point for academics and practitioners who are working towards the development of a better understanding of this complex area. Furthermore, it presents a case for criminologists to engage more fully with the cyber and to integrate cyber concerns and life into the mainstream of criminological research and writing.

2 In the face of overwhelming evidence the great majority of subjects fully admitted the offences and pleaded guilty. Of the 11 sentenced all were found guilty and sentenced to various terms in custody ranging from 18 months to five years. All were now required to sign on the sex offender register for varying periods (10 years to life). Most were also made subjects of sex offender prevention orders (SOPOs), with stringent conditions in relation to their computer/internet use and their contact with children.

3 Police interviews were conducted to gather further evidence for prosecution and not for research purposes. Therefore, the questions asked were exploratory which, at times, required answers of a descriptive nature. During the interviews, respondents were asked to describe their offence and, where applicable, to explain their use of child abuse images, their *modus operandi* and the tools used to groom children online. These insights contributed to enhance the understanding of both sex offenders' online behaviour and their own subjective understandings of their behaviour. However, the validity of some of the respective data can be questioned on the basis that issues such as conflict in adult relationships or denial were not thoroughly explored during the interviews. Given the qualitative, open nature of the interviews, other relevant information emerged at various points. Following Silverman (2004), qualitative counts are reported where appropriate.

References

Abel, G., Becker, G., Mittelman, J. V., Cunningham-Rathner, J., Rouleau, J. L. and Murphy, W. D. (1987) Self-reported sex crimes of non-incarcerated paraphiliacs. *Journal of Interpersonal Violence*, 2, 3–25.

BBC News Online. (11 September 2000) *Blair Unveils Internet Plans*; http://news.bbc.co.uk/1/hi/uk_politics/919903.stm, accessed on 2/3/2009.

Calder, M. (2004). *Child Sexual Abuse and the Internet: Tackling New Frontiers*, Lyme Regis, Russell House Publishing.

Cooper, A., McLaughlin, I. P. and Campbell, K. M. (2000) Sexuality in Cyberspace: Update for the 21st Century. *Cyber Psychology and Behaviour*, 3(4), 521–36.

Davidson, J. and Martellozzo, E. (2004) *Educating Children about Sexual Abuse and Evaluating the Metropolitan Police Safer Surfing Programme*, London, University of Westminster and Metropolitan Police.

Davidson, J. and Martellozzo, E. (2008a) Policing the Internet: Protecting Vulnerable Children From Sex Offenders In Cyberspace. *Police Investigations Police Practice & Research: An International Journal*.

X Davidson, J. and Martellozzo, E. (2008b) Protecting Children in Cyberspace, in G. Letherby, P. Birch, M. Cain and K. Williams (eds), *Sex Crime*, Cullompton, Willan Publishers.

Davidson, J. and Martellozzo, E. (2009) Internet Sex Offenders: Risk, Control and State Surveillance, in M. Johnson and S. Scalter (eds), *Individual Freedom, Autonomy and the State*, Cambridge, Hart Press.

Davidson, J., Grove-Hills, J., Bifulco, A., Gottschalk, P., Caretti, V., Pham, T., et al. (2009) Online Abuse: Literature Review and Policy Context. *Prepared for the European Commission Safer Internet Plus Programme*.

Davidson, J., Lorenz, M. and Martellozzo, E. (2010) Evaluation of CEOP ThinkUKnow. Internet Safety Programme and Exploration of Young People's Internet Safety Knowledge. *Centre for Abuse and Trauma Studies*.

Davidson, J. C. (2008) *Child Sexual Abuse: Media Representations and Government Reactions*, London, Routledge-Cavendish.

Franko Aas, K. (2006) Beyond the 'Desert of the Real': Crime Control in a Virtual(ised) Reality, in Y. Jewkes (ed), *Crime Online*, Cullompton, Willan.

Gallagher, B. (2007) Internet-Initiated Incitement and Conspiracy to Commit Child Sexual Abuse (CSA): The Typology, Extent and Nature of Known Cases. *Journal of Sexual Aggression. An International, Interdisciplinary Forum for Research, Theory and Practice*, 13(2), 101–19.

Gallagher, B., Fraser, C., Christmann, K. and Hodgson, B. (2006) *International and Internet Child Sexual Abuse and Exploitation. Research report*, Huddersfield, Centre for Applied Childhood Studies, University of Huddersfield.

Gillespie, A. (2008) *Child Exploitation and Communication Technologies*, Dorset, Russell House Publishing.

Goodman, M. (1997) Why the Police don't Care about Cybercrime. *Harvard Journal of Law and Technology*, 10, 465–94.

Greer, C. (2003) *Sex Crime and the Media. Sex Offending and the Press in a Divided Society*, London, Willan Publishing.

Grubin, D. (1998) Sex Offending against Children: Understanding the Risk. *Police Research Series*, 99.

Hernandez, A. E. (2009) *Psychological and Behavioural Characteristics of Child Pornography Offenders in Treatment*. Paper presented at the Global Symposium: Examining the Relationship between Online and Offline Offences and Preventing the Sexual Exploitation of Children.

Jewkes, Y. (2003a) *Dot.cons: Crime, Deviance and Identity on the Internet*, Cullompton, Willian.

Jewkes, Y. (2003b) Policing Cybercrime, in T. Newburn (ed), *Handbook of Policing* (pp. 501–24), Collompton, Devon: Willan.

Kelly, L. (1988) *Surviving Sexual Violence*, Oxford, Polity Press.

Lanning, K. (2005) Compliant Child Victims: Confronting an Uncomfortable Reality, in E. Quayle and M. Taylor (eds), *Viewing Child Pornography on the Internet. Understanding the Offence, Managing the Offender, Helping the Victims* (pp. 49–60), Lyme Regis, Russell House Publishing.

Livingstone, S. and Bober, M. (2005) *Internet Literacy Among Children and Young People*, LSE.

Martellozzo, E. (2010) Sex Offenders Use of the Internet, in J. Davidson and P. Gottschalk (eds), *Internet Child Abuse: Current Research & Practice*, London, Routledge.

Platt, A. (1969) *The Child Savers: The Invention of Delinquency*, Chicago, University of Chicago Press.

Prime, J., White, S., Liriano, S. and Patel, K. (2001) *Criminal Careers of Those Born Between 1953 and 1978 March 2001*, London, Home Office.

Sanderson, C. (2007) *The Seduction of Children. Empowering Parents and Teachers to Protect Children from Child Sexual Abuse*, London, Jessica Kingsley Publishers.

Silverman, D. (2004) *Interpreting Qualitative Data: Methods for Analysing Talk, Text and Interaction* (2nd edn), London, Sage.

Smallbone, S. and Wortley, R. (2001) Child Sexual Abuse: Offender Characteristics and Modus Operandi. *Trends and Issues in Crime and Criminal Justice*, 193, 1–6.

Soothill, K. and Walby, S. (1991) *Sex Crime in the News*, London, Routledge.

Spindler, P. (2003) *Policing Paedophiles on the Internet*, The John Grieve Centre.

Stanko, E. (1990) *Everyday Violence*, London, Unwin Hyman.

Sullivan, J. (2008) Interviewing Child Sex Offenders. Unpublished Lecture. CEOP.

Taylor, J. (2005) *Just an Epidemic or Another Crime?* Paper presented at the Criminology Lecture.

Wall, D. (2007) Policing Cybercrimes: Situating the Public Police in Networks of Security within Cyberspace. *Police Practice and Research: An International Journal*, 8(2), 183–205.

West, D. (1996) Sexual Molesters, in N. Walker (ed), *Dangerous People*, London, Blackstone Press Limited.

Wolak, J., Finkelhor, D. and Mitchell, K. (2005) Internet-Initiated Sex Crimes Against Minors: Implications for Prevention Based on Findings from a National Study. *Journal of Adolescent Health*, 35(5), 424–37.

Wolak, J., Finkelhor, D. and Mitchell, K. J. (2009) Trends in Arrests of 'Online Predators'. *Crime Against Children Research Centre*.

Young, K. (2008) Understanding Sexually Deviant Online Behaviour from an Addiction Perspective. *International Journal of Cyber Criminology*, 2(1), 298–307.

Young, K. S. (2001) *Tangled in the Web: Understanding Cybersex from Fantasy to Addiction*, Bloomington, IN, Authorhouse.

Chapter 8

Conclusion

Introduction

In this book I have sought to explore the policing of child sexual abuse (CSA) online, with particular emphasis on the problem of online grooming. As a result, this work has produced a significant amount of in-depth empirical data regarding police perceptions of sex offenders' behaviour and police practice. The key aim was to develop a theoretical and empirical understanding of the perpetration and policing of online CSA that would have direct relevance at the levels of policy and practice. I achieved this in a number of ways. With respect to researching the perpetration of online CSA, I explored sex offenders' online grooming tactics through the observation of their interaction with undercover police officers and the analysis of their case files. With respect to researching the policing of online CSA, I explored covert and overt police activities through a combination of ethnographic observations, semi-structured interviews and documentary analysis.

A full immersion in the field of research

The mixed methods approach I selected sought to generate a more comprehensive understanding of online CSA than had previously been available in the existing academic literature. Moreover, this study is the first qualitative research conducted at the Metropolitan Police High Tech Crime Unit (HTCU) and Paedophile Unit, one of the best-equipped police units in the Western world. Here I secured unprecedented access to staff, facilities and to confidential and highly sensitive documents. This material has facilitated insights into policing procedures, police officers' perceptions and offenders' understanding of CSA which so far have not been available in the academic literature. At the same time, this study forms part of a long-standing tradition of criminological and sociological research of the processes and dynamics through which deviant behaviour is socially constructed in particular settings (Humphreys 1970; Douglas 1976; Hammersley and Atkinson 1983). The experience of this study has confirmed the usefulness of a qualitative, ethnographically informed approach for providing a holistic understanding of policing online CSA and sex offenders' *modus operandi*.

Primary data include data derived from participant observation, online communication between undercover officers and alleged sex offenders, police interviews with alleged sex offenders post arrests, my interviews with police officers and the analysis of official documents. Through this process of triangulation, the findings contribute significantly to theory, methods and epistemology.

With my empirical study, I seek to understand the process in which sex offenders use the internet to groom children and the way in which the police also make use of technology to protect children from being harmed. When the observational fieldwork began it comprised of:

- observing officers engaged in the surveillance of and real time online chatting with suspected child abusers
- involvement in discussions around the effectiveness of existing techniques and the development of new ones
- observing first-hand the processes and practices of policing CSA online
- studying relevant documents and legislation.

Over time, I felt I developed what seemed to me to be solid relationships with some detectives, who subsequently emerged as 'key informants' (Ericson et al. 1987: 91). These individuals were revisited at frequent intervals, sometimes acting as 'sounding boards' against which ideas about the nature of policing online abuse could be tested, and sometimes being asked to clarify issues of organisational policy and practice. On the one hand, the frequent meetings and conversations with some officers may have increased levels of trust between us. This, in turn, may have promoted a more open discussion of the policing process. On the other hand, it was important to guard against compromising the integrity of the research by giving too much weight to the views of a few particularly helpful and cooperative individuals. This was managed by seeking as representative a sample as possible in terms of rank, work experience and gender.

Nevertheless, it was not my objective to generate findings that would allow empirical generalisations as to the nature of online grooming and respective policing practices in the UK and beyond. The research design I employed was not geared towards this task. Rather, I wish to argue that the principal merit of my case study lies in establishing a baseline of empirical knowledge and conceptual tools for the study of online grooming. In line with well established traditions of qualitative case study research, this is an exploratory piece of research that arguably fulfils an important heuristic function in its field.

The theoretical framework used as an aid to analyse the data collected and understand the phenomenon of online CSA is that of Finkelhor (Finkelhor 1984a; Finkelhor 1984b; Finkelhor et al. 1986). As argued in the literature, although theoretical approaches to study CSA have focused singularly upon physiological, sociological, structural and psychological factors by way of explanation, the eclectic approach has the greatest support amongst academics and practitioners. This is because eclecticism incorporates the central themes of psychoanalytic, behavioural, sociological and feminist approaches. For this reason, Finkelhor's approach was the most desirable. Finkelhor (1984) created a framework which describes who is more at risk of offending in both a familial and extra-familial environment. Therefore, Finkelhor's theoretical model has contributed in an innovative and comprehensive manner to the understanding of CSA and has thus been used in this research as a theoretical framework to aid the understanding of the problem of online CSA.

Furthermore, the originality of this work derives from being able to explore offenders' behaviour in its natural virtual environment, avoiding the constraints that researchers commonly face during the interviews with offenders after their detection and conviction. The research has been conducted in tandem with the development of new policing techniques and practices. It has therefore presented me with the unique opportunity not only to engage with practitioners in the field, but also to observe and reflect on sex offenders' grooming tactics.

Summary of main research findings

Whilst there is no such thing as a typical online child groomer, it is nevertheless both possible and instructive to identify a range of distinctive child grooming behaviours. The research explores a spectrum of grooming behaviours from online fantasists, who groom for immediate sexual gratification in the virtual world, to persistent predators, who groom online to lay the foundations for CSA in the physical world. The police must prioritise in order to allocate their limited resources to dealing with those online groomers who are perceived to pose the greatest risk in the physical world. Informed prioritisation is a process that requires undercover officers entering the world of the online groomers and interacting over time to develop an understanding of their intentions. This research explores the complex, multi-faceted and at times counterintuitive relationships between online grooming behaviours, risk assessment, police practices and the actual danger of subsequent abuse in the physical world.

Development of new techniques, processes and practices in policing online CSA

The study portrays a virtual world in which sex offenders can anonymously and simultaneously target large numbers of victims within a very short period of time. The findings highlight that the anonymous nature of cyberspace makes the policing of online CSA challenging in a number of ways.

First, the generation of children's profiles to be used for undercover police investigations is extremely complicated. The identity of the child portrayed in the image has to be protected so that the child cannot be identified. Therefore, to protect the child's identity the images obtained need to be altered electronically. However, obtaining a profile image for other proactive police operations is not always so straightforward. The police have to rely on volunteers (preferably working for criminal justice agencies) to provide photos of when they were young to be used for undercover investigations. Whilst the quality of the photos obtained is often poor, obtaining a photo of a child that fits a particular suspect's interests is even more challenging, from both moral and legal perspectives.

Undercover police officers need to immerse themselves fully in the profile they have created and research what children do and like. They need to know what, for example, 13-year-old children may enjoy in terms of music or fashion; how children may spend time on the internet and their computer language; what games they may play; what sites they may use and what they may study at school. Police officers acknowledge that undercover online investigations are very costly and labour intensive. Time and resources need to be invested as follows: first, in researching and preparing for the operation; secondly, in the interaction with the suspects and the gathering of evidence; thirdly, in the surveillance and arrest; and finally in the preparation of the case to present in the criminal courts.

Online CSA is becoming increasingly more difficult to police as the internet and technologies develop rapidly. Police practitioners expressed the view that 'hyper-cautious' sex offenders are aware that the internet is policed and, as a result, they request increasingly more evidence to ascertain that the child to whom they are talking is a real child. During the interaction, these types of offenders ask for more pictures of the child, ask to speak to the child, to see the child via webcam or, if they are posing as like-minded adults, they are asked to distribute indecent images. However, the police may not have the tools necessary to satisfy the requests of the most hyper-cautious offenders.

Undercover policing: officer interview findings

The majority of police practitioners interviewed in this study acknowledged that it would be difficult to identify a 'typical online groomer' using a 'typical profile'. Sex offenders who target young children form a diverse group that cannot be characterised with one-dimensional labels as behaviour varies enormously from case to case. Some offenders spend long periods of time grooming young people; others express their sexual interests immediately. Online behaviour and the risk that a suspect may pose to a child can only be understood and analysed through individual online interaction and on a case-by-case basis. It is dangerous to assume that collectors of indecent images or those who fantasise online are high-risk contact abusers, for example. However, all practitioners supported the notion that, regardless of the levels of confidence and despite the fluidity of grooming behaviours, it is possible to distinguish certain characteristics that are common to all groomers explored in this study. It has been found, for example, that they share an element of suspiciousness and they often lie about their age.

Sex offenders: findings from online observations and case studies analysis[1]

The majority of sex offenders in this study started to satisfy their fantasy by exploring cyberspace in a recreational manner. However, the fantasy theme developed very rapidly until the discovery of the anonymous and abundant availability of chat rooms and social networking groups. They quickly realised that these sites would make their imagination more tangible by allowing them actively to engage in erotic dialogues with children or people who are also attracted to children and download pornography and indecent images.

Therefore, sex offenders' exploratory behaviour becomes more ingrained and develops into a compulsive obsession (Young 2008). It emerged that sex offenders' lives seem to be dependent on their interaction with their virtual targets or virtual like-minded friends. The great majority of sex offenders in this study recognised their dependence on both the internet and their online relationships. In their interviews with police officers, some sex offenders discussed the process of how their behaviour escalated from discovery or boredom to the point of becoming entangled in the web of the internet. They felt that the internet could continuously feed their curiosity and alleviate their boredom without risks. It emerged that all groomers were found to be in possession of pornography or indecent images of children (sometimes both) after having been arrested. Almost two-thirds of the subjects exposed themselves to the undercover officer via photograph or webcam. However, whilst some suspects used indecent images as a grooming tool, most of them used indecent images principally for sexual gratification.

Observation by undercover officers operating online has shown that, when a profile of a young girl is posted in social networking groups, it initially attracts hundreds of adult males. Of these, some may start prolonged and persistent contact on MSN but may decide not to keep it within the realm of cyberspace. Others may go beyond the discovery and exploration stages after their first few interactions and allow their fantasy to escalate through the whole cycle of abuse (Sullivan and Beech 2004), eventually committing offences contrary to the Sexual Offences Act 2003. It is, however, impossible to identify who is more likely to commit contact offences on the basis of an online profile.

Conceptualising online CSA: Future directions

As indicated earlier, conceptual debates about online CSA in some ways seem to be at an impasse. To begin with, debates among practitioners and academic criminologists are very much constrained by narrowly essentialist understandings of sexual contact between adult and children, focusing on supposed social, biological and psychological dysfunctions in offenders, rather than the social and cultural dynamics that constitute the interaction between offenders, victims, controlling agents of the state, therapists and so forth and through which the offender and his crime come into being in the first place. Moreover, critical sociological analyses of CSA often focus on its representational dimensions in politics and popular media and the consequences of such representations for penal policy, to the exclusion of the events of actual 'abuse' studied by practitioners and criminologists.

In this section, I wish to examine possible future directions of enquiry that might point a way through this impasse. In particular, I wish to argue that an integrated perspective on the power relations that are embedded in the various interactional dimensions of CSA merits consideration.

Gender, power, sexuality

In order to move debates on CSA forward, it seems important to draw them into the horizon of broader sociological arguments about the social constructedness of gender and sexuality. In line with arguments put forward by scholars such as Connell (1987, 2002), both gender and sexuality can be understood as social structures, which pattern the interaction between human beings in enduring ways, but are historically and culturally variable and not biologically or psychologically fixed. In this sense, the sexual differences that seem unquestionable to contemporary Western common sense have only emerged in fairly recent years and are not culturally invariant. It therefore seems important to acknowledge the openness and heterogeneity of what sex may mean.

In order to understand the social nature of CSA, it is important to examine it from the perspective of gendered and sexualised power relations. Power relationships in historically patriarchal Western societies work to establish the gendered and sexualised authority of men over women, but are also constitutive of hierarchies among men and women of different sexual orientations, among generations, among social classes and so forth. Radical feminists have been among the first to write critically about the problem of CSA. They recognise the psychological and at times physical oppression of patriarchy and consider the sexual abuse of children a manifestation of the oppression of females inherent in patriarchy (Wearing 1989). Finkelhor and Russell (1984) argue that patriarchy, and the power that derives from it, provide an explanation as to why most abusers are men and most victims are women. Thus, power is central in the sense that men have power over women and objectify them; adults (independent of gender) have a power over children and objectify them. As argued by Nelson and Oliver: 'Sexual abuse is seen as a product of adult motivation to have sexual contact with children coupled with factors that eliminate internal and external barriers to acting on the motivations. Male dominance affects both the capacity to act on motivations and the creation of those motivations in the culture and gender roles' (1998: 559). The prevalence of girls being victims of sexual abuse highlights the lower status as females and, at the same time, men's greater power over young women and men.

Such arguments correspond to long lines of enquiry in feminist scholarship and sociology, which have sought to de-essentialise understanding of gender and sexuality in the Western world since the late 1970s. The question thus must be raised why contemporary research on CSA either defers to common sense by essentialising gender and sexuality or treats both categories as 'black boxes' beyond its purview. In relation to this question, I here wish to focus particularly on the way in which contemporary politics and policy-making, as well as discourses in the mass media and popular culture, work to establish gendered and sexualised hierarchies that frame 'paedophiles' as a distinctive category of socially excluded men (and, to a much more limited extent, women) deviant in scholarly legal, moral and cultural terms.

The common media coverage of CSA occurring via new technologies promotes the perception that children are at greatest risk from online abusers: a new form of threat to society. Online sex offenders are 'collectively designed as the enemy of respectable society, their behaviour is seen as harmful or threatening to the values, the interests, possibly the very existence of society, or at least a sizable segment of society' (Goode and Ben-Yehuda 1994). Paedophiles have been identified in the popular media as a threat to society. However, what is interesting to note is that online CSA scandals have paid scant attention to the institution of the family, or the role of the father, the brother, the uncle or the close family friend and have focused instead on online predators. Although incidents concerning sexual abuse and neglect have taken place in the home, these have been considerably muted by the 'stranger abuse' argument. It is widely acknowledged that the vast majority of CSA is carried out by those within the immediate family (Nelson and Oliver 1998; Finkelhor et al. 1986; Finkelhor 1984a; Corby 2000; Jenks 1996); however, no form of media has created a moral panic around the institution that many people feel is the most important in society. The focus of abuse outside the home, in particular in cyberspace, therefore protects, in part anyhow, the majority of abusers. As argued by Chris Jenks: 'We are nor seeking explanation in terms of occasional, random occurrences or shadowy, hyperbolic figures of evil, rather we are seeking the routine and the commonplace – the normal type of people who have mundane relationship with children' (1996: 91). The primary source of threat for children is not cyberspace, public parks or playgrounds but the family and people known to the family. There is a clear danger of over-prioritising online CSA over CSA that takes place in the home, where children are at greater risk of being abused by someone they know. Myths such as this should be challenged rather than reinforced and allowed to prevail.

As I have suggested in previous chapters, the cultural figure of the paedophile in its present form has emerged from a combination of various cultural and political developments over the past four decades, with the neoliberal turn towards the punitive state playing a pivotal role, particularly in the 1990s and 2000s.

There needs to be a greater recognition that the police officers, legal practitioners, social workers, therapists and psychiatrists etc who deal with abusers and their victims on a daily basis cannot be divorced from this cultural field. Rather, the meaning and consequences of their activities need to be re-examined as part and parcel of the political and cultural discourses to which I have alluded above. This raises important and thorny questions about the relationship between, on the one hand, practitioners' efforts to avert or minimise harm inflicted upon the victims of CSA and, on the other hand, the eminently problematic public discourses that have invented 'paedophiles' as demonic figures and that provide the cultural fundament for practictioners' activities.

At the same time, there is an urgent need to re-examine the perspectives which the academic literature provides on offenders themselves. In order to contribute to prevention and rehabilitation, rather than simply punishment, it is essential to consider how offenders themselves construct their understandings, motivations and experiences with children in the context of the aforementioned discourses and cultural hierarchies. Offenders themselves are immersed in public narratives of CSA on a daily basis and it may be expected that their perceptions of self and self-identities will be strongly shaped by them, particularly in the absence of communities that would allow them to formulate alternative narratives of self (Plummer 1995). If we are interested in the prevention of harm, child safety and rehabilitation it is important that we take an interest in what exactly they are about, both online and offline: we need to understand offenders' communities, their motivations and behaviour.

In this sense, the lens of power relations may make it possible to arrive at an integrative, sociologically informed perspective on the way in which macro-structures of politics and culture intersect to shape the practices of the various categories of individuals involved in CSA, as well as their underlying experiences of self. This perspective, therefore, might constitute an important way forward for current academic debate.

Concluding remarks

In this book, I have sought to present an in-depth analysis of policing strategies implemented to combat online CSA. I have also sought critically to evaluate sex offenders' online behaviour, focusing particularly on grooming tactics. The data presented in this book have shed some much-needed light on the debate by ascertaining the extent to which offending behaviour is influenced by the internet – that is, the extent to which the internet can be conceptualised as a causative factor in offending behaviour – and, as such, in the need to separate theorisation – or the extent to which online offending is simply another manifestation of pre-existing motivations that is explicable in terms of 'real world' theories of sexual abuse. The significance of this question is fundamental, for it carries important implications for the development both of treatment programmes aimed at reducing offending behaviour and for strategies designed and targeted at reducing the sexual abuse of children online and in the real world.

Very little up-to-date research has been conducted in the context of cyberspace. Therefore, this book has contributed to the development of the theory of online CSA and practice. This research broadly supports the theoretical context that explains what motivates sex offenders to abuse children sexually and, in order to validate the claims made throughout this project, evidence from previous research is cited here.

The evidence presented has shown that online CSA is a growing problem and that the global nature of the internet makes this problem even more difficult to control. The Metropolitan Police invest a great amount of resources in undercover investigations which have proved to be effective, albeit difficult and expensive to sustain.

Other important issues raised by this research include the relationship the police have with the media. It has been shown that the media have been central in the process of increasing social awareness. However, despite these undeniable benefits, the media are problematic and potentially damaging in a number of ways (Kitzinger and Skidmore 1995).

This work is significant to a number of key constituencies of the private and public sector, all concerned with the safety of children and young persons. This includes organisations dealing with young people, organisations that work with offenders towards a better understanding of online offending motivations, as well as practices and law enforcement agencies responsible for public safety. This wide-ranging significance stems from two central tenets of this study. First, as I have shown, this research is based on unprecedented access to so far largely invisible settings in which CSA is committed and comes under surveillance by the police. In this sense, this study offers innovative and unprecedented insights into the empirical dynamics of CSA that may inform the work of academics and practitioners in a variety of fields. Secondly, this study, based on a comprehensive overview of achievements in the field, offers a novel conceptual perspective on online CSA that transcends the accomplishments of prior research. Therefore, it is hoped that it will inspire the thinking and future work of scholars and practitioners in the field.

Whilst this work has not purported to demonstrate direct causal relationships between media forms and deviant behaviour, the problem of online CSA is already pressing, increasing and unlikely to decrease in the future.

As global access to the internet rapidly expands (Franko Aas 2006) and the mediatised sexualisation of society proceeds apace (Greer and Jewkes 2005), the policing of online CSA will retain a central importance in everyday police work and the wider projects of public safety and child protection. It is hoped that this research will help cast some much needed light on this dark corner of contemporary social life.

Note

1 A more in-depth discussion on groomers' motivations has been published in Martellozzo, E. (2010) 'Sex Offenders' Use of the Internet' in J. Davidson and P. Gottschalk, *Internet Child Abuse: Current Research & Practice*, London, Routledge.

References

Connell, R. (1987) *Gender and Power*, Cambridge, Polity Press.

Connell, R. (2002) *Gender*, Cambridge, Polity Press.

Corby, B. (2000) *Child Abuse: Towards a Knowledge Base*, Buckingham, Open University Press.

Douglas, J. D. (1976) *Investigative Social Research: Individual and Team Field Research*, Beverly Hills, Sage.

Ericson, R., Baranek, P. and Chan, J. (1987) *Visualising Deviance: A Study of News Organisation*, Milton Keynes, Open University Press.

Finkelhor, D. (1984a) *Child Sexual Abuse; New Theory and Research*, New York, Free Press.

Finkelhor, D. (1984b) *Four conditions: A model. Child Sexual Abuse: New Theories and Research*, New York, The Free Press.

Finkelhor, D., Araji, S., Baron, L. and Browne, A. (1986) *A Sourcebook on Child Sexual Abuse*, California, Sage.

Finkelhor, D. and Russell, D. (1984) Women as perpetrators: Review of the Evidence. *Child Sexual Abuse: New Theory and Research*.

Franko Aas (2006) *The Body does not lie; Identity, Risk and Trust in Technoculture*, Crime, Media, Culture, vol. 2(2): 143–158.

Goode, E. and Ben-Yehuda, N. (1994) *Moral Panics. The Social Construction of Deviance*, Oxford, Blackwell.

Greer, C. and Jewkes, Y. (2005) *Extremes of Otherness: Media Images of Social Exclusion*, Social Justice, 32, 20–31.

Hammersley, M. and Atkinson, P. (1983) *Ethnography Principles in Practice*, London, Routledge.

Hammersley, M. (1991) On Feminist Methodology. *The Journal of the British Sociological Association*, 26, 187–206.

Hobbs, D. (2000) Researching Serious Crime, in R. King and E. Wincup (eds), *Doing Research on Crime and Justice*, Oxford, Oxford University Press.

Humphreys, L. (1970) *Tearoom Trade: Impersonal Sex in Public Places*, Chicago, Aldine.

Jenks, C. (1996) *Childhood: Key Ideas*, London, Routledge.

Kitzinger, J. and Skidmore, P. (1995) *Playing Safe: Media Coverage of the Prevention of Child Sexual Abuse*. Child Abuse Review, 4, 47–56.

Murphy, D., Durkin, J. and Joseph, J. (2011) Growth in Relationship. A Post-Medicalized Vision for Positive Transformation, in N. Tehrani (ed.), *Managing Trauma in the Workplace. Supporting Workers and Organisations*, East Sussex, Routledge.

Nelson, A. and Oliver, P. (1998) Gender and the Construction of Consent in Child-Adult Sexual Contact. Beyond Gender Neutrality and Male Monopoly. *Gender and Society*, 12, 554–77.

Plummer, K. (1995) *Telling Sexual Stories: Power, Change and Social Worlds*, London, Routledge.

Sullivan, J. and Beech, A. (2004) *Are Collectors of Child Abuse Images a Risk to Children?*, London, The John Grieve Centre for Policing and Community Safety.

Tehrani, N. (2011) Supporting Employees at Risk of Developing Secondary Trauma and Burn-Out, in N. Tehrani (ed), *Managing Trauma in the Workplace. Supporting Workers and Organisations*, East Sussex, Routledge.

Wearing, B. (1989) The Role of Gender in Socialisation, in T. Jagtenberg and P. D'Alton, (eds), *Four dimensional social space*, Sydney, Harper and Row.

Young, K. S. (1996) *Internet Addiction: the Emergence of a New Clincial Disorder*, 104th Annual Meeting of the American Psycological Association, Toronto, Canada.

Index

Note: The reference 24n3 refers to chapter end-note 3 on page 24. Child sexual abuse is abbreviated to CSA.